Buddhist Beliefs and Practices

Buddhist Beliefs and Practices

K N Tiwary

MD Publications Pvt Ltd
New Delhi
www.mdppl.com

Published by :

MD Publications Pvt Ltd
"MD House", 11, Darya Ganj,
New Delhi-110 002
Phone : +91-11-45355555
E-mail : contact@mdppl.com
Website : www.mdppl.com

ISBN : 978-81-7533-288-1

Published and Printed by Mr. Pranav Gupta on behalf of
MD Publications Pvt Ltd at Printext, New Delhi.

Preface

Buddhism is considered by some to be more of a philosophy than a religion. Buddha never declared Himself to be God. Almost all the other religions essentially entail some form of theism. However, Buddhism, in itself, is considered to be non-theistic or atheistic. It does not emphasize the existence or non-existence of a God or Gods any point of time. In addition to that, Buddhism does not have doctrines in the same sense as other religions do.

One of the basic tenets of Buddhism is the Buddhist belief that everyone, everywhere, can achieve good fortune and happiness. It isn't something that can be achieved by only a small group of people - or people of some certain culture. This happiness is available to everyone regardless of background, race, gender or age. It doesn't matter who you are, or where you're from.

Buddhism, as a religion, lays great emphasis on the adherence to the basic beliefs. The basic Buddhist belief comprise of the basic teachings and concepts of Buddhism. Lord Buddha urged His followers to concentrate on the Four Noble Truths, which helps in attaining freedom from suffering.

One of the basic Buddhist beliefs is the belief that happiness and good fortune can be achieved by everyone, irrespective of their age, race or background. Buddhists believe that by using meditation all negative states of mind can be overcome. Meditation can help humans to develop positive, peaceful states of mind and through meditation are able to solve all types of problems which they face daily.

The belief in reincarnation is also a basic belief of

Buddhism. Buddhists believe that everyone is re-born after dying by going through many cycles of birth, life and rebirth, the cycles only end when a state of freedom and liberation from suffering is achieved; this is called the state of Nirvana and the desired outcome for all Buddhists.

There are many different schools of Buddhism, but the one Buddhist Belief that runs through all of them is that meditation is one of the best Sways to overcome those thoughts and behaviors that are negative in nature. Once people have developed a regular, daily practice of meditation they can achieve positive, peaceful states of mind. People who meditate find that dealing effectively with the daily hassles that come up is accomplished with much greater ease. Of great importance among the Buddhist Belief system is the understanding and willingness to follow the Five Precepts. These Precepts are often referred to as the curriculum of Buddhist teaching.

I am very grateful to Mr. Pranav Gupta, Director of MD Publications Pvt Ltd, New Delhi, for his cooperation and support for this book.

K N Tiwary

CONTENTS

1

The Buddha and his Teachings

In about the sixth century B.C. Siddhartha Gautama was born into a royal family. When he was a young adult his experiences with the outside world drove him to seek out a greater understanding of life and spiritual fulfilment. Through seeking guidance and meditation, Siddhartha achieved Enlightenment. From that point, he was known as the Buddha, which means 'Enlightened One'. For the rest of his life, the Buddha travelled great distances teaching people about one path to salvation. Siddhârtha Gautama (Sanskrit; Pali: Siddhattha Gotama) was a spiritual teacher in the northern region of the Indian subcontinent who founded Buddhism.

He is generally seen by Buddhists as the Supreme *Buddha* (Sammâsambuddha) of our age. The time of his birth and death are uncertain: most early 20th-century historians date his lifetime from c. 563 BCE to 483 BCE; more recently, however, at a specialist symposium on this question, the majority of those scholars who presented definite opinions gave dates within 20 years either side of 400 BCE for the Buddha's death, with others supporting earlier or later dates. Gautama, also known as *Úâkyamuni* or *Shakyamuni* ("sage of the Shakyas"), is the key figure in Buddhism, and accounts of his life, discourses, and monastic rules are believed by Buddhists to have been summarized after his death and memorized by his followers.

Various collections of teachings attributed to Gautama were passed down by oral tradition, and first committed to writing about 400 years later. Early Western scholarship tended to accept the biography of the Buddha presented in the Buddhist scriptures as largely historical, but currently "scholars are increasingly reluctant to make unqualified claims about the historical facts of the Buddha's life and teachings."

The primary sources of information regarding Siddhârtha Gautama's life are the Buddhist texts. The Buddha and his monks spent four months each year discussing and rehearsing his teachings, and after his death his monks set about preserving them. A council was held shortly after his death, and another was held a century later.

At these councils the monks attempted to establish and authenticate the extant accounts of the life and teachings of the Buddha following systematic rules. They divided the teachings into distinct but overlapping bodies of material, and assigned specific monks to preserve each one. From then on, the teachings were transmitted orally.

From internal evidence it seems clear that the oldest texts crystallized into their current form by the time of the second council or shortly after it. The scriptures were not written down until three or four hundred years after the Buddha's death. By this point, the monks had added or altered some material themselves, in particular magnifying the figure of the Buddha.

The ancient Indians were generally not concerned with chronologies, being far more focused on philosophy. The Buddhist texts reflect this tendency, providing a clearer picture of what Shakyamuni may have taught than of the dates of the events in his life.

These texts contain descriptions of the culture and daily life of ancient India which can be corroborated from the Jain scriptures, and make the Buddha's time the earliest period in Indian history for which substantial accounts exist. According to Michael Carrithers, there are good reasons to doubt the traditional account, though the outline of "birth, maturity, renunciation, search, awakening and liberation, teaching, death" must be true.

CONCEPTION AND BIRTH

Siddhartha was born in Lumbini and raised in the small kingdom or principality of Kapilvastu, both of which are in modern day Nepal. At the time of the Buddha's birth, the area was at or beyond the boundary of Vedic civilization; it is even possible that his mother tongue was not an Indo-Aryan language. His community does not seem to have had a caste system, and their society was not structured according to Brahminical theory. It was not a monarchy, and seems to have been structured either as an oligarchy, or as a form of republic.

According to the traditional biography, however, his father was King Suddhodana, the chief of the Shakya nation, one of several ancient tribes in the growing state of Kosala; Gautama was the family name. His mother, Queen Maha Maya (Mâyâdevî) and Suddhodana's wife, was a Koliyan princess. On the night Siddhartha was conceived, Queen Maya dreamt that a white elephant with six white tusks entered her right side, and ten lunar months later Siddhartha was born. As was the Shakya tradition, when his mother Queen Maya became pregnant, she left Kapilvastu for her father's kingdom to give birth. However, she gave birth on the way, at Lumbini, in a garden beneath a sal tree.

The day of the Buddha's birth is widely celebrated in Theravada countries as Vesak. Various sources hold that the Buddha's mother died at his birth, a few days or seven days later. The infant was given the name Siddhartha (Pâli: Siddhatta), meaning "he who achieves his aim". During the birth celebrations, the hermit seer Asita journeyed from his mountain abode and announced that the child would either become a great king (chakravartin) or a great holy man. This occurred after Siddhartha placed his feet in Asita's hair and Asita examined the birthmarks. Suddhodarna held a naming ceremony on the fifth day, and invited eight Brahmin scholars to read the future.

All gave a dual prediction that the baby would either become a great king or a great holy man. Kaundinya (Pali: Kondanna), the youngest, and later to be the first arahant, was the only one who unequivocally predicted that Siddhartha would become a Buddha. While later tradition and legend characterized Suddhodana as a hereditary monarch, the descendant of the Solar Dynasty of Ikcvâku (Pâli: Okkâka), many scholars believe that Úuddhodana was the elected chief of a tribal confederacy.

THE LIFE OF THE BUDDHA

Buddhism has its roots in India around 2,500 years ago and was founded by an Indian Hindu prince, Siddhartha Gautama, who became known as 'the Buddha' i.e. 'the Enlightened One'. Siddhartha Gautama was born in what is now Nepal near the border of India. He lived for 80 years, and his life, like that of other founders of religion, has become a profound example to millions of his fellow people. Actually, he was born Siddhartha Gautama and the term Buddha was a title meaning "the awakened one", or "the one who knows", and was used from the age of thirty-five.

There are two aspects of the Life of Siddhartha Gautama - the historical way and the legend, which has embroidered the story of this amazing man. We will cover the three main parts of his life, the early years as a prince, his search for the truth, and the years spreading his teaching, and some of the details are no doubt part legend. The historical fact is that around 563BC, in Lumbini, in Nepal near the present border of Northern India, Siddhartha was born. The family name was Gautama and they were the rulers of a small feudal kingdom of the Sakya clan. Increasing urbanisation and trade meant that that there was increasing affluence in that era.

His mother died seven days after the birth, and he was raised by his aunt, the King's second wife. Legend has it that, soon after Siddhartha was born, he was examined by the holy men, who announced that he would become either, a great political leader and would unify India, or a great religious leader. As the story goes, the king, his father wanted his son to follow in his footsteps. So he set about to provide a life of luxury without any hardships for the boy.

Siddhartha wore clothes made of silk, and he grew up in palaces and gardens. Musicians and dancers were there to amuse him. Fearful of the prediction, his father ordered that he be shielded from contact with ugliness, sickness, old age and death. From about the age of seven, he was trained in athletic skills and was instructed in the spiritual disciplines of the day, and, by the standards of the day, well educated although it is not known whether he could read or write. At that time in India, Hinduism was the orthodox religion, and this was dominated by the Brahmins who controlled the religious process.

The teaching was based on the Vedas and ritual was important. The Vedas are a collection of over a thousand hymns, some of which date back to 1200 BC. The Vedas present the world mythologically rather than philosophically. Siddhartha would have been schooled in the Hindu faith and introduced to the many Hindu gods. When he turned sixteen, the council decided that it was time for him to marry. A young woman named Yasodhara was found and the couple married. Yasodhara soon had a son who was named Rahula. At this point, he had everything it seemed possible to have in life, but despite all this affluence, Siddhartha in his early twenties, became discontent. The basis for this is a famous legend of the four encounters, or passing sights. If Siddhartha went out of the palace, the king had always first ordered that all those with any disability be hidden from view.

The story is told that, one day, Siddhartha saw an old man, bent and trembling, and discovered old age. On the second encounter, he saw a sick man suffering from disease, and on the third journey, he witnessed a funeral procession and a corpse. Finally, on the fourth journey, he met a wandering monk who had an inner tranquillity despite living an austere life, suggesting to Siddhartha that he had come to terms with old age, sickness and death.

The king then called for more festivities to entertain his son, however on the night of his 29th birthday, the young prince renounced his regal life, left his sleeping family, and set out with a servant. Once he was far enough away, he cut off his long black hair, exchanged his fine clothes for simple cloth and sent back his servant and horse. This decision was not an easy one for Gautama, and in making this choice, he took it upon himself to find out about the origin of suffering and how to overcome it. He did this for his own understanding and for all people.

THE BUDDHA

In the forests of northern India in around 560 B.C., there was a rich county ruled by an important King, Suddhodana. One night the Queen, Maha Maya, had a very strange dream. She dreamed that she saw a huge white elephant come into the room, carrying a lotus flower. The elephant trumpeted while it walked around her bed three times and pierced her right side with one of its tusks. In the morning, the King called the wise men of the land to the palace, to find out the meaning of this dream. The wise men said that a great and noble son will be born to the Queen. The King and Queen were very happy. Soon the Queen gave birth to the prince, and it was said he walked seven steps as soon as he was born. His skin was the colour of gold.

The King was so happy and proud that he called his little son Siddhartha, which means 'a wish fulfilled.' When Siddhartha was a few days old the King asked eight famous fortune-tellers to examine the baby. They looked on his body for special signs - such as if his ears were long, if there was hair between his eyebrows, if round marks appeared on the soles of his feet. Seven of the fortune-tellers agreed with each other and said that this child was no ordinary boy - it was written in the stars that if he stayed in the palace he will become a great emperor, but if he left the court he will be a Buddha, a fully awakened one, overflowing with wisdom and goodness. (A Buddha means an enlightened person.) Kondanna, the eighth fortune-teller said that the markings on the child showed that his future can go in only one way - a time will come when he will see four special signs. He will become a Buddha.

After a few years Siddhartha was sent to school. He becomes good at languages and arithmetic. In sport he loved archery and wrestling. He was tall, strong and handsome. His kindness and good manners made everybody like him. Siddhartha loved all living creatures. One day he was walking in the woods with his cousin, Devadatta, who carried a bow and arrows with him. Seeing a swan fly overhead, he took aim and shot it. Both boys ran quickly to where the swan had fallen, Siddhartha reaching it first. The swan was still alive and Siddhartha gently drew the arrow out of its wing. Taking some leaves he squeezed the juice from them on to the wound to stop the bleeding. Then he spoke comforting words to calm the frightened bird.

Devadatta came up and said the swan was his and that he must have it. Siddhartha refused. 'If you had killed it, it would have been yours,' he said, 'but it is only wounded and since I have saved its life it belongs to me.' They argued on and on until Siddhartha suggested asking the wise men of the palace. When they heard the story, the verdict was: 'A life must belong to him who tries to save it. A life cannot be claimed by one who wants to destroy it. Siddhartha has the right to take the wounded swan.' So Siddhartha looked after the swan until it flew away.

THE YOUNG MAN

When Siddhartha was grown up, the King became worried about the four signs which the fortune-teller had predicted. He did not want Siddhartha to become a Buddha 'I will not allow my son to be a holy man, a homeless wanderer. He must rule the world, not forsake it', he said to himself. So one day he sent for seven of the fortune-tellers. The eight, Kondanna became one of the five disciples. They told him, 'Your son will become a Buddha if he sees four things - an old man, a sick man, a dead man and a forest monk.'

The King thought 'I must make sure my son does not see these things.' At once he ordered that no old or sick people and no sign of death should be allowed near the prince. Special guards were posted to enforce this. No monk was allowed within a mile of him. Even fading flowers and leaves were removed from gardens and parks so that the prince should not see anything that might make him think of death. At the same time everything he could possibly want was given to him. Three palaces were built for him, one for the hot season, one for the rainy season and one for the cool months of winter. Beautiful parks, with ponds decorated with water-lilies and full of fish, were made.

GETTING MARRIED

Even in such happy surroundings Siddhartha became a young man of great intelligence, strength and beauty, but still he was unsettled and restless so the King decided he should marry. All the loveliest girls in the kingdom were called to the palace for Siddhartha to make his choice. Among them was his cousin, Yasodhara, a pretty and charming girl. Siddhartha fell in love with her and they were married with much ceremony and rejoicing. Some years went by and Yasodhara had baby boy. The King began to think that everything was turning out, after all, as he wanted. But in spite of his pleasant life, Siddhartha continued to be thoughtful and troubled. Were parties and feasts what life was about? Was that all? Was all this splendid luxury to be the whole meaning of his life?

THE FOUR SIGNS

In spite of having everything he wanted, Siddhartha became bored and restless. One day, when he was 29, he asked his coachman, Channa, to take him for a drive in to the city. They had not gone far before they saw a hunched-up, weary-looking old man. At last the King's precautions had failed. Siddhartha asked Channa to stop. 'What is that? It looks like a man but his hair is white, he has no teeth, his skin is wrinkled, and his back so bent that he has to lean on a stick. What kind of man is he?' 'He is an old man,' said Channa, 'bowed down by years.' 'Does this happen to everyone, Channa? Or is it only this man who grows old?' 'Time lets no man escape old age, my lord. He was once a young man and full of energy as yourself.'

Siddhartha returned home full of thought, too troubled to speak. The next day he ordered Channa to take him out again. This time they saw a sick man who was so ill that he rolled and writhed on the ground. His mouth foamed and his eyes were bloodshot. Once more the prince asked if any person could become ill. When Channa said yes, he returned home full of heaviness and doubt. A third time they went out and came upon a funeral procession. The body lay still and lifeless and the mourners were weeping and wailing. Channa told the prince, 'Death is the end of life. Your body dies when it can go on no longer. But there is nothing strange about it, for everyone who is born must sooner or later die.'

Siddhartha and Channa drove out a forth time and, as before, an unusual sight awaited them. This time it was not a sad scene. It was a man with a shaven head, dressed in a yellow robe, standing barefoot, and holding a bowl in his hands. His face was calm and peaceful. 'Who is this?' asked Siddhartha. 'Can it be a god who stands there, so serene and happy? He looks as if the sorrows of life do not touch him.' 'He is a wandering monk. He has no home, but shelters in caves and woods. He begs for his food. He tries to be pure-hearted and seeks the truth of life.' 'How I would like to follow such a way as that,' said Siddhartha. 'That way will be my way, the forests will be my shelter, my only home. I will leave the palace tonight, Channa. Have my horse saddled and ready.'

DEPARTURE AND ASCETIC LIFE

At the age of 29, Siddhartha left his palace in order to meet his subjects. Despite his father's effort to remove the sick, aged and suffering from the public view, Siddhartha was said to have seen an old man. Disturbed by this, when told that all people would eventually grow old by his charioteer Channa, the prince went on further trips where he encountered, variously, a diseased man, a decaying corpse, and an ascetic.

Deeply depressed by these sights, he sought to overcome old age, illness, and death by living the life of an ascetic. Siddhartha escaped his palace, accompanied by Channa aboard his horse Kanthaka, leaving behind this royal life to become a mendicant.

That night there was a great feast and the dancing girls performed before the prince. But he was weary of such sights and he fell asleep. When the lamps of scented oil were nearly out and the rest of the palace slept, Siddhartha awoke. He went to look on his sleeping wife and baby for the last time. He then rode out of the palace on his horse with Channa riding by his side. They crossed a river. At the other side Siddhartha took off his rich silk robes and put on humble yellow cotton ones. He gave his jewels to Channa. Then he took out his sword and cut off his long flowing hair. 'Take my clothes, jewels and sword back to my father, Channa. Tell him that I am going away to find the real meaning of life and death. When I have found it, I will come back to see him and my wife and son.'

It is said that, "the horse's hooves were muffled by the gods" to prevent guards from knowing the Bodhisatta's departure. This event is traditionally called "The Great Departure". Siddhartha initially went to Rajagaha and began his ascetic life by begging for alms in the street. Having been recognised by the men of King Bimbisara, Bimbisara offered him the throne after hearing of Siddhartha's quest. Siddhartha rejected the offer, but promised to visit his kingdom of Magadha first, upon attaining enlightenment. Siddhartha left Rajagaha and practised under two hermit teachers. After mastering the teachings of Alara Kalama (Skr. Ârâ a Kâlâma), Siddhartha was asked by Kalama to succeed him, but moved on after being unsatisfied with his practices. He then became a student of Udaka Ramaputta (Skr. Udraka Râmaputra), but although he achieved high levels of meditative consciousness and was asked to succeed Ramaputta, he was still not satisfied with his path, and moved on. Siddhartha and a group of five companions led by Kaundinya then set out to take their austerities even further.

They tried to find enlightenment through near total

deprivation of worldly goods, including food, practising self-mortification. After nearly starving himself to death by restricting his food intake to around a leaf or nut per day, he collapsed in a river while bathing and almost drowned. Siddhartha began to reconsider his path. Then, he remembered a moment in childhood in which he had been watching his father start the season's plowing and he had fallen into a naturally concentrated and focused state that was blissful and refreshing, the *jhana*.

LONELINESS AND STARVATION

For the next six years Siddhartha wandered through the plains and forests of northern India. Sometimes he was afraid of the great woods, where tigers roamed: 'How hard it is to be a lonely forest-dweller. The silent trees bear heavily on the man who has not yet found his true self.' But yet he went on, for he knew he must find out the truth about his own existence. He found two religious teachers, who taught him yoga, concentration and meditation, but he did not find enlightenment there. Then he joined a group of five other wanderers like himself. They told him he should fast - eat very little food - and then he would find the truth. So Siddhartha ate just one bean a day, or one grain of rice.

He became very weak and ill. One day a milkmaid went past and offered him a bowl of milk. He drank it. Then he ate some food and began to feel strong again. 'From now on I will take the middle way. I shall neither starve my body nor feed it too richly, but will eat just what is needed and no more.' The five wanderers could not believe that Siddhartha had broken his fast and left him.

THE BODHI TREE

He went on alone. He thought of the six years that had passed since he left his father's palace. He had still found no answer to all the suffering in life, why it is there and how it can be overcome. At last he came to a great tree, later to be called the bo-tree (from 'bodhi' which means wisdom). 'I shall sit beneath this tree and though my flesh and bones should waste away and my life-blood dry up, I shall not move again until I have found the truth.' He sat and meditated. Day turned to night and the full moon of May came up. Now Mara, the evil one, came to him. According to legend, Mara tempted him with many things of the world including a great longing to go back to his wife and child and give up his long search. But, although Siddhartha was tired and discouraged, his will to find enlightenment was stronger.

Then, it is said, Mara hurled thunderbolts at him but they turned to sweet-scented petals as they neared him. And Mara caused huge jagged lighting flashes which turned to soft sounds of music in his ears. Last of all, Mara shouted, 'Even if you find out the truth, which do you think will ever believe you? What right do you have to claim the throne of enlightenment? Siddhartha touched the ground with his hand and replied, 'The earth will bear witness, to all my past action of purity.' Mother earth rose from the ground and brought forth a great flood which swept Mara and his hosts away.

ENLIGHTENMENT

After asceticism and concentrating on meditation and Anapanasati (awareness of breathing in and out), Siddhartha is said to have discovered what Buddhists call the Middle Way-a path of moderation away from the extremes of self-indulgence and self-mortification. He accepted a little milk and rice pudding from a village girl named Sujata, who wrongly believed him to be the spirit that had granted her a wish, such was his emaciated appearance.

One happy Vesak night, as he was seated under the famous Pippala tree at Buddha Gaya, with mind tranquilized and purified, in the first watch he developed that supernormal knowledge which enables him to remember his past lives *Pubbenivasanussati Nana - Reminiscence of Past Births*. In the middle watch he developed vision dealing with the death and rebirth of beings *Cutupapata Nana - Perception of the Disappearing and Reappearing of Beings*. In the last watch of the night he developed the supernormal knowledge with regard to the *destruction of passions - Asavakkhaya Nana*, and comprehending things they truly are, attained *Perfect Enlightenment - Samma Sambodhi.*

Then, sitting under a pipal tree, now known as the Bodhi tree in Bodh Gaya, India, he vowed never to arise until he had found the Truth. Kaundinya and the other four companions believing that he had abandoned his search and become undisciplined left him. After 49 days meditating, at the age of 35, he attained Enlightenment; according to some traditions, this occurred approximately in the fifth lunar month and according to others in the twelfth. Gautama, from then on, was known as the *Buddha* or "Awakened One." Buddha is also sometimes translated as "The Enlightened One." Often, he is referred to in Buddhism as Shakyamuni Buddha or "The Awakened One of the Shakya Clan."

At this point, he is believed to have realized complete awakening and insight into the nature and cause of human suffering which was ignorance, along with steps necessary to eliminate it. This was then categorized into 'Four Noble Truths'; the state of supreme liberation-possible for any being-was called Nirvana. He then allegedly came to possess the Nine Characteristics, which are said to belong to every Buddha. According to one of the stories in the *Âyâcana Sutta* (Samyutta Nikaya VI.1), a scripture found in the Pâli and other canons, immediately after his Enlightenment, the Buddha was wondering whether or not he should teach the *Dharma* to human beings.

He was concerned that, as human beings were overpowered by greed, hatred and delusion, they would not be able to see the true *dharma,* which was subtle, deep and hard to understand. However, Brahmâ Sahampati interceded and asked that he teach the *dharma* to the world, as "there will be those who will understand the *Dharma*". With his great compassion to all beings in the universe, the Buddha agreed to become a teacher.

Having in his 35th year attained Buddhahood - that supreme state of Perfection, He devoted the remainder of that precious life to serve humanity both by example and precept dominated by no personal motive. The Buddha was a human being. As a man He was born, as a man He lived, and as a man His life came to an end. Though human, He became *an extraordinary man - Acchariya Manussa.* The Buddha laid stress on this fact and left no room for anyone to fall into the error of thinking that He was an immortal being. There is no deification in the case of the Buddha. Nor does the Buddha claim to be an incarnation of Vishnu, nor does He call himself a "Saviour" who freely saves others by His personal salvation.

The Buddha exhorts His disciples to depend on themselves for their salvation, for both defilement and purity depend on oneself. *"You yourselves should make the exertion. The Tathagatas are only teachers,"* says the Buddha. The Buddhas pointed out the path, and it is left for us to follow that path to save ourselves. *"To depend on others for salvation is negative, but to depend on oneself is positive."* Dependence on others means a surrender of one's effort. Furthermore, the Buddha does not claim a monopoly of Buddhahood, which as matter of fact is not the perogative of any specially graced, chosen person. He reached the highest possible state of perfection any person could aspire to; and without the closed fist of a teacher, He revealed the only straight path that leads thereto.

According to the teachings of the Buddha anybody may be aspire to that supreme state of perfection if he makes the necessary aspiring determination and necessary exertion. As a man He attained Buddhahood and proclaimed to the world the latent possibilities and the creative power of man. Instead of placing an unseen almighty God over man, and making him subservient to such belief, He raised the worth of mankind. It was He who taught that man could obtain his Deliverance from sorrow by his own exertion, without depending on a God and mediating priests, or on sacrifices and prayers.

It was He who taught the ego-centric world the noble ideal of selfless service. It was He who revolted against the degrading caste system and taught the equality of mankind. He declared that the gates of success and prosperity were open to all, in every condition of life, high and low, saint and sinner, who would care to turn over a new leaf and aspire to Perfection. Irrespective of caste, colour or rank, he established for both deserving men and women a celibate order which was "democratic in constitution and communistic in distribution". He gave complete freedom of thought and wanted us to open our eyes to see things as they truly are. He comforted the bereaved by His consoling words. He ministered to the sick that were deserted. He helped the poor who were neglected.

He ennobled the lives of sinners and purified the corrupted lives of criminals. He encouraged the feeble, united the divided, enlightened the ignorant, clarified the mystic, guided the deluded, elevated the base, and dignified the noble. Rich and poor, saint and sinner, loved Him alike. Despotic and righteous kings, glorious princes and nobles, generous and miserly millionaires, haughty and humble scholars, destitute paupers, downtrodden scavengers, wicked murderers, despised courtesans - all benefited by His words of wisdom and compassion. His noble example was a source of inspiration to all. His Message of Peace was hailed by all with indescribable joy, and was of eternal benefit to everyone who had the fortune to come under its benign influence.

THE SEARCH

So now we come to the second part of his life. Gautama took on the life of a wandering monk, accepting food as it was offered to him. He pursued his spiritual quest and studied under the well-known teachers of his day. He learned of deep meditation and followed the yogic practices, but in the end discovered that he reached a point where the teachers could offer him no more. So he left with five followers and he was now called Sakyamuni, sage of the Sakyas, the clan of his father.

It was widely accepted by the holy men of the era, that the body and its desires were an obstacle to spiritual development and that these should be subdued. For six years, Sakyamuni starved and punished his body and lived the most austere life imaginable. In the end, he vowed to try even harder to limit his physical body. However, at the point of near death, he saw a three stringed lute, a musician's instrument. He was shown that if the string is too loose, no sound is produced, too tight and it breaks, and tuned just right it will produce pleasant sound. He saw that the austere way would not take him to enlightenment.

Gautama gave up his extreme life and began to eat normally again. His five followers now left him, disgusted that he had, in their opinion, been defeated. All alone now, he decided to tackle the quest once again, and he sat himself under a Bodhi tree at a place called Bodh Gaya and determined not to move until he had found the answers he sought. His meditation was deep, and, on the night of the full moon in May, complete Enlightenment came to him. His mind became calm and clear and he understood the cycle of birth, death and the wheel of life. He understood his true nature and that of all living beings. This was the end of his spiritual journey, and at that moment he became "the Buddha".

The Buddha continued to sit under the Bodhi tree for some time, enjoying the supreme experience and contemplating the future. At first, he doubted whether others could grasp what he now knew, but then he decided that there were those who could be shown the way, and he would dedicate the rest of his life to teaching what he had discovered. He chose the path of greatest compassion for all his fellow men and women.

FORMATION OF THE SANGHA

After becoming enlightened, two merchants whom the Buddha met, named Tapussa and Bhallika became the first lay disciples. They are given some hairs from the Buddha's head, which are believed to now be enshrined in the Shwe Dagon Temple in Rangoon, Burma. The Buddha intended to visit Asita, and his former teachers, Alara Kalama and Uddaka Ramaputta to explain his findings, but they had already died. The Buddha thus journeyed to Deer Park near Vâranasî (Benares) in northern India; he set in motion the Wheel of Dharma by delivering his first sermon to the group of five companions with whom he had previously sought enlightenment.

They, together with the Buddha, formed the first *sangha*, the company of Buddhist monks, and hence, the first formation of Triple Gem (Buddha, Dharma and *Sangha*) was completed, with Kaundinya becoming the first stream-enterer. All five soon become arahants, and with the conversion of Yasa and fifty four of his friends, the number of arahants swelled to 60 within the first two months. The conversion of the three Kassapa brothers and their 200, 300 and 500 disciples swelled the *sangha* over 1000, and they were dispatched to explain the dharma to the populace. It is unknown what language the Buddha spoke, and no conclusive documentation has been made at this point. However, some modern scholars, primarily philologists, believe it is most likely that the Buddha spoke a vulgate then current in eastern India, Mâgadhî Prakrit.

TRAVELS AND TEACHING

The third part of the life of the Buddha covers the most years. Gautama was now thirty-five years old. For the next forty-five years, until his death at about eighty years of age, he pursued his life's mission. The Buddha accepted many men as followers. He even accepted some from the lowest caste, called the Untouchables, which set a new precedent and angered many people who suggested that this would disrupt the existing order of the society. Despite opposition, the Buddha founded an order of monks and for nine months each year, walked the roads of India, to towns, villages and cities, teaching to whoever would listen. For the remaining three months of every year, corresponding to the wet season, he retreated from public life with his monks.

Unlike the Brahmin priests, he would teach in the local dialects, and spoke to all castes, even those at the lowest levels, as well as to both men and women. While controversial, his words appealed to both beggars and kings. With royal patronage and assistance from some wealthy landowners, his monasteries grew and became permanent places for the monks. After the dead of his father, his aunt asked Buddha to allow her to become a nun in the Buddhist order. The Buddha first refused saying that it was not yet time for women to become nuns.

She then shaved her head, put on the orange robes of a monk, and, together with fifty other women, went again to the Buddha. After discussing the situation with his advisors, the Buddha allowed the women to join, although they were subject to an additional set of rules. This was a most revolutionary idea for this era, as women had low status in the community. The Buddhist philosophy was then open to all, rich and poor, men and women of all levels of society, and all were equal in the community. Many others of the Buddha's own family also became his followers. And, in his own day, he became the best known and loved of all the spiritual teachers in India.

The Buddha never set himself up as an authority figure and there were incidents of internal squabbles between groups of his followers, but most were resolved in due course. His personality was a combination of dignity and friendliness, wisdom and kindliness. He had both a cool and logical mind and a warm heart. In debate, he was courteous and had a strong sense of irony. The Buddha himself wrote nothing. His teaching was communicated entirely orally and the details we have today are from the writings many years after his death. When he was about to die, at the age of eighty, he lay down on his right side, and urged his followers to ask him questions. At this point, however, they were all silent. Then he spoke his final words, which were: "All component things decay, work on your own salvation with diligence."

Some scholars believe that some portions of the Pali Canon and the Agamas could contain the actual substance of the historical teachings (and possibly even the words) of the Buddha. This is not the case for the later Mahayana sutras. The scriptural works of Early Buddhism precede the Mahayana works chronologically, and are treated by many Western scholars as the main credible source for information regarding the actual historical teachings of Gautama Buddha.

For the remaining 45 years of his life, the Buddha is said to have traveled in the Gangetic Plain, in what is now Uttar Pradesh, Bihar and southern Nepal, teaching his doctrine and discipline to an extremely diverse range of people- from nobles to outcaste street sweepers, mass murderers such as Angulimala and cannibals such as Alavaka. This extended too many adherents of rival philosophies and religions. The Buddha founded the community of Buddhist monks and nuns (the *Sangha*) to continue the dispensation after his *Parinirvâna* (Pâli: Parinibbâna) or "complete Nirvâna", and made thousands of converts. His religion was open to all races and classes and had no caste structure. He was also subject to attack from opposition religious groups, including attempted murders and framings.

The *sangha* travelled from place to place in India, expounding the dharma. This occurred throughout the year, except during the four months of the vassana rainy season. Due to the heavy amount of flooding, travelling was difficult, and ascetics of all religions in that time did not travel, since it was more difficult to do so without stepping on submerged animal life, unwittingly killing them.

During this period, the *sangha* would retreat to a monastery, Public Park or a forest and people would come to them. The first vassana was spent at Varanasi when the *sangha* was first formed. After this, he travelled to Rajagaha, the capital of Magadha to visit King Bimbisara, in accordance with his promise after enlightenment.

It was during this visit that Sariputta and Mahamoggallana were converted by Assaji, one of the first five disciples; they were to become the Buddha's two foremost disciples. The Buddha then spent the next three seasons at Veluvana Bamboo Grove monastery in Rajagaha, the capital of Magadha. The monastery, which was of a moderate distance from the city centre, was donated by Bimbisara. Upon hearing of the enlightenment, Suddhodana dispatched royal delegations to ask the Buddha to return to Kapilavastu. Nine delegations were sent in all, but the delegates joined the *sangha* and became arahants. Neglecting worldly matters, they did not convey their message.

The tenth delegation, led by Kaludayi, a childhood friend, resulted in the message being successfully conveyed as well as becoming an arahant. Since it was not the vassana, the Buddha agreed, and two years after his enlightenment, took a two month journey to Kapilavastu by foot, preaching the dharma along the way. Upon his return, the royal palace had prepared the midday meal, but since no specific invitation had come, the *sangha* went for an alms round in Kapilavastu. Hearing this, Suddhodana hastened to approach the Buddha, stating "Ours is the warrior lineage of Mahamassata, and not a single warrior has gone seeking alms", to which the Buddha replied:

That is not the custom of your royal lineage. But it is the custom of my Buddha lineage. Several thousands of Buddhas have gone by seeking alms. Suddhodana invited the *sangha* back to the royal palace for the meal, followed by a dharma talk, after which he became a sotapanna. During the visit, many members of the royal family joined the *sangha*. His cousins Ananda and Anuruddha were to become two of his five chief disciples. His son Rahula also joined the *sangha* at the age of seven, and was one of the ten chief disciples. His half-brother Nanda also joined the *sangha* and became an arahant. Another cousin Devadatta also became a monk although he later became an enemy and tried to kill the Buddha on multiple occasions.

Of his disciples, Sariputta, Mahamoggallana, Mahakasyapa, Ananda and Anuruddha comprised the five chief disciples. His ten foremost disciples were completed by the quintet of Upali, Subhoti, Rahula, Mahakaccana and Punna. In the fifth vassana, the Buddha was staying at Mahavana near Vesali. Hearing of the impending death of Suddhodana, the Buddha went to his father and preached the dharma, and Suddhodana became an arahant prior to death. The death and cremation led to the creation of the order of nuns. Buddhist texts record that he was reluctant to ordain women as nuns.

His foster mother Maha Pajapati approached him asking to join the *sangha*, but the Buddha refused, and began the journey from Kapilavastu back to Rajagaha. Maha Pajapati was so intent on renouncing the world that she led a group of royal Sakyan and Koliyan ladies, following the *sangha* to Rajagaha. The Buddha eventually accepted them five years after the formation of the *Sangha* on the grounds that their capacity for enlightenment was equal to that of men, but he gave them certain additional rules (Vinaya) to follow. This occurred after Ananda interceded on their behalf. Yasodhara also became a nun, with both becoming arahants.

During his ministry, Devadatta (who was not an arahant) frequently tried to undermine the Buddha. At one point Devadatta asked the Buddha to stand aside to let him lead the *sangha*? The Buddha declined, and stated that Devadatta's actions did not reflect on the Triple Gem, but on him alone. Devadatta conspired with Prince Ajatasattu, son of Bimbisara, so that they would kill and usurp the Buddha and Bimbisara respectively. Devadatta attempted three times to kill the Buddha. The first attempt involved the hiring of a group of archers, whom upon meeting the Buddha became disciples.

A second attempt followed when Devadatta attempted to roll a large boulder down a hill. It hit another rock and splintered, only grazing the Buddha in the foot. A final attempt by plying an elephant with alcohol and setting it loose again failed. Failing this, Devadatta attempted to cause a schism in the *sangha*, by proposing extra restrictions on the vinaya. When the Buddha declined, Devadatta started a breakaway order, criticising the Buddha's laxity. At first, he managed to convert some of the bhikkhus, but Sariputta and Mahamoggallana expounded the dharma to them and succeeded in winning them back. When the Buddha reached the age of 55, he made Ananda his chief attendant.

THE FUNDAMENTAL TEACHINGS

Some of the fundamentals of the teachings of Gautama Buddha are:

- The Four Noble Truths: that suffering is an inherent part of existence; that the origin of suffering is ignorance and the main symptoms of that ignorance are attachment and craving; that attachment and craving can be ceased; and that following the Noble Eightfold Path will lead to the cessation of attachment and craving and therefore suffering.
- The Noble Eightfold Path: right understanding, right thought, right speech, right action, right livelihood, right effort, right mindfulness, and right concentration.
- Dependent origination: that any phenomenon 'exists' only because of the 'existence' of other phenomena in a complex web of cause and effect covering time past, present and future. Because all things are thus conditioned and transient (anicca), they have no real independent identity (anatta).
- Rejection of the infallibility of accepted scripture: Teachings should not be accepted unless they are borne out by our experience and are praised by the wise.
- *Anicca* (Sanskrit: *anitya*): That all things are impermanent.
- *Anatta* (Sanskrit: *anâtman*): That the perception of a constant "self" is an illusion.
- *Dukkha* (Sanskrit: *dukkha*): That all beings suffer from all situations due to unclear mind.

However, in some Mahayana schools, these points have come to be regarded as more or less subsidiary. There is some disagreement amongst various schools of Buddhism over more esoteric aspects of Buddha's teachings, and also over some of the disciplinary rules for monks. According to tradition, the Buddha emphasized ethics and correct understanding. He questioned the average person's notions of divinity and salvation.

He stated that there is no intermediary between mankind and the divine; distant gods are subjected to karma themselves in decaying heavens; and the Buddha is solely a guide and teacher for the sentient beings who must tread the path of NirvâGa (Pâli: Nibbâna) themselves to attain the spiritual awakening called *bodhi* and see truth and reality as it is. The Buddhist system of insight and meditation practice is not believed to have been revealed divinely, but by the understanding of the true nature of the mind, which must be discovered by personally treading a spiritual path guided by the Buddha's teachings.

THE INDIAN BACKGROUND

In the sixth century BCE, north India was home to a dozen or more kingdoms and oligarchies, including the kingdom of Koysala, which in the Ramayana is described asbeing ruled by Dasaratha and his son Rama at one time, their capital located at Ayodhya. The Sakya tribe, which ruled over Koysala in the sixth century, had its capital at Sravasti in the Himalayan foothills, and it is at nearby Lumbini (now in Nepal) that Siddhartha Gautama was born in or around 563 BCE on a full moon night. His birth, like that of Christ, is supposed to have been miraculous, and the sage Asita is said to have declared that the boy would become the greatest monarch of all times or a great renouncer, the teacher of humankind.

Anxious lest Siddhartha take to the life of a saint, his father and aunt, in whose care he had been placed after the death of his mother in his infancy, endeavored to hide the realities of life from Siddharta. In his young manhood, Siddhartha was married to Yasodhara, who soon bore him a son. One day, resolved that he should see more of the world, Siddhartha ordered a chariot to take him out to witness the life led by his subjects. There, for the first time, he encountered an old man bent with age, and so came to the realization that with advancing years one's strength diminishes.

On subsequent trips, he saw an ill man, and was brought to an awareness of disease, and finally a corpse, which brought home the inescapable conclusion that no one can escape death. Upon his return to the palace, Siddhartha resolved to find the cause for the sorrow that afflicts humans, as well as the way to bring the sorrow to an end. Accompanied only by his faithful servant Channa, he set out from the palace one night;

and then sending Channa back to Kapilavastu with his jewel, Siddharta cut off hair and assumed the life of a mendicant. In his quest for the 'truth', Siddhartha engaged with the teachings of various sages, and practiced the austerities counseled by these spiritual teachers. Weak from hunger and the pain inflicted on his body, Siddhartha came to the conclusion that extreme deprivation and exposure of the body to pain would in no manner bring him closer to self-realization.

Moving underneath a bodhi tree in Sarnath, outside the vicinity of present-day Benares, he resolved to sit and meditate until he achieved enlightenment. Though visions of affluence, power, opulent food, and sexual fulfillment swept past him, Siddhartha remained untempted by all these deviations from the path. It is then that he became the exponent of a specific set of teachings, henceforth known as the "Four Noble Truth", namely: all existence is suffering (*dukha*); the cause of suffering is ignorance (*avidya*) or desire; if there is suffering, there is a cure for it; and the cure for suffering lies in the eight-fold path of right beliefs, right speech, right conduct, right mode of livelihood, right effort, right mindedness, right meditation, and right aspirations. Siddhartha, or the Buddha, "The Enlightened One", as he became known, preached his first sermon in the deer park at Sarnath in or around 527 BCE.

The very first disciples he acquired became the members of the Buddhist *sangha* or association, and slowly his fame spread. It is said that Kasshyapa, a renowned Brahmin sage, came to realize the futility of worshipping the fire (*Agni*) upon encountering the Buddha, and similarly the Buddha was able to persuade king Bimbisara, who would become his patron, that the sacrificial killing of innocent animals could not be construed as adding merit or happiness to one's life. The Buddha became the great exponent of *ahimsa* or non-violence, but he resolutely refused to claim for himself any miraculous powers.

One of the most famous episodes in Buddha's life relates how, since his fame had spread, a woman once came to him with her dead child, and asked him to bring him back to life.

While consoling her, the Buddha asked her to bring him a few mustard seeds from any house where no death had taken place; and though she went from door to door, this woman had to return to the Buddha with the news that she had not been able to find any such house. This would be the great teaching of the Buddha: whatever is born must die, and there is no permanence except sorrow; and to free us from this sorrow, one must become free from desire itself. The Buddha's last words, in paraphrase, are said to have been, "Growing old is the dharma of all composite things." Over the years, though his father endeavored to restore to him the kingdom that he had renounced, the Buddha could not be tempted to abandon his calling; eventually, his own son, Rahula, became his disciple.

The oral sources relate how some people conspired to kill him: a huge boulder was thrown down upon him and some disciples gathered around him, but it is said that the boulder split in two, and a piece fell on either side of the Buddha. A wild elephant was set loose in the Buddha's path, and though it caused havoc everywhere, it knelt at the Buddha's feet. The Buddha lived to the age of eighty, when he is described as having achieved mahanirvana, or absolute spiritual emancipation. In less than two centuries after his death, his teachings had spread not only in India but over large parts of Asia. The emperor Ashoka, who was to establish the greatest empire India was to know until the advent of the Mughals in the sixteenth century, himself became a convert to Buddhism. Some people have associated the Buddha's teachings with an excessive intellectualism and agnosticism; others have charged that Buddhism is a form of quietism.

Representation of Buddha's human form amidst the lines and curves of Indian sculptures appeared much later than the construction of stupas. His presence was originally depicted by footprints, his birth was depicted by a standing woman, a tree was initially the symbol of his enlightenment and the stupa represented his death. It was in Gandhara and Mathura in the midst of the art of lines, carves and colours of Indian sculpture Buddha as human was depicted.

The Mathura Buddha is therefore just not a diachronic sculpture but a medieval Indian sculptural descriptor where Buddha is depicted as just not a historical figure but a figure worthy of bowing down. Putting a date to the origin of this standing Mathura Buddha sculpture is almost impossible however; historians believe that it was in the last century BCE - about 500 years after the Buddha's death Mathura Buddha was sculpted in the Mathura style at the central India. The standing Mathura Buddha is a colossal statue wearing monastic robes. The transparent robes which is carved with circular lines once again points at his masculine body. The right shoulder is bare as the left shoulder is draped elegantly.

Apart from the standing posture another Mathura Buddha sculpture represents Buddha in his Yogic posture. Buddha is seated with his legs crossed and hands lay in the lap. The robes, worn over the left shoulder and arm, cover a part of the chest and most of the lower part of the body, a twisted coil of hair or bun corresponding to the later cranial bump on the head complements with the yogic posture of the Mathura Buddha. The serene smile of the face and the pair of eye looking directly at the viewer makes it a remarkable piece of art. The soles of Buddha's feet are turned upward and are marked with Buddha's symbols.

The halo behind his head stands as the logo of his ultimate divinity and is delicately marked with scalloped design on the edge. The celestial background representing his enlightenment is treated with magnificent brilliance. The lively naturalism of the rres at the background of the Mathura Buddha once again reminds of the artistry of the Indian artists. The rich red hue of the scarlet sand stones spotted and veined with yellow further makes this Mathura Buddha a rare sculpture to define Indian artistry.

DEATH OF THE BUDDHA

After nearly a half century of teaching, the Enlightened One predicted that He would pass away in three months time on the full moon of May. The news hurriedly spread over the land. The Venerable Ananda, who had yet to realize Enlightenment, begged the Blessed One to remain on earth longer. With great compassion, the Master gently reminded him it is in the nature of all composite things to pass away, to separate ourselves from all that is near and dear. Everything that is born, or brought into being, and organized, contains within itself the inherent propensity for dissolution. On one occasion, when the Order was gathered about the ailing Blessed One, He noticed that Ananda was not among them, but stood apart, weeping bitterly because the Buddha would soon pass away and he had not realized Enlightenment.

After sending for him, the Buddha said, "For a long time, Ananda, you have been very near to me by acts of love in word, deed and thoughts. You have done well, Ananda! Be earnest in your efforts and you, too, shall know Liberation." When the Blessed One had journeyed to Kusinara, the Awakened One felt His long life was drawing to a close. He addressed the Order, assuring them He had not withheld any spiritual instruction regarding the Path leading to the end of sorrow and to Enlightenment. The Buddha stated He would not appoint a successor but, rather, He bequeathed the Holy Dhamma (the Truth) as the ultimate guide for their lives. Counseling the Order, He said:

"Hold fast to the Truth and the Discipline as a lamp. Seek deliverance alone in the Truth. Strive on with diligence. Free yourself from the tangled net of sorrow and dissatisfaction. Look not for assistance to anyone besides yourself. In regard to the body and the mind, let one be mindful and overcome the greed which arises from the body's craving, which arises from craving for sensations, which arises from craving due to ideas, reasons and emotions. If one is mindful, seekers of Truth shall surely reach the top- most pinnacle of Emancipation. But they must be willing to learn."

The Buddha gave special exhortation to members of the Order: to practice and meditate on the Truth, and to spread it abroad so that the teachings would last long and be perpetuated for the good and happiness of great multitudes, out of compassion for the world and the good of every living being. He gave those in the Order, the teachers of many, the last chance to ask questions to resolve doubts or misunderstandings, noting this would be the final opportunity to question the Master face-to-face. All remained silent.

The Compassionate One said:

"It may be that you do not speak out of reverence for me as your teacher. If that is so, then speak to me as my friends.

Still, they remained silent. The Buddha, with His Wisdom-mind, saw into their inmost hearts that, indeed, no one had misgivings and that everyone assembled would surely realize Liberation. Finally, before passing away, the Buddha said:

"Perishable are all conditioned things, but the Truth will live forever! Work out your Liberation with diligence!"

The Buddha lay on a couch spread between two giant sal trees. The ancient texts say the trees blossomed out of season and sweet-smelling flowers scattered over His couch. Then, lying on His right side, calm and composed, the Great Being entered a profound state of deep meditative bliss and passed away (entered *Parinibbana,* the final decease of an All-Enlightened Buddha). A light spread over His face and then His body. There occurred a mighty earthquake and from the depths of the earth a great roar arose, and from the heavens peal after peal of hair-raising thunder was heard. Those who were emancipated from sorrow bore their grief, collected and composed. Those who were not yet set free covered their faces and wept in anguish.

Those who were liberated comforted the bereaved. After the Buddha passed away, prominent monks spent the rest of the night discussing the teachings. At dawn, the Venerable Ananda informed the Mallas of Kusinara of the death of the Master. For seven days the Mallas and throngs of people paid respect to the body of the Blessed One with lights, incense, garlands of flowers, instrumental music and religious songs. For the cremation ceremonies, a pyre of perfumed wood and flowers was prepared. The body of the Buddha was cremated with honor due the Greatest King. His relics were distributed to Kings in equal portion. They were enshrined in burial mounds (stupas) which have become sites of pilgrimage for the faithful. Thus the Buddha Sakyamuni passed from earthly eyes, yet His teachings of Truth, the way to end sorrow and life's pain, remains in our hearts and minds forever!

MAHAPARINIRVANA

According to the Maha *Parinibbana* Sutta of the Pali canon, at the age of 80, the Buddha announced that he would soon reach Parinirvana or the final deathless state abandoning the earthly body. After this, the Buddha ate his last meal, which he had received as an offering from a blacksmith named Cunda. Falling violently ill, Buddha instructed his attendant Ânanda to convince Cunda that the meal eaten at his place had nothing to do with his passing and that his meal would be a source of the greatest merit as it provided the last meal for a Buddha.

Metta nando and von Hinüber argue that the Buddha died of mesenteric infarction, a symptom of old age, rather than food poisoning. The precise contents of the Buddha's final meal are not clear, due to variant scriptural traditions and ambiguity over the translation of certain significant terms; the Theravada tradition generally believes that the Buddha was offered some kind of pork, while the Mahayana tradition believes that the Buddha consumed some sort of truffle or other mushroom. The Mahayana Vimalakirti Sutra claims, that the Buddha doesn't really become ill or old but purposely presents such an appearance only to teach those born into *samsara* about the impermanence and pain of defiled worlds and to encourage them to strive for Nirvana.

"Reverend Ánanda, the Tathágatas have the body of the Dharma-not a body that is sustained by material food. The Tathágatas have a transcendental body that has transcended all mundane qualities. There is no injury to the body of a Tathágata, as it is rid of all defilements. The body of a Tathágata is uncompounded and free of all formative activity. Reverend

Ánanda, to believe there can be illness in such a body is irrational and unseemly!' Nevertheless, since the Buddha has appeared during the time of the five corruptions, he disciplines living beings by acting lowly and humble."

Ananda protested Buddha's decision to enter Parinirvana in the abandoned jungles of Kuúinâra (present-day Kushinagar, India) of the Malla kingdom. Buddha, however, reminded Ananda how Kushinara was a land once ruled by a righteous wheel-turning king that resounded with joy:

Kusavati, Ananda, resounded unceasingly day and night with ten sounds-the trumpeting of elephants, the neighing of horses, the rattling of chariots, the beating of drums and tabours, music and song, cheers, the clapping of hands, and cries of "Eat, drink, and be merry!"

Buddha then asked the entire attendant Bhikshus to clarify any doubts or questions they had. They had none. He then finally entered Parinirvana. The Buddha's final words were, "All composite things pass away. Strive for your own liberation with diligence." The Buddha's body was cremated and the relics were placed in monuments or stupas, some of which are believed to have survived until the present. For example, The Temple of the Tooth or "Dalada Maligawa" in Sri Lanka is the place where the relic of the right tooth of Buddha is kept at present. According to the Pâli historical chronicles of Sri Lanka, the DîpavaCsa and MahâvaCsa, the coronation of Aúoka (Pâli: Asoka) is 218 years after the death of Buddha.

According to one Mahayana record in Chinese, the coronation of Aœoka is 116 years after the death of Buddha. Therefore, the time of Buddha's passing is either 486 BCE according to Theravâda record or 383 BCE according to Mahayana record. However, the actual date traditionally accepted as the date of the Buddha's death in Theravâda countries is 544 or 543 BCE, because the reign of Aœoka was traditionally reckoned to be about 60 years earlier than current estimates. At his death, the Buddha told his disciples to follow no leader, but to follow his teachings (dharma). However, at the First Buddhist Council, Mahakasyapa was held by the *sangha* as their leader, with the two chief disciples Mahamoggallana and Sariputta having died before the Buddha.

PHYSICAL CHARACTERISTICS

Buddha is perhaps one of the few sages for whom we have mention of his rather impressive physical characteristics. A *Kshatriya* by birth, he had military training in his upbringing, and by Shakyan tradition was required to pass tests to demonstrate his worthiness as a warrior in order to marry. He had a strong enough body to be noticed by one of the kings and was asked to join his army as a general. He is also believed by Buddhists to have "the 32 Signs of the Great Man". The Brahmin Sonadanda described him as "handsome, good-looking, and pleasing to the eye, with a most beautiful complexion. He has a godlike form and countenance; he is by no means unattractive."(Digha Nikaya, I: 115).

"It is wonderful, truly marvellous, how serene is the good Gotama's appearance, how clear and radiant his complexion, just as the golden jujube in autumn is clear and radiant, just as a palm-tree fruit just loosened from the stalk is clear and radiant, just as an adornment of red gold wrought in a crucible by a skilled goldsmith, deftly beaten and laid on a yellow-cloth shines, blazes and glitters, even so, the good Gotama's senses are calmed, his complexion is clear and radiant." (Anguttar Nikaya, I: 181) A disciple named Vakkali, who later became an Arahant, was so obsessed by Buddha's physical presence that Buddha had to tell him to stop and reminded Vakkali to know Buddha through the Dhamma and not physical appearances.

Although the Buddha was not represented in human form until around the 1st century CE, the physical characteristics of fully-enlightened Buddhas are described by the Buddha in the Digha Nikaya's *LakkhaGa Sutta* (D,I:142). In addition, the Buddha's physical appearance is described by Yasodhara to their son Rahula upon the Buddha's first post-Enlightenment return to his former princely palace in the non-canonical Pali devotional hymn, *Narasîha Gâthâ* ("The Lion of Men").

2

The Dharma

The Law of Life

Dharma may be defined as the highest good. Its idea is not limited to sense perception, and requires a proper teacher to explain it. It arises from action, which is the law of life. Success arises from action; and action cannot be renounced. There is action even when we do not see it, which is both eternal and universal. However, there is a difference between natural and deliberate action; and the subject matter of the Vedas is action. The idea of dharma does not arise from sense-perception, because the latter is limited to what is present, while the idea of dharma goes beyond the present. As it is conceived to be the highest good.

Which is a valid means of acquiring knowledge, and does not require the authority of a Badarayana to prove it? (Badarayana is the name of the celebrated author of the Vedanta Sutras). Some people say that dharma arises from action, and prove their point by referring to the actual facts of life. And so believe that the idea of dharma is not permanent.

Dharma is indeed linked with action, for we often say that a person does his dharma, and that implies action. Action is part of our nature, as all of us are engaged in some kind of action or the other at the same time, and we see it in prakrti (or nature) in all its modifications.

We also see that success in action is often the result of a number of persons acting together. At the same time we find that there are some who believe that we should be indifferent to all that is in the world but, even he who is said to be indifferent acts. He might appear to be inactive, but is not really so. And we believe that he has not acted, because he has not succeeded in achieving his object (or objective). We have to go beyond the commencement of an action to understand all this. As the sun may appear to be inactive, but it is in fact acting all the time; and so are all the creatures on this world acting accordingly.

There is an immutable law of action at work within all forms of life, according to which all must act. For instance, we see things growing in size, but without apparent action; yet there is sound, motion and vibration within them which is unperceived. Action is eternal, because it is meant to be performed for the sake of something else; and also because we see it all the time everywhere. The number of creatures engaged in action is so large, that it cannot be counted; and it is not necessary to refer to the same creature again, because all are acting at the same time. We say so because we know the manner in which action takes place; and if we take necessary evidence or observe the working of prakrti or nature, we shall find that it is so.

It may be argued that action, performed in the ordinary course of nature, is of little importance as it does not serve any special purpose; and those who believe that all action should be of this kind would naturally argue in this fashion. But we see that when people have a purpose or aim in action, it is the result of deliberate intention or precise thinking. According to some, the Vedas deal with the problem of the soul as their principal subject matter.

However, this is not correct, as we find that they deal with the world of prakrti or nature, which is not permanent. This has been stated to be their subject matter; and that is how they are taught and explained. Further, all Vedic literature is of the same kind, as they deal with the problem of action. They tell us what actions to perform and how to perform them. We find that man is always engaged in action; and this should enable us to acquire definite knowledge in regard to the law of action. Any contradiction of the fact that there is action everywhere should be disregarded; for we know that it is impossible.

But every action is not dharma. We cannot say that an action of the body, performed by a healthy man in the ordinary course of nature is dharma. The sacred books have their won idea of dharma, and are based on certain principles, admitted by all to be true. There is no inconsistency or contradiction in the sacred books. And if there is any inconsistency anywhere, we should take it to be in our own thought or interpretation rather than in them. We should therefore, accept what is contained in these books. The action of a healthy body, performed spontaneously or in the ordinary course of nature, is obviously the result of impulse. This is not the idea of dharma as given in the sacred books. It would be an incorrect application of the rules laid down by them to think that it is so.

Their statement regarding dharma is definite and complete, and leaves no gaps to be filled. Further, we can verify this for ourselves by making an experiment and a careful study of the sacred books. If we do so, we shall find that there is only one inescapable conclusion. That there is action everywhere, and all things are subject to it. This is proved by the fact that we can find nothing in the world that is eternal. Action means that there is a material contact of an object with a place. This however, does not limit the idea of action to make it local; for the same object can be at different places at different times. Just as when we say that a person belongs to Mathura, we do not confine him to that place. The law of action or of the doer of deed,- for both are the same.

This may be illustrated by the action of a person who is devoted to something for a while; and this is not inconsistent with the law of universal action described in the sacred books. Since, they speak of continuous action, we have to understand the sense in which the term is used, or otherwise we might commit a mistake. We can understand the real meaning, if we make a special effort; and our inability to do so arise from the fact that we take only the form of words, and neglect their real meaning. The entire meaning of the text would be changed by changing the form of a word in a particular place; and this can be done because there is no fixed rule regarding the combination of words or their parts. But if we adopt a single meaning, we cannot distinguish between things; and that will render the whole idea worthless. It is possible to look at the text in different ways, but the best meaning is that which refers to action.

There are some who believe that there is no reference to action; that there is no possibility of any other meaning than the common one and that the words refer to one particular object only. All that we can say is that the meaning does refer to action, and there is no break in the continuity of its idea. Dharma is an Indian term that is understood to mean simply the law of life. Within Buddhism, the Dharma means more specifically the teachings of Buddha. Following Buddha's death his followers convened to create a system of doctrines that they could all agree on. These teachings were then handed down orally over future generations through Buddhist monks.

In 80 B.C., Buddhist scribes finally compiled the teachings of the Buddha on paper, which became the Pali Canon, also called the Tripitaka. The teachings contained rules for conduct, methods for spiritual attainment, and the ethics taught by the Buddha. Contrary to Hinduism's caste system which required a series of rebirths to move up through the different castes, the Buddhists recruited disciples from all castes. According to Buddha, nirvana, or deliverance from suffering, is extended to everyone who strictly obeys the laws of a monastic life. However, he did feel that the caste system was important for the framework of a temporal life. It was a step away from the strict caste system of India.

The Buddha rejected subservience of any kind to a supreme God and denied belief in an eternal self. While he believed that karma would determine the kind of rebirth and quality of life one would have at rebirth, he didn't believe it was a self or soul that was reborn. He taught instead that there is a rearrangement of the elements of a person's identity, which are called "self". In other words the new self is still comprised of the same parts. Where the Brahmins of India taught that nirvana was attained when the soul becomes one with the Universal soul, Buddha held that nirvana is actually the termination of rebirths. That is, you finally get to get off the wheel.

You've reached Nirvana, you're done, you cease to exist. It's hard to see where the hope lies in this, but rebirth after rebirth could, I suppose, make your complete elimination from existence sound appealing. Buddha believed that we are temporal creations born to lives of sorrow and suffering. This suffering is a result of selfish desires that chain people to the wheel of insubstantial impermanent things. Living according to the Dharma will help one eliminate these desires thus leading you to Nirvana. According to Buddha, the way to deliverance is summed up in four noble truths:

1. The universality of suffering - People discover through rebirth, aging, and death that life is full of sorrow. We suffer this sorrow until deliverance is achieved.
2. The origin of suffering - Suffering is caused by the false desires of the senses that have been deceived into clinging to the impermanent world. The quest for immortality further aggravates human suffering.
3. The overcoming of suffering - If false desires cause suffering, then the desires need to be suppressed, abandoned, or rejected in order to nullify their effects. Ignorance of the way of deliverance and the delusion that there is a permanent self are the primary cause of suffering.
4. The way leading to the suppression of suffering - The noble eightfold path is a sacred path with eight branches called right views of understanding, right aspirations, right speech, right conduct or action, right livelihood, right effort or endeavor, right mind control or concen-tration, and right mindfulness. These eight branches are not stages that can be lived out in succession or isolation from one another. They are different dimensions of a total way of life.

While Buddha did not deny the existence of gods, he taught that the worship of gods obstructed one's quest for nirvana. To him the gods inhabit the cosmos and are impermanent like all of us, so they too must escape rebirth through nirvana. And how long will it take to follow these truths to deliverance and reach this state of spiritual suicide? According to the Buddha several lives are required to attain it. He taught that the journey to nirvana is long and difficult. And the reward for all your efforts is inner peace and harmony with all beings right before you reaches Nirvana. And then.....nothing.

Dhamma or Dharma in Buddhism has two primary meanings:

- The teachings of the Buddha which lead to enlightenment.
- The constituent factors of the experienced world.

In East Asia, the character for Dharma is pronounced fî in Mandarin and hô in Japanese. The Tibetan translation of this term is chos. In Mongolian *dharma* is translated as *nom,* which is noteworthy since it ultimately derives from the Greek word íîìïò (*nomos*) (law). The term dharma (Sanskrit: *dhárma,* Pali *dhamma*), is an Indian spiritual and religious term, that means one's righteous duty or any virtuous path in the common sense of the term. In Indian languages it can be equivalent simply to "religion", depending on context. Throughout Indian philosophy, Dharma is presented as a central concept that is used in order to explain the "higher truth" or ultimate reality of the universe.

The word *dharma* literally translates as *that which upholds or supports,* and is generally translated into English as *law.* The word "dharma" can also be translated as "the teachings of the Buddha". The various Indian religions and philosophy (Hinduism, Buddhism, Jainism, and Sikhism, among others) have all accorded a central focus to Dharma and advocate its practice. Each of these religions emphasizes Dharma as the correct understanding of reality in its teachings. In these traditions, beings that live in accordance with Dharma proceed more quickly toward Dharma Yukam, Moksha or Nirvana (personal liberation).

Dharma also refers to the teachings and doctrines of the founders of these traditions, such as those of Gautama Buddha and Mahavira. In traditional Hindu society with its caste structure, Dharma constituted the religious and moral doctrine of the rights and duties of each individual. Dharma in its universal meaning shares much in common with the way of Tao or Taoism. The antonym of dharma is *adharma* meaning unnatural or immoral.

In the Rigveda, the word appears as an *n*-stem, *dhárman*- with a range of meanings encompassing "something established or firm" (in the literal sense of prods or poles), figuratively "sustainer, supporter" (of deities), and semantically similar to the Greek *ethos* ("fixed decree, statute, law"). In Classical Sanskrit, the noun becomes thematic, *dharma*. It is from an Indo-Iranian root *dhar* ("to fasten, to support, to hold"), in turn from Proto-Indo-European *dher*, which is related to the Latin *frçnum* ("rein, horse tack"); OHG "tarni" and "latens" ("hidden, held back"); and, extended to "dher-gh", OCS "drúžë, drúžati" ("to hold, possess"). Etymological identity of *dharma* with Latin *firmus* (the source of the English word *firm*) has been suggested, but remains uncertain.

From the Atharvaveda and in Classical Sanskrit, the stem is thematic, *dhárma*, and in Pâli, it takes the form *dhamma*. It is also often rendered *dharam* in contemporary Indian languages and dialects. It is used in most or all philosophies and religions of Indian origin-sometimes summarized under the umbrella term of *Dharmic faiths*-including Hinduism, Buddhism, Jainism, and Sikhism.

It is difficult to provide a single concise definition for *dharma*, as the word has a long and varied history and straddles a complex set of meanings and interpretations. In most of the modern Indian languages, such as Hindi or Bangla, *dharma* can also contextually mean simply "religion". Hinduism, Buddhism, Jainism, and Sikhism are called *Hindu Dharma*, *Bauddha-Dharma*, *Jain-Dharma* and *Sikh dharma*, respectively.

DEVELOPMENT

In the *Rig Veda*, the belief (or observation) that a natural justice and harmony pervades the natural world becomes manifest in the concept of rta, which is both 'nature's way' and the order implicit in nature. Thus rta bears a resemblance to the ancient Chinese concept of tao and the Heraclitan or stoic conception of the logos. This "power" that lies behind nature, and which keeps everything in balance became a natural forerunner to the idea of *dharma* as one can see in this early Vedic prayer. This idea laid the cornerstone of Dharma's implicit attribution to the "ultimate reality" of the surrounding universe, in classical Hindu.

The following verse from the Rig-Veda is an example where *rta* finds mention:

"*O Indra, lead us on the path of Rta, on the right path over all evils.*" (RV 10.133.6)

The transition of the rta to the modern idea of Dharma occurs in the Brihadaranyaka Upanishad. The Upanishads saw dharma as the universal principle of law, order, harmony, all in all truth that sprang first from Brahman. It acts as the regulatory moral principle of the Universe. It is *sat*, truth, a major tenet of Hinduism. This hearkens back to the conception of the Rig Veda that "Ekam Sat," (Truth Is One), of the idea that Brahman is "*Sacchidananda*" (Truth-Consciousness-Bliss). Dharma is not just law, or harmony, it is pure Reality. In the Brihadaranyaka's own words:

"*Verily, that which is Dharma is truth.*

Therefore they say of a man who speaks truth, 'He speaks the Dharma,'

or of a man who speaks the Dharma, 'He speaks the Truth.'

Verily, both these things are the same."

(Brh. Upanishad, 1.4.14)

In the Mahabharata, Krishna defines Dharma as: "Dhaaranaad dharma ity aahur dharmena vidhrtaah prajaah,

Yat syaad dhaarana sanyuktam sa dharma iti nishchayah," or, "Dharma upholds both this-worldly and other-worldly affairs" (Mbh 12.110.11).

DHARMA AS A PURUSARTHA

In moving through the four ashrams, or stages of life, viz. Brahmacharya, Grihastha, Vaanprastha, Sanyaasa, a person also seeks to fulfill the four essentials (purusartha) of Kama (sensual pleasures), Artha (worldly gain), Dharma, and Moksha (liberation from reincarnation or rebirth). Moksha, although the ultimate goal is emphasized more in the last two stages of life, while Artha and Kama are considered primary only during Grihastha and Dharma, however is essential in all four stages.

As a purusartha (human goal), Dharma can also be considered to be a lens through which humans plan and perform their interactions with the world. Through the Dharmic lens, one focuses on doing what is right and avoiding what is wrong, while the Kama perspective focuses on doing what is pleasurable (in many senses, not just sex) and avoiding pain, and the Artha perspective focuses on doing what is profitable (in many senses, not just money) and avoiding loss.

THE DEITY NAMED DHARMA

Dharma is also the name of a deity or "Deva" in charge of Dharma. Mythologically, he is said to have been born from the right breast of Brahma, is married to ten daughters of Daksha and fathers Shama, Kama and Harahsa. He is also the father of the celebrated Rishis Hari, Krishna, and Nara-Narayana. In the epic *Mahabharata,* he is incarnate as Vidura. Also, Dharma is invoked by Kunti and she begets her eldest son Yudhisthira from him. As such Yudhisthira is known as Dharmaputra. There is also an assimilation of God Dharma and Yama, the God responsible for the Dead.

IN TECHNICAL LITERATURE

In technical literature, e.g., in Sanskrit grammar, *dharma* also means "property" and *dharmin* means "property-bearer". In a

Sanskrit sentence like *shabdo 'nityah,* "sound is impermanent", "sound" is the bearer of the property "impermanence". Likewise, in the sentence *iha ghatah,* "here, there is a pot", "here" is the bearer of the property "pot-existence" - this shows that the categories of property and property-bearer are closer to those of a logical predicate and its subject-term, and not to a grammatical predicate and subject.

For many Buddhists, the Dharma most often means the body of teachings expounded by the Buddha. The word is also used in Buddhist phenomenology as a term roughly equivalent to phenomenon, a basic unit of existence and/or experience. In East Asia, the translation for Dharma pronounced *fǐ* in Mandarin, *beop* in Korean, *hô* in Japanese, and *pháp* in Vietnamese. However, the term Dharma can also be transliterated from its original form as well.

The tradition says that the Buddha spent forty-nine days in the neighborhood of the Bodhi Tree. Then the two merchants en route from Orissa passed close by and were advised by the spirit of a dead relative to make offerings to the new Buddha, who was sitting at the foot of a certain tree. They offered honey cakes and sugar cane and "took refuge in the Buddha and his Dharma, thus becoming the first Buddhists and the first lay devotees in the world." In this case, Gautama did not preach Dharma to the two men, but merely received their reverence and offerings. Worship of holy persons is nonsectarian, and does not involve subscribing to their ideas. The Buddhist lay cult is here shown developing naturally out of pre-Buddhist practices.

BUDDHA'S TEACHINGS

For practicing Buddhists, references to "Dharma" or *Dhamma* in Pali, particularly as "the" Dharma, generally means the teachings of the Buddha, commonly known throughout the East as Buddha-Dharma. The status of Dharma is regarded variably by different Buddhist traditions. Some regard it as an ultimate truth, or as the font of all things which lies beyond the 'three realms' (Sanskrit: *tridhatu*) and the 'wheel of becoming' (Sanskrit: *bhavacakra*), somewhat like the Christian logos: this is known as Dharmakaya (Sanskrit).

Others, who regard the Buddha as simply an enlightened human being, see the Dharma as the essence of the '84,000 different aspects of the teaching' (Tibetan: *chos-sgo brgyad-khri bzhi strong*) that the Buddha gave to various types of people, based upon their individual propensities and capabilities. "Dharma" usually refers not only to the sayings of the Buddha, but also to the later traditions of interpretation and addition that the various schools of Buddhism have developed to help explain and to expand upon the Buddha's teachings. For others still, they see the Dharma as referring to the "truth" or the ultimate reality of "the way that things really are" (Tib. Cho).

The Dharma is one of the Three Jewels of Buddhism in which practitioners of Buddhism seek refuge, or that upon which one relies for his or her lasting happiness. The Three Jewels of Buddhism are the Buddha, meaning the mind's perfection of enlightenment, the Dharma, meaning the teachings and the methods of the Buddha, and the *Sangha*, meaning those awakened beings who provide guidance and support to followers of the Buddha.

QUALITIES OF BUDDHA DHARMA

The Teaching of the Buddha also has six supreme qualities:

1. Svakkhato (Pali) The Dharma is not a speculative philosophy, but is the Universal Law found through enlightenment and is preached precisely. Therefore it is Excellent in the beginning (Sîla - Moral principles), Excellent in the middle (*Samadhi* - Concentration) and Excellent in the end (Pañña - Wisdom).
2. Samditthiko (Pali) The Dharma is testable by practice and known by direct experience.
3. Akâliko (Pali) The Dharma is able to bestow timeless and immediate results here and now, for which there is no need to wait until the future or next existence.

4. Ehipassiko (Pali) The Dharma welcomes all beings to put it to the test and to experience it for themselves.
5. Opâneyiko (Pali) The Dharma is capable of being entered upon and therefore it is worthy to be followed as a part of one's life.
6. Paccattam veditabbo viññûnhi (Pali) The Dharma may be perfectly realized only by the noble disciples (Pali: *Ariyas*) who have matured and who have become enlightened in supreme wisdom.

Knowing these attributes, Buddhists hold that they will attain the greatest peace and happiness through the practice of their own Dharma. Each person is therefore fully responsible to engage in their own practice and commitment.

DHARMAS IN BUDDHIST PHENOMENOLOGY

Other uses include *dharma,* normally spelled with a small "d" (to differentiate), which refers to a *phenomenon* or *constituent factor* of human experience. This was gradually expanded into a classification of constituents of the entire material and mental world. Rejecting the substantial existence of permanent entities which are qualified by possibly changing qualities, Buddhist Abhidharma philosophy, which enumerated seventy-five dharmas, came to propound that these "constituent factors" are the only type of entity that truly exists.

This notion is of particular importance for the analysis of human experience: Rather than assuming that mental states inhere in a cognizing subject, or a soul-substance, Buddhist philosophers largely propose that mental states alone exist as "momentary elements of consciousness" and that a subjective perceiver is assumed.

One of the central tenets of Buddhism, is the denial of a separate permanent "I", and is outlined in the three marks of existence. The three signs:

1. Dukkha - Suffering (way to end) (Pali: Dukkha),
2. Anitya - Change/Impermanence (Pali: Anicca),

3. Anatman - No-I (Pali: Annatta).

At the heart of Buddhism, is the denial of an "I" (and hence the delusion) as a separate self-existing entity. Later, Buddhist philosophers like Nâgârjuna would question whether the dharmas (momentary elements of consciousness) truly have a separate existence of their own. (i.e., Do they exist apart from anything else?) Rejecting any inherent reality to the dharmas, he asked (rhetorically):

When all dharmas are empty, what is endless? What has an end?

What is endless and with an end? What is not endless and not with an end?

What is *it*? What is *other*? What is permanent? What is impermanent?

What is impermanent and permanent? What is neither?

Auspicious is the pacification of phenomenal metastasis, the pacification of all apprehending;

There is no dharma whatsoever taught by the Buddha to whomever, whenever, wherever.—Mûlamadhyamakakârikâ, nirvanânaparîksâ, 25:22-24

DHARMA AS RIGHTEOUSNESS

According to S. N. Goenka, teacher of Vipassana Meditation, the original meaning of dhamma is "dhareti ti dhamma", or "that which is contained". Dharma in the Buddhist scriptures has a variety of meanings, including "phenomenon" and "nature" or "characteristic". Dharma also means "mental contents," and is paired with citta, which means heart-mind.

The pairing is paralleled with the combining of kaya (body) and vedana (feelings or sensations which arise within the body but are experienced through the mind), in major sutras such as the Mahasatipatthana sutra. Dharma is also used to refer to the teachings of the Buddha, especially the discourses on the fundamental principles (such as the Four

Noble Truths and the Noble Eightfold Path), as opposed to the parables and to the poems.

What is called Buddhism in the west has been referred to in India (the teachings' place of origin) and the east generally for many centuries as buddha-dharma. This term has no sectarian connotations but simply means "Path of Awakening" and thus conforms to a universal understanding of dharma.

- "Dharma" usually refers inclusively not just to the sayings of the Buddha but to the later traditions of interpretation and addition that the various schools of Buddhism have developed to help explain and expand upon the Buddha's teachings. The 84,000 different teachings (the Kangyur/ bka.'gyur) that the Buddha gave to various types of people based on their needs. The teachings are expedient means of raising doubt in the hearer's own cherished beliefs and view of life; when doubt has opened the door to the truth, the teaching can be put aside.
- Alternately, "dharma" may be seen as an ultimate and transcendent truth which is utterly beyond worldly things, somewhat like the Christian logos, seeing the dharma as referring to the "truth" or ultimate reality or "the way things are".

The Dharma is one of the Three Jewels of Buddhism of which practitioners of Buddhism seek refuge in (what one relies on for his/her lasting happiness). The three jewels of Buddhism are the Buddha (mind's perfection of enlightenment), the Dharma (teachings and methods), and the *Sangha* (awakened beings who provide guidance and support).

THE BUDDHA'S DHARMA BODY

The quality of the Dharma (Law, truth) are the same as the qualities of the Buddha and forms his "truth body" or "Dhamma Kaya": In the Samyutta Nikaya, Vakkali Sutta, Buddha said to his disciple Vakkali that,

"Yo kho Vakkali dhammam passati so mam passati"

O Vakkali, whoever sees the Dhamma, sees me [the Buddha]

Another reference from the Agganna Sutta of the Digha Nikaya, says to his disciple Vasettha:

"Tathâgatassa h'etam Vasettha adivacanam Dhammakayo iti pi..."

O Vasettha! The Word of Dhammakaya is indeed the name of the Tathagata

QUALITIES OF BUDDHA DHARMA

The Teaching of the Buddha also has six supreme qualities:

1. Svâkkhâto (Sanskrit: Svâkhyâta "well proclaimed"). The Dhamma is not a speculative philosophy, but is the Universal Law found through enlightenment and is preached precisely. Therefore it is excellent in the beginning (sîla - Sanskrit úîla - moral principles), excellent in the middle (samâdhi - concentration) and excellent in the end (paññâ - Sanskrit prajñâ... Wisdom).
2. Sanditthiko (Sanskrit: Samdrstika "able to be examined"). The Dhamma can be tested by practice and therefore he who follows it will see the result by himself through his own experience.
3. Akâliko (Sanskrit: Akâlika "immediate"). The Dhamma is able to bestow timeless and immediate results here and now, for which there is no need to wait until the future or next existence.
4. Ehipassiko (Sanskrit: Ehipaœyika "which you can come and see" — from the phrase ehi, paœya "come, see!"). The Dhamma welcomes all beings to put it to the test and come see for themselves.
5. Opanayiko (Sanskrit: Avapranayika "leading one close to"). The Dhamma is capable of being entered upon and therefore it is worthy to be followed as a part of one's life. In the "Vishuddhimagga" this is also referred to as "Upanayanam."
6. Paccattam veditabbo viññûhi (Sanskrit: Pratyâtmam veditavyo vijñaih "To be personally known by the wise").

The Dhamma can be perfectly realized only by the noble disciples (Ariyas) who have matured and enlightened enough in supreme wisdom.

Knowing these attributes, Buddhists believe that they will attain the greatest peace and happiness through the practice of the Dhamma. Each person is therefore fully responsible for himself to put it in the real practice. Here the Buddha is compared to an experienced and skilful doctor, and the Dhamma to proper medicine.

However efficient the doctor or wonderful the medicine may be, the patients cannot be cured unless they take the medicine properly. So the practice of the Dhamma is the only way to attain the final deliverance of Nibbâna. These teachings ranged from understanding karma (Pâli: kamma) (cause and effect) and developing good impressions in one's mind, to reach full enlightenment by recognizing the nature of mind.

3

The Sangha

The *Sangha* and the development of Buddhism; the Buddhas first sermon; the beginnings of the Sangh; the First Council 483 BCE; the Second Council 383 BCE; the emergence of the Mahayana; the Third Council; the decline of Buddhism in India and its development elsewhere. Buddhists have always recognized the importance of community life, and over the centuries there has developed a distinctive symbiotic relationship between monks (and in some cases nuns) and the lay community. The relationship between the monastics and the laity has differed from place to place and from time to time, but throughout most of Buddhist history both groups have played an essential role in the process of constituting and reconstituting the Buddhist world.

Moreover, both the monastics and the laity have engaged in a variety of common and complementary religious practices that have expressed Buddhist orientations and values, structured Buddhist societies, and addressed the soteriological and practical concerns of individuals. The *sangha* is the assembly of Buddhist monks (and in some contexts nuns) that has, from the origins of Buddhism, authoritatively studied, taught, and preserved the teachings of the Buddha.

In their communities monastics have been responsible for providing an example of the ideal mode of Buddhist life, for teaching Buddhist principles and practices to the laity, for generating and participating in basic ritual activities, for offering "fields of merit" that enable lay members of the community to improve their spiritual condition, for providing protection against evil forces (particularly though not exclusively supernatural forces), and for maintaining a variety of other services that have varied over time and place.

In exchange for their contributions, the monastics have received veneration and support from the laity, who thereby earn merit, advance their own well-being, and contribute to the well-being of others (including, in many cases, the ancestors of the living). Besides serving as the centre of Buddhist learning, meditation, ritual activity, and teaching, the monastery offers the monk or nun an opportunity to live apart from worldly concerns, a situation that has usually been believed necessary or at least advisable in order to follow the path that leads most directly to release.

According to scholars of early Buddhism, at the time of the Buddha there were numerous mendicants in northeastern India who wandered and begged individually or in groups. They had forsaken the life of a householder and the involvement with worldly affairs that this entails in order to seek a pattern of belief and practice that would meaningfully explain life and offer salvation. When such a seeker met someone who seemed to offer such a salvific message, he would accept him as a teacher (guru) and wander with him. The situation of these mendicants is summed up in the greeting with which they met other religious wanderers.

This greeting asked, "Under whose guidance have you accepted religious mendicancy? Who is your master (*sattha*)? Whose *dhamma* is agreeable to you?" According to early Buddhist texts, the Buddha established an order of male monastics early on in his ministry and outlined the rules and procedures for governing their common life. These texts also report that later in his career he reluctantly agreed to a proposal made by his aunt Mahapajapati and supported by his favourite disciple, Ananda, to establish an order of nuns.

The Buddha then set down rules and procedures for the order of the nuns and for the relationship between the order of nuns and the order of monks. (In the discussion that follows, the emphasis will be on the order of monks.) The various mendicant groups interrupted their wanderings during the rainy season (*vassa*) from July through August. At this time they gathered at various rain retreats (*vassavasa*), usually situated near villages, where they would beg for their daily needs and continue their spiritual quest. The Buddha and his followers may well have been the first group to found such a yearly rain retreat.

After the Buddha's death his followers did not separate but continued to wander and enjoy the rain retreat together. In their retreats the Buddha's followers probably built their own huts and lived separately, but their sense of community with other Buddhists led them to gather at the time of the full and new moons to recite the *patimokkha,* a declaration of their steadfastness in observing the monastic discipline. This occasion, in which the laity also participated, was called the *Uposatha.*

Within several centuries of the Buddha's death, the *sangha* came to include two different monastic groups. One group, which retained the wandering mode of existence, has been a very creative force in Buddhist history and continues to play a role in contemporary Buddhism, particularly in Sri Lanka and Southeast Asia. The other, much larger group gave up the forest life and settled in permanent monastic settlements (*viharas*); it is the earliest truly cenobitic monastic group about which any knowledge exists.

There appear to be two major reasons for the change in the mode of living of most Buddhist monks. First, the Buddha's followers were able, through their common loyalty to the Buddha and his teachings, to build up a certain coherent organization. Second, as acts of piety, the laity gave gifts of land and raised buildings in which the followers of the Buddha might live permanently, assured of a supply of the staples of life and also able to fulfill the Buddha's directive to minister to the laity. In this manner small *viharas* were established in northeastern India and adjoining areas into which Buddhism spread.

Already in the period prior to the reign of King Asoka, the Buddhist monastic community had become a strong, widely dispersed religious force. The support of Asoka encouraged further expansion, and in the post-Asokan period the number, wealth, and influence of the monasteries increased. As Buddhism continued to develop, many kinds of monastic centres were established throughout India, several of which received lavish support from royal courts or from wealthy merchants, who were among the strongest supporters of Buddhism.

Among the most interesting centres were the magnificent cave monasteries-for example, at Ajanta and Ellora-which contain some of the greatest examples not only of Buddhist art but of Indian art more generally. Perhaps the most influential monasteries were the great university-like *mahaviharas* that developed somewhat later in northeastern India. In all Buddhist countries monasteries served as centres of teaching, learning, and outreach. Different types of monastic establishments developed in particular areas and in particular contexts. In several regions there were at least two types of institutions.

There were a few large public monasteries that usually functioned in greater or lesser accord with classical Buddhist norms. There were also many smaller monasteries, often located in rural areas that were much more loosely regulated. Often these were hereditary institutions in which the rights and privileges of the abbot were passed on to an adopted disciple. In areas where clerical marriage was practiced-for example, in medieval Sri Lanka, in certain Tibetan areas, and in post-Heian Japan-a tradition of blood inheritance developed.

The transformation of the *sangha* from a group of wandering mendicants, loosely bound together by their commitment to the Buddha and his teachings, to monks living closely together in a permanent monastery necessitated the development of rules and a degree of hierarchical organization. It appears that the earliest organization within

Indian monasteries was democratic in nature. This democratic character arose from two important historical factors. First, the Buddha did not, as was the custom among the teachers of his time, designate a human successor. Instead, the Buddha taught that each monk should strive to follow the path that he had preached.

This decision placed every monk on the same footing. There could be no absolute authority vested in one person, for the authority was the *dhamma* that the Buddha had taught. Second, the region in which Buddhism arose was noted for a system of tribal democracy, or republicanism that had existed in the past and was preserved by some groups during the Buddha's lifetime. Within this tradition each polity had an elected assembly that decided important issues.

This tradition, which was consonant with the antiauthoritarian nature of the Buddha's teaching, was adopted by the early *sangha*. When an issue arose, all the monks of the monastery assembled. The issue was put before the body of monks and discussed. If any solution was forthcoming, it had to be read three times, with silence signifying acceptance. If there was debate, a vote might be taken or the issue referred to committee or to arbitration by the elders of a neighbouring monastery. As the *sangha* developed, a certain division of labour and hierarchical administration was adopted. The abbot became the head of this administrative hierarchy and was vested with power over monastic affairs.

In many countries there are developed state-controlled hierarchies, which enabled kings and other political authorities to exert a significant amount of control over the monks and their activities. The antiauthoritarian character of Buddhism, however, continued to assert itself. In China, for instance, the abbot referred all important questions to the assembled monks, who had elected him their leader. Similarly, in Southeast Asian countries there has traditionally been a popular distaste for hierarchy, which makes it difficult to enforce rules in the numerous almost-independent monasteries.

As the Buddhist *sangha* developed, specific rules and rites were enacted that differ very little in Buddhist monasteries even today. The rules by which the monks are judged and the punishments that should be assessed are found in the *vinaya* texts (*vinaya* literally means "that which leads"). The *Vinaya Pitaka* of the Theravada canon contains precepts that were supposedly given by the Buddha as he judged a particular situation. While in many cases the Buddha's authorship may be doubted, the attempt is made to refer all authority to the Buddha and not to one of his disciples. The heart of the *vinaya* texts is the *patimokkha*, which became a list of monastic rules.

Ideally, the *patimokkha* is recited by the assembled monks every fortnight, with a pause after each one so that any monk who has transgressed this rule may confess and receive his punishment. While the number of rules in the *patimokkha* differs in the various schools, with 227, 250, and 253, respectively, in the Pali, Chinese, and Tibetan canons, the rules are essentially the same. The first part of the *patimokkha* deals with the four gravest sins, which necessarily lead to expulsion from the monastery. They are sexual intercourse, theft, murder, and exaggeration of one's miraculous powers. The other rules, in seven sections, deal with transgressions of a lesser nature, such as drinking or lying.

In the Theravada countries-Sri Lanka, Myanmar, Thailand, Cambodia, and Laos-the Buddhist monastic community is composed primarily of male monks and novices (the order of nuns died out in the Theravada world more than a millennium ago, and contemporary efforts to reestablish it have met with only minimal success), white-robed ascetics (including various types of male and female practitioners who remain outside the *sangha* but follow a more or less renunciatory mode of life), and laymen and laywomen.

In some Theravada countries, notably in mainland Southeast Asia, boys or young men were traditionally expected to join the monastery for a period of instruction and meditation. Thus, the majority of men in these areas were (and to a lesser extent still are, especially in Myanmar) directly involved with the monastic ethos. This practice has fostered a high degree of lay participation in monastic affairs. In the Mahayana and Vajrayana countries of China and Tibet, there was traditionally a stage of one year before the aspirant could become a novice.

This was a year of probation, during which the aspirant did not receive tonsure and remained subject to governmental taxation and service while receiving instructions and performing menial tasks within the monastery. At the end of this period, the aspirant had to pass a test, which included the recitation of part of a well-known sutra-the length depending upon whether the applicant was male or female-and a discussion of various doctrinal questions. In China usually only those who were of exceptional character or who were affiliated with the government progressed beyond the novice stage.

According to *vinaya* rules, entry into the *sangha* is an individual affair that depends on the wishes of the individual and his family. In some Buddhist countries, however, ordination was often under the control of the state, which conducted the examinations to determine entry or advancement in the *sangha*. In certain situations ordination could be obtained through the favour of high officials or through the purchase of an ordination certificate from the government. At times the government engaged in the selling of ordination certificates in order to fill its treasury. The life of a Buddhist monk originally involved wandering, poverty, begging, and strict sexual abstinence.

The monks were supposed to live only on alms, to wear clothes made from cloth taken from rubbish heaps, and to possess only three robes, one girdle, an alms bowl, a razor, a needle, and a water strainer for filtering insects from drinking water (so as not to kill or imbibe them). Most Buddhist schools still stress celibacy, though some groups, particularly in Tibet and Japan, have relaxed the monastic discipline, and some Vajrayana schools have allowed sexual intercourse as an esoteric ritual that contributes to the attainment of release. In all schools, however, begging has become merely a symbolic gesture used to teach humility or compassion or to raise funds for special purposes.

Also, the growth of large monasteries has often led to compromises on the rule of poverty. While the monk might technically give up his property before entering the monastery-though even this rule is sometimes relaxed-the community of monks might inherit wealth and receive lavish gifts of land. The acquisition of wealth has often led to the attainment of temporal power. This factor, in addition to the self-governing nature of Buddhist monasteries and the early Buddhist connection with Indian kingship, has influenced the interaction of the *sangha* and the state. Buddhism is sometimes inaccurately described as a purely monastic, otherworldly religion.

In the earliest phases of the tradition, the Buddha was pictured as a teacher who addressed not only renouncers but lay householders. Moreover, although he is not depicted in the early texts as a social reformer, the Buddha does address issues of social order and responsibility. Perhaps the most famous early text on this topic is the *Sigalovada Sutta,* which has been called the "householder's *vinaya.*" Throughout their history Buddhists have put forth varying forms of social ethics based on notions of karmic justice (the "law" that good deeds will be rewarded with happy results while evil deeds will entail suffering for the one who does them); the cultivation of virtues such as self-giving, compassion, and evenhandedness; and the fulfillment of responsibilities to parents, teachers, rulers, and so on.

Moreover, Buddhists have formulated various notions of cosmogony, cosmology, and soteriology that have provided legitimacy for the social hierarchies and political orders with which they have been associated. For the most part, Buddhism has played a conservative, moderating role in the social and political organization of various Asian societies, but the tradition has also given rise to more radical and revolutionary movements. Over the course of Buddhism's long history, the relationship between the Buddhist community and state authority has taken many forms.

The early Buddhist *sangha* in India appears to have been treated by Indian rulers as a self-governing unit not subject to their power unless it proved subversive or was threatened by internal or external disruption. Asoka, the king whose personal interest in Buddhism contributed to the religion's dramatic growth, appears to have been applying this policy of protection from disruption when he intervened in Buddhist monastic affairs to expel schismatics. He came to be remembered, however, as the Dharmaraja, the great king who protected and propagated the teachings of the Buddha.

In Theravada countries Asoka's image as a supporter and sponsor of the faith has traditionally been used to judge political authority. In general, Buddhism in Theravada countries has been either heavily favoured or officially recognized by the government. The *sangha*'s role in this interaction, at least ideally, has been to preserve the *dhamma* and to act as spiritual guide and model, revealing to the secular power the need for furthering the welfare of the people. While the *sangha* and the government are two separate structures, there has been some intertwining; monks (often from elite families) have commonly acted as governmental advisers, and kings-at least in Thailand-have occasionally spent some time in the monastery. Moreover, Buddhist monastic institutions have often served as a link between the rural peoples and the urban elites, helping to unify the various Theravada countries.

In China, Buddhism has been seen as a foreign religion, as a potential competitor with the state, and as a drain on national resources of men and wealth. These perceptions have led to sharp persecutions of Buddhism and to rules curbing its influence. Some of the rules attempted to limit the number of monks and to guarantee governmental influence in ordination through state examinations and the granting of ordination certificates. At other times, such as during the early centuries of the Tang dynasty (618–907), Buddhism was virtually a state religion. The government created a commissioner of religion to earn merit for the state by erecting temples, monasteries, and images in honour of the Buddha.

In Japan, Buddhism experienced similar fluctuations. From the 10th to the 13th century, monasteries gained great landed wealth and temporal power. They formed large armies of monks and mercenaries that took part in wars with rival religious groups and in struggles for temporal power. By the 14th century, however, their power had begun to wane. Under the Tokugawa regime in the 17th century, Buddhist institutions were virtually instruments of state power and administration.

Only in Tibet did Buddhists establish a theocratic polity that lasted for an extended period of time. Beginning in the 12th century, Tibetan monastic groups forged relationships with the powerful Mongol khans that often gave them control of governmental affairs. In the 17th century the Dge-lugs-pa school, working with the Mongols, established a monastic regime that was able to maintain almost continual control until the Chinese occupation in the 1950s.

During the premodern period the various Buddhist communities in Asia developed working relationships of one kind or another with the sociopolitical systems in their particular areas. As a result of Western colonial incursions, and especially after the establishment of new political ideologies and political systems during the 19th and 20th centuries, these older patterns of accommodation between Buddhism and state authority were seriously disrupted.

In many cases bitter conflicts resulted-for example, between Buddhists and colonial regimes in Sri Lanka and Myanmar, between Buddhists and the Meiji reformers in Japan, and between Buddhists and many different communist regimes. In some cases, as in Japan, these conflicts were resolved and new modes of accommodation established. In other cases, as in Tibet, strong tensions remained.

Many people, especially in the West, are drawn to Buddhism because they want to meditate. That is a healthy impulse-we invest so much effort in caring for our bodies, but usually very little effort in caring for our minds. And the Dharma does indeed present meditation as a crucial aspect of mental development. But it does not present meditation as sufficient in itself.

The way of life that the Buddha taught is generally understood to consist of eight components, known collectively as the Noble Eightfold Path. These components are named after the ideals embodied in them. Just to give you a sense of what the Path involves, here is a version of those names.

Perfect Vision

Perfect Emotion

Perfect Speech

Perfect Action

Perfect Livelihood

Perfect Effort

Perfect Awareness

Perfect Concentration

"Perfect" is the author's rendering of Sanskrit *samyaka* frequently translated as "right." *Sangha*rakshita offers several other possibilities-"whole," "integral," "complete"-but settles on "perfect."

Even if you have never seen this list before, it's probably evident that these categories must overlap or merge in various ways. The overlaps help to make the Path a coherent whole. They also have a reinforcing effect: Progress in one category facilitates progress in others. It may be less evident where meditation is to be found. One standard approach locates it in that final component, which is sometimes translated as "right meditation." (The Sanskrit term in question is *Samadhi.*)

But it might be more useful to construe the three final categories as all relevant to meditation, and the final one as more or less exclusively concerned with it. However that point is interpreted, it is clear that the Path involves far more than meditation. It should also be clear that the Path is intended to engage the entirety of one's life-that it is concerned, not just with what one perceives or thinks, but with what one does.

The Buddhist Path leads to wisdom and compassion, and both of these faculties seek to comprehend life as a whole. Buddhist practice is intended to develop two functions of the mind: Wisdom and compassion. "Wisdom" in this context is not primarily a matter of intellectual achievement, but a kind of direct awareness of things as they are. (Forgive the awkward formula-this experience is a very difficult subject to write about.) Within the human personality, wisdom and compassion are essential complements to each other; to pursue one of these qualities without the other is to risk a kind of mental deformity.

The pursuit of wisdom without compassion tends towards selfishness, complacency, and reluctance to act. The pursuit of compassion without wisdom invites confusion, anxiety, and misplaced effort. Wisdom and compassion complement each other because they share some essential qualities. Perhaps the most obvious similarity is that they are both "boundless," in the sense that a person seriously cultivating either faculty is likely to grow increasingly unwilling to recognize any limitation of it. The notion of "a little wisdom" or "a little compassion" is likely to seem increasingly absurd.

And in Buddhist practice, wisdom and compassion are both ways of coming to terms with what the Dharma portrays as basic features of existence: That the self, as we usually conceive of it, is a kind of mirage, that all things arise and pass away, and that all life is profoundly interdependent. As our awareness of this interdependence grows stronger, our capacity for empathy grows wider and deeper.

At some point in the course of this development, the serious student of Buddhism is liable to discover that it no longer makes sense to think of one's practice as purely a personal quest. One ceases to practice just for oneself-and that is when practice really begins. One can begin to practice for-and with-all beings.

All beings become the wisdom that practice seeks and expresses. All beings are inexhaustibly marvelous just as they are, without the perceptual confusion that our own appetites and fears project upon them. This is not some sort of utopian, Peaceable Kingdom experience. It's not a matter of "making friends" with pathogens, invasive alien species, or other organisms that humanity, with good reason, is attempting to eradicate or control. Instead, it's a way of experiencing people, trees, birds, fish, mosquitoes, diseases-all beings-as at once both themselves and as me rging within the entire, immense fabric of life, of living and dying, of existence itself.

And beyond that, it's a way of experiencing this fabric as it is constantly weaving and reweaving itself; and beyond even that, it's a way of seeing that there is no fabric apart from this weaving and reweaving. And beyond that too-trees are trees and mosquitoes are mosquitoes. We have arrived at Green Buddhism. Green Buddhism is merely an effort to act on this process, in a practical and systematic way, for the benefit of all the other species with which we share this world.

One final proposition:

Green Buddhism should not confuse gestures or symbols with practical action.

Buddhism, like other religions, has fostered the development of myriad ceremonies, great works of art, and other forms of expression that have immense spiritual value. Such spiritual expressions, Buddhist or otherwise, offer great comfort to billions of people. But the spiritual value of such things does not make them panaceas. If you have appendicitis, it may be a good idea to pray or chant, but it's an even better idea to call a doctor, and doing so won't diminish your spirituality.

It's a similar situation with spiritually-motivated environmental work. Traditional forms of religious practice may be crucial to the development of one's spiritual or environmental awareness, but when the time comes to act, it's important to do so in a way that will really be effective. That is why, in our view, religious environmental programs should hold themselves accountable to the same standards that apply to secular programs. Green spiritual effort should produce tangible, measurable benefits. It should make sense in terms of whatever criteria-ecological, social, political-are relevant to the efforts involved.

This type of accountability is a basic feature of the Earth *Sangha*'s environmental programs, and it has served both our programs and our volunteers very well. Our programs benefit because regular evaluation, in one form or another, allows us to learn relatively quickly what works and what does not. Our volunteers benefit because they gain direct access to the work itself, without any interpretative baggage, beyond what is necessary for understanding field procedures. We believe that this is one of the most useful things that we can do for our colleagues in the field: We want them to experience for themselves the challenges of working with the soil and water, and the plants and animals that make up our landscapes. There is nothing added or extraneous in this way of working. And that is what makes it effective.

In 1991, the Thai Buddhist monk Phrakhru Pitak Nanthakhun sponsored a tree ordination in Nan Province. The ritual-conducted by twenty northern Thai monks and attended by close to 200 villagers, district officials, and journalists-formally established and sanctified a protected community forest for ten adjoining villages. The hour-long ceremony included chanting, sanctification of water, and wrapping a monk's orange robes around the largest remaining tree in the forest. The ten village headmen drank the holy water to seal their pledge to protect the forest.

This ritual was one of numerous tree ordinations conducted by Buddhist monks in the 1990s in an effort to preserve the nation's rapidly depleting forest and protect people's livelihoods within it. "Environmentalist monks" (*phra nak anuraksa* in Thai) form a small percentage of the total number of monks in Thailand. Nevertheless, their actions are visible in Thai society. They tackle urgent and controversial issues, such as deforestation and the construction of large dams, using modified Buddhist rituals and an ecological interpretation of Buddhist teachings.

The effectiveness of environmentalist monks' projects remains unclear. Because these monks have only been active in Thailand over the past decade, not enough time has passed to assess projects aimed at stopping deforestation or cleaning polluted rivers. Their projects do not have sufficient scope to change what most environmentalists perceive as the destructive patterns of deforestation and growth-oriented economic and industrial development that have been dominant in Thailand since the 1960s.

Despite their small numbers and limited effectiveness, this group represents a case of people within a specific cultural setting who are implementing their own environmental concepts. They reinvent human relationships with nature in the face of what Arturo Escobar (1996) criticizes as the capitalization of nature worldwide.

Their environmental seminars and their relations with local people illustrate the processes through which this small group of monks challenges the dominant trend of "ecological capital". Despite a historical link between the Buddhist *Sangha* (the community of monks) and the Siamese state, these monks reject the state's definition of development and how it is implemented.

A high degree of environmental degradation has accompanied the government's growth and export-oriented development policies. The Thai forest has been cut down at one of the fastest rates in Asia. (According to official figures, forest cover in Thailand decreased from 72 per cent of the total land in 1938 to 53 per cent in 1961 and 29 per cent in 1985 [England 1996:60]. Most environmental non-government organizations [NGOs] estimate that less than 15 per cent of the country's total land area can be considered forest today.) Activist monks join a growing, popular environmental movement that questions the government's priorities and policies.

The contemporary development concept was first formulated in the mid-1800s when King Mongkut brought his kingdom into the global economy and restructured the Buddhist *Sangha* to legitimize the central government. Changing Thai governments have continued to use Buddhism to support their development agendas, especially since the 1960s. This process resulted in the rise of independent "development monks" in the 1970s and "environmental monks" in the late 1980s who challenged the government's concept of development, Buddhism's legitimation of it, and the suffering that they believed it caused the Thai people.

Ironically, engaged Buddhism in Thailand emerged out of the same political-economic situation and close relationship with the state that it seeks to change. Engaged Buddhism and Buddhist environmentalism are significant less because of their use of Buddhist principles than because they incorporate people's culture, values, and concerns for their livelihood and an understanding of historical, social, and political context into a creative approach to dealing with social problems.

DEVELOPMENT IN THAILAND

Siam, as Thailand was formerly known, remained a small, relatively isolated kingdom until 1855 when the Bowring Treaty with Great Britain formally brought it into the emerging global economy. Even as the Siamese attempted to limit foreign access to their markets, the colonial economies being developed in neighboring countries forced them to rethink their relations with the international community and begin to modernize. Initiated by King Mongkut, Siam introduced modern scientific concepts, economic practices, and education.

Mongkut also instituted religious reform in the 1830s and 1840s, and established the Thammayut Order of the *Sangha*. Similar to the modernization of other aspects of Thai society that Mongkut initiated, he rationalized the religion, aiming to eliminate practices that he felt were too ritualistic, metaphysical, or overly influenced by local or regional culture.

Mongkut attempted to develop an interpretation of Buddhism consistent with Western science and learning and this attempt marked the beginning of a fundamental epistemological shift in doctrinal Thai Buddhism. The theoretical shift, which continues to have significant religious implications today, involved the rejection of the layered or hierarchical notion of truth which underlay traditional Buddhist teachings and its replacement with the notion of a single, universal, and all-encompassing truth.

Mongkut linked the *Sangha* hierarchy with the absolute monarchy based in Bangkok, using it to legitimize the central government and weaken the influence of regional forms of religion and the power of regional political leaders. The legitimizing role that the *Sangha* played toward the state was strengthened as Bangkok expanded its control to the peripheral regions, using wandering forest monks to forge relations with remote rural peoples. During the modernization period, Siam-renamed Thailand in 1932-established the three-fold concept of religion, monarchy, and nation, formalizing the connection between religion and state even further.

Three *Sangha* Acts enacted by the Thai government in 1902, 1941 and 1962 brought the *Sangha* formally under the government's control. Each of these Acts created a state-imposed organizational structure for the *Sangha* that paralleled the current forms of government: in 1902, Siam was still a monarchy, and the hierarchical, centralized *Sangha* was headed by a Supreme Patriarch; in 1941, a decentralized *Sangha* structure was established that paralleled the democratic, constitutional monarchy in place at the time; in 1962, a top-down structure was reintroduced to match the autocratic government of Field Marshall Sarit Thanarat.

Underlying the Acts, especially that of 1962, was an effort to garner support not only for the current government, but to legitimize its development policies as well. The 1962 Act, in particular, aimed to use the *Sangha* to foster Prime Minister Sarit Thanarat's development agenda. After coming to power through a coup in 1958, Sarit aggressively pushed Thailand into an intensive development policy. Based on a Western model, Sarit promoted agricultural intensification and expansion toward an export-oriented, industrial economy.

He encouraged a shift toward cash-cropping, bringing more forest land under cultivation, thus "civilizing" the wild forest and making it useful for humans. He also drew on traditional cultural values to promote his development agenda. Yoneo Ishii comments that Sarit thought that national integration must be strengthened to realise national development. To attain this goal he planned to start with fostering the people's sentiment for national integration through the enhancement of traditional values as represented by the monarchy and Buddhism.

Using the concept of a single, absolute truth and a centralized *Sangha* organization, Sarit incorporated Buddhism into his development campaign through community development and missionary programs involving monks. These programs included *thammathud,* which sent monks to missionize in politically sensitive and economically poor border provinces, *thammacarik,* through which monks worked with the Department of Public Welfare among minority hill peoples to convert them from animism and to develop them, as well as community development programs sponsored by the two national Buddhist universities.

Their aim was to strengthen the sense of national identity of peripheral peoples through Buddhism. These programs were-and are still today-supported and overseen by the government rather than the *Sangha*. Governments following Sarit's have continued his aggressive industrial and export-oriented development and agricultural intensification policies.

The results have been mixed: Thailand's growth until the economic crisis of 1997 was phenomenal, but the rate of environmental degradation, especially forest loss and pollution levels were among the highest in Asia. The gap between rich and poor widened and consumerism spread and symbolized by the growth of malls and McDonald's restaurants. Rural people's quality of life deteriorated as they moved from subsistence to market farming or left the countryside to seek work in urban factories. Through the use of a national, centralized concept of Buddhism, local culture and regional diversity were devalued.

DEVELOPMENT MONKS

Not all members of the *Sangha* agreed with either the government's development agenda or the involvement of monks in it. Beginning in the early 1970s, a handful of monks began independent rural development projects based on their interpretations of Buddhist teachings and in opposition to the capitalism promoted by the government. Of particular concern was the impact of the government's rapid development program on rural people's lives, and because of the government's emphasis on Buddhism as a form of nationalism, the erosion of traditional local Buddhist values.

These monks feared the effects of growing consumerism and the dependence of farmers on outside markets. Working in specific villages and addressing localized concerns and problems, these self-proclaimed "development monks" (*phra nak phatthana*) began conducting alternative development projects. One of the first development monks, Phra Dhammadilok, (formerly Phra Thepkavi) formed his own NGO, the Foundation for Education and Development of Rural Areas (FEDRA), in 1974 just outside of Chiang Mai city in Northern Thailand (Darlington 1990). He realized that if people are hungry, cold, and sick, they will not and cannot devote their energy toward religious ends.

Similarly, without spiritual development and commitment, they cannot overcome material suffering. FEDRA was established with the goal of developing spirituality and economics simultaneously. The organization has four major objectives: 1) to support agriculture; 2) to encourage education (specifically that which is appropriate for the rural occupation of the farmers); 3) to promote religion; and 4) to develop local areas. "Local areas" means the people, land, institutions, traditions, and cultures of the rural Northern Thai.

FEDRA's projects, located in over thirty-five villages today, include rice banks, buffalo banks (which provide buffaloes for poor farmers to plow their fields), credit unions, small revolving funds for agricultural development initiatives, integrated agriculture projects, and training for rural women in traditional handicrafts and sewing to enable them to supplement their agricultural incomes. Unlike most government programs, the projects of Phra Dhammadilok and other development monks are aimed at local, rather than national or regional, development. They respond to immediate needs identified by the rural peoples themselves.

Most of the development monks are from the areas in which they work, making them aware of the problems that rapid economic change has brought to rural people. They initiate projects designed for a specific location and problem using local cultural concepts and beliefs rather than pulling people into a national agenda that often ignores their needs and wants. The emergence and growth of development monks paralleled and accompanied the rise of NGOs engaged in alternative development. NGOs since the 1970s have become a major social opposition movement within Thai society. Both secular NGOs and development monks emerged because of concern over the negative impacts of government development policies toward Thai society, culture, and environment. Together they have fostered the rise of a national environmental movement.

RISE OF THE ENVIRONMENTAL MOVEMENT

While development monks worked on a local level, the environmental movement grew on a national level in response to the government's economic development agenda. Many of the NGOs that were engaged in a search for alternative forms of development moved into environmental activism because of their concerns about the rate of environmental destruction and degradation caused by the policies of the central government.

The causes for environmental degradation in Thailand are numerous, multifaceted, and virtually impossible to verify, but the coincidence of the nation's rapid economic growth from the 1960s until the mid-1990s and its high rate of forest loss and environmental problems during the same period fuel fierce debate. The government, supported by international organizations such as the World Bank, argues that environmental destruction is primarily due to poverty, making economic growth imperative to solving environmental problems. Environmentalists, on the other hand, point to the inequalities underlying the government's development agenda as the root of much of the country's poverty.

The government's policies, they argue, further promote destruction of the forest by encouraging agricultural intensification and capital growth through the exploitation of natural resources. The arguments are complex and beyond the scope of this paper, but it are critical to note the range of positions surrounding environmental issues, even within the environmental movement. The case of forest reserves and national parks illustrates the complexity of environmentalism in Thailand. Forests represent a major natural resource for the nation. Thailand invested heavily in logging until a ban was passed in 1989 after 300 people died in floods caused by deforestation and erosion.

Debates still rage concerning the best way to manage the country's forests and the role of local people. The creation of national parks and forest reserves points to an environmental sensitivity on the part of the government. Few of the parks have been well managed, however. No one agrees, even within the environmental movement, on the best way to manage the forest reserves and parks. On one side, local peoples living within the forests are blamed for destructive agricultural practices such as the slash-and-burn method. Advocates of this perspective argue that to preserve the remaining forest land these people should be moved out of the forest and trained in more environmentally-friendly methods.

Others argue that it is the local people who can best look after the forest because their livelihoods depend on the natural resources that they contain. Therefore, rather than moving them out and allowing illegal loggers, hunters, and developers to take advantage of the changes, forest dwellers should be granted titles to the land that they have used for generations. Environmentalist monks are also caught up in this debate. The majority takes the position that local forest dwellers will best protect the forest. A few others argue strongly that people must be removed from forests, especially watersheds, if there is to be any chance of protecting the remaining forested land.

Thai environmentalism cannot be simplified into a two-sided debate. It entails multiple perspectives that are grounded, according to Philip Hirsch (1996), in a variety of material and ideological bases. As seen in the debate over forests, "environmentalism in Thailand needs to be seen as a multi-faceted discourse that deals with key social, economic and political issues, including questions of control over resources by empowered and disempowered groups" (1996:15–16). The environmental movement is composed of both a growing middle class with the time, resources, and influences to engage in environmental debates and rural farmers whose livelihoods depend on a healthy environment.

Many middle-class Thais were educated abroad and therefore tend to approach these issues informed by a Northern concept of environmentalism. They see the need to protect and preserve nature from human impact. Most farmers see themselves as caretakers intimately familiar with and dependent upon a natural environment that includes people as part of a whole ecological system. Activist monks often use the latter argument as an example of the Buddhist concept of dependent origination, showing the interdependence of all things. Even within the environmental movement, with its diverse interpretations supporting a wide range of economic and ideological interests, the influence of the concept of environmentalism in Thai society cannot be denied. NGOs carry significant weight within environmental discourse and influence government policy.

Crucial environmental legislation was enacted due to NGO activism and its popular support. For example, environmentalists won a major case in 1988 when the government decided to shelve the Nam Choen Dam in Kanchanaburi Province in response to protests by a diverse "coalition of local groups, farmers, journalists, Buddhist monks, students and foreign environmentalists". This event, early in the environmental movement, demonstrated its potential, even though several other controversial dams have since been built.

EMERGENCE OF ENVIRONMENTALIST MONKS

It is within the context of debates over development and the rise of a diverse yet influential environmental movement that the self-proclaimed environmentalist monks emerged. Just as the environmental movement in Thailand grew out of the concerns of the NGOs about the ecological impact of government development policies and global ecological capitalism, the work of environmentalist monks evolved from that of independent development monks with concerns about local people's lives and spirituality. The first case in which Buddhist monks took an environmental position *as monks* involved the 1985 proposal to build a cable car up Doi Suthep mountain and through Doi Suthep-Pui National Park in Chiang Mai to promote tourism and economic development. Chayant describes the importance of the site for Northern Thai Buddhists:

> Doi Suthep is a mountain lying at the outskirts of the town of Chiang Mai, named for a seventh-century Lawa chieftain who converted to Buddhism, became a monk, and retreated from the world to the mountain which now bears his name. It is the location of an important Buddhist monastery, Wat Pra That, which houses a relic of the Buddha. Local people revere the mountain temple as a destination of spiritual significance for Buddhists. Since the construction of the temple in the fourteenth century, Doi Suthep has been an important pilgrimage site. Reflecting the emerging environmental movement as a whole, opposition to the cable car project included students, people's organizations, social action groups, local media, and the general public of the city.

Buddhist monks joined the protests as the cause gained publicity, and the full ecological and cultural impacts of building the cable car became apparent. Concerns were raised over the deforestation of the mountainside, especially in a national park that contained diverse plant, bird, and animal species. Arguments focused on environmental conservation versus economic development, but the motivation of the monks involved was mostly framed in terms of concepts of sanctity and the threat to a sacred Buddhist heritage site. One monk in particular, Phra Phothirangsi, district head of the *Sangha* for the city of Chiang Mai, took a leading role in the fight against the cable car.

He articulated a link between Buddhism and preserving trees and the forest beyond the immediate religious concern for a pilgrimage site. He argued that Buddhism and the forest cannot be separated. The cable-car case was the first time that Buddhist monks concerned about development incorporated environmental concerns in their actions. It is not typical of the kinds of actions in which environmentalist monks engage, however, because their fears involved the threat to a sacred Buddhist site as much as to Doi Suthep's ecosystem. Nevertheless, it was the first time that Thai monks articulated the relationship between Buddhism and the natural environment as a motivation for social and political activism.

They responded to a local social and historical situation as much as to an ecological issue; the threat to the sacred sites of Doi Suthep and Wat Pra That should not be underestimated as a powerful motivation for monks to move into political activism. As a result of this initial action, the Thai public was less surprised by other monks' more explicit environmental actions that followed. Environmentalist monks cannot be described as forming a coherent social movement, although the potential for effecting social change clearly exists within their actions.

Many of the monks engaged in environmental projects participate in an informal network that periodically brings them together to share their activities, concerns, obstacles, and successes and generate new ideas. It is through these Buddhist environmental seminars, sponsored by NGOs from five to ten times a year and involving from twenty to two hundred monk participants at a time that a new concept of human relations with nature and human responsibility toward nature is being constructed. Despite the importance of the dialogue and exchange of ideas that take place at these seminars, the real construction of knowledge occurs through the interaction between monks and villagers as they implement their ecological projects within local environments and informed by local histories.

The new social relations forged between monks and villagers, local officials and businessmen are as important as the localized ecological conservation efforts enacted. The work of two monks in Nan Province, northern Thailand, illustrates the process and the potential of the knowledge created by environmentalist monks. The first monk is Phrakhru Pitak Nanthakhun. He was born and raised in the village of Giew Muang, deep in the mountainous forest north of Nan City. His introduction to both environmental concerns and Buddhism arose out of an incident that occurred when he was a child. Phrakhru Pitak witnessed his father shoot a mother monkey while hunting. Its baby clung to the mother's body, allowing itself to be captured.

For three days, it cried from its cage, and when the boy finally released it, it went, still crying, straight to the skin of its mother hanging out to dry. This experience contributed not only to Phrakhru Pitak's later conservation work, but also was part of the reason that he ordained as a novice and has remained in the *Sangha* for almost 30 years. He realized that the teachings of the Buddha could help prevent such human-induced suffering. Growing out of his childhood experience with the baby monkey, Phrakhru Pitak incorporated a message of the environmental responsibility of humans into his teachings. The urgency of preaching an environmental ethic became clearer to him as he witnessed the continual deforestation of the mountainous province.

This was caused by logging concessions, illegal logging, slash-and-burn agriculture, overuse of the land by villagers, and the introduction of cash cropping. In the late 1980s, Phrakhru Pitak realized that preaching alone was not enough, that he needed to become actively engaged in conservation work. He visited Phrakhru Manas of Phayao Province, the monk generally credited with first performing tree ordinations to raise awareness of the value of the forests. Symbolically ordaining large trees in an endangered forest by wrapping monks' orange robes around them serves several purposes.

First, the action draws attention to the threat of deforestation. Second, the ritual provides the opportunity for the ecology monks and the laity who work with them (predominantly non-government environmentalists and development agents) to teach about the impact of environmental destruction and the value and means of conserving nature. Finally, the monks use the ritual to teach the *Dhamma* and to stress its relevance in a rapidly changing world. After visiting Phrakhru Manas, Phrakhru Pitak returned to Nan and began actively teaching villagers about environmental conservation, presenting slide shows, and holding discussions with people about the problems that they face due to deforestation.

In 1990, he helped his home village formally establish a community forest encompassing about 400 acres of land. The community forest was officially consecrated, and the villagers' commitment to preserving it was marked by the ordination of the largest remaining tree. Letters were sent to the surrounding villages announcing the creation of the protected area and making clear that it was forbidden to cut trees or hunt within it. The villagers also performed a ceremony requesting the local tutelary spirit to help them protect the forest and its wildlife. Phrakhru Pitak's work is not limited to his home village, but instead is constantly being expanded.

Since 1990, he has sponsored several tree ordinations and *phâ pâ* ceremonies, which are traditionally used to give "forest robes" to monks, but in these cases they include giving seedlings for reforestation. Lay people make religious merit through their donations and participation. In May 1993, an adapted traditional ceremony was held to preserve and lengthen the life of the Nan River in conjunction with a seminar to highlight the problems of desiccation and pollution that the province faces. A fish sanctuary was established at the site of the ceremony as well. By 1999, over thirty-nine community forests and 100 fish sanctuaries had been established by Phrakhru Pitak's NGO, the We Love Nan Province Foundation.

Phrakhru Pitak emphasizes basic Buddhist principles such as dependent origination and an interpretation of the Buddha's life that highlights a close relationship with the forest. His work is significant less because it incorporates Buddhism with ecological conservation principles than because he works closely with local villagers to identify and develop ways of dealing with the problems that they face. Phrakhru Pitak also encourages sustainable development practices such as integrated agriculture and growing food for subsistence rather than for sale.

Villagers are willing to try his approaches because of their respect for him as a monk and their awareness of his concern for their well-being. He is outspoken in his criticism of government-sponsored economic development promoting cash crops and the use of chemical fertilizers. Although Phrakhru Pitak has become famous and his NGO has grown to work in several villages and on multiple conservation projects, his work is still based in the specific environmental context of Nan Province. He has also inspired several other environmental projects, some sponsored by monks, others by lay people in their own villages.

The case of Phra Somkit represents the second example of an environmentalist monk engaged in the construction of new knowledge. Phra Somkit, unlike Phrakhru Pitak, only works in his home village. Similarly concerned with deforestation around his village, Phra Somkit began in the early 1990s to protect the village's forest. He went *bindabat* for forest, which is traditionally the practice of going on alms rounds providing lay people with the opportunity to make merit through giving food to monks. Phra Somkit's innovation entailed offering villagers the opportunity to make merit by donating land to the village temple. His father was the first to make an offering, presenting approximately an acre of hilly land that had been denuded through intensive cultivation of corn as a cash crop.

As a means to protect the forest, Phra Somkit began a model integrated-agriculture farm on land belonging to his temple. With the help of his younger brother, he maintains two fish ponds, raises free range chickens, and plants natural rice plots behind the temple. In the chaotic garden, pigs feed among numerous varieties of fruit trees. (Phra Somkit does not kill the fish, chickens, or pigs, raising them only to show villagers integrated agricultural methods.) He uses no chemical fertilizers, pesticides, or herbicides to demonstrate the benefits of natural farming to the villagers. On the land donated by his father, Phra Somkit has allowed the forest to regenerate naturally. In the almost ten years since the original gift, the forest has again grown dense.

When I visited him in October 1999, Phra Somkit told me that he had counted close to 100 separate species of plants in the area. A steady train of visitors come to see Phra Somkit's natural farm. In 1999, he received more than 1000 people from both Thailand and abroad. In September, ten British students spent one week volunteering on the farm to learn about integrated agriculture and sustainable development. Even more important is Phra Somkit's claim that all but about ten of the more than 100 families in the village have begun to implement some form of integrated agriculture.

Phra Somkit strongly believes in the importance of education in the protection of the natural environment. Using the mountainous terrain surrounding the village, he regularly takes children on ecology meditation walks. He works with them to consider the value of the plants and wildlife with which they share their environment. His belief is that through teaching children about human responsibility toward nature, they will take their lessons home and teach their parents. Phra Somkit undertakes all this work as part of what he perceives as his own responsibility as a Buddhist monk.

Both Phra Somkit and Phrakhru Pitak illustrate ways in which environmentalist monks respond to changing national, regional, and global agendas concerning development and the environment within local contexts. Their motivation comes from witnessing environmental degradation and the suffering that it creates. Actively seeking out the causes of this suffering has led them to redefine the underlying concepts of development and progress. Their awareness has led them to reexamine Buddhist teachings to support their work rather than follow any inherent ecological principles within the scriptures.

As Buddhists have done since the Buddha's time, they adapt their interpretations and practices of the religion to fit a changing sociopolitical-and natural-environment, in this case, a result of modernization. Their work is an example of the concept of environmental imaginary formulated by Peet and Watts (1996), which they describe as follows:

> There is environmental imaginary, or rather whole complexes of imaginaries, with which people think, discuss, and contend threats to their livelihoods. Notions like 'environmental imaginary,' which draw on the Marxist conception of consciousness, poststructural ideas about imagination and discourse, and, dare we add, environmental determinism from early-modern geography, open political ecology to considerations so different that we propose a new term to describe them-liberation ecology.

The intention is to raise the emancipatory potential of environmental ideas and to engage directly with the larger landscape of debates over modernity, its institutions, and its knowledges. While environmentalist monks do not form a united, coherent movement, the collective implication of their work illustrates the concept of liberation ecology described by Peet and Watts.

Their emergence within a particular historical, political, economic, and environmental context enables them to reassess Buddhism to fit that context and engage in debates over modernity and one of its primary institutions: development. They demonstrate a willingness to confront the traditional mutual support of the *Sangha* hierarchy and the state-a relationship that was itself a product of modernization.

The impact of their individual projects may be impossible to assess, but the potential of their activism to challenge Thai Buddhists to rethink their religion, their society, and their place in both the political and the natural world cannot be denied.

4

Sharing Christ with Buddhists

When sharing your faith with a Buddhist, remember that there are many different branches of Buddhism. While they all share many of the same core beliefs, they can vary greatly in other beliefs and some may involve more animistic superstitions than others. The Buddha taught that speculation about spiritual beings hinders one from achieving spiritual enlightenment; however, many Buddhist groups are very concerned with appeasing evil spirits and are very much enslaved by spiritual bondage. Though the different sects within Buddhism may differ in beliefs, all of their beliefs conflict in every way with the teachings of Christ. Below are some tips to keep in mind when sharing the Bible and the message of Christ with Buddhists.

1. Certain religious terms or phrases that you might use while witnessing to a Buddhist may have a completely different meaning to a person of a different heritage, culture, or belief system. For example, you wouldn't want to suggest to a Buddhist without much explanation that they should accept Christ and be 'born again'. To the Buddhist, being born again equals a failure. Buddhism teaches that through a cycle of rebirths you can reach Nirvana, therefore being born again may confuse them and give them a negative view of what accepting Christ means. You might use the term 'new birth'. Explain to them that by accepting Christ we are born as a new person

spiritually and are saved eternally. It isn't a physical rebirth, but a spiritual one.

2. Also, be careful when explaining that we are saved through grace. The Buddhist has been taught that you must work for anything good. They feel to attain something as desired as nirvana, one must practice meditation, observe the required rituals, live a life free from wrong desires and actions, and perform many other traditions and works. The idea that salvation is a free gift will seem very foreign to them and perhaps too simplistic and illogical. It will take time for them to understand God's love and forgiveness, and to accept their own inability to resist sin. Explain that salvation is not a gift handed out to anyone, there is an action on the part of the seeker, but the value of the gift is found in God's love for us. Spend a lot of time reading the Bible with them to help them understand this concept.
3. When explaining Christ's crucifixion and the role it plays in salvation, don't be surprised if Buddhists find this idea abhorrent. They may ask "How can an all-powerful God allow himself to be killed in such a humiliating way?" There may also be a cultural barrier if the person you're speaking with is of Japanese descent. To them, Jesus' death on the cross possesses none of the qualities they admire in their society, such as serenity, strength, and honor. Point out to them that Christ is a living God and He conquered death. His death paid the price for our sins. Christ died for us because He loves and cares for us. Only a God who has suffered as He had can identify with our inner torments; only a God who really cares for us would allow himself to be so cruelly afflicted; and only a God who truly is God could rise from the dead and give eternal life to those who follow Him. Paul prophesied that some would stumble over the cross in Galatians 5:11. We are also instructed not to be ashamed of it.
4. Buddhists do not believe in heaven or in an eternity anywhere for that matter. They believe that by following the teaching of Buddhism strictly and leading a perfect

life they will escape a cycle of rebirths and cease to exist. This end to the soul is called Nirvana. It might seem hard to believe that anyone would look forward to a gift of nothing, but it's important to understand that family traditions, an attachment to earthly pursuits and worldly pleasures, and a strong disbelief in God can blind them to how much better the hope Christ gives us is. Use your personal experiences and your own life as an example of the hope they can have. But, also keep in mind many Buddhists will look at Christians who are wrapped up in worldly things as an example of Christianity and they may not understand how people so focused on their earthly lives could really believe in a better place. Explain to them that some people have fallen short, while others are true to God's calling, but all who repent and seek God are forgiven. We have a loving God.

5. When witnessing to a Buddhist, be prepared for spiritual warfare! We can always expect to be attacked when we're sharing our faith. Satan never wants to see us succeed. But, spiritual warfare may be especially intense in this case because Buddhists participate in idol worship, the veneration of the spirits of deceased ancestors, and ceremonial rituals for the purpose of appeasing evil spirits. If they are actively interacting with evil spirits, we can expect to be attacked. As Christians, we need not fear evil. Explain to the Buddhist that we don't need to appease evil spirits because we have power over them through Christ. Jesus already won that battle, and we can resist them, and cast them out as Christ did. Use examples from the Gospels of Jesus and His disciples doing just this. I John 4:4 "You, dear children, are from God and have overcome them (evil spirits), because the one who is in you is greater than the one who is in the world."

6. Most importantly, love them. You have an opportunity to share with them the greatest gift they could ever receive, a relationship with Jesus Christ. Share the love of Christ with them in what you say and how you treat them. They have been deceived and they need your help.

In Deuteronomy 10:19 God instructed the Jews saying, "And you are to love those who are aliens, for you yourselves were aliens in Egypt." We should also love those who are different from us while not being afraid or ashamed to share the hope that is within us.

There has been much speculation regarding a possible connection between both the Buddha and the Christ, and between Buddhism and Christianity. Buddhism is usually assumed to have originated about 500 years before the Apostolic Age and the origins of Christianity. Scholars have explored connections between Buddhism and Christianity. Elaine Pagels, professor of religion at Princeton University, believes that some of the early Christian teachings show similarities to Buddhism. According to Pagels, texts like the Gospel of Thomas "may have in fact been influenced by a well-established Buddhist tradition".

Author Godfrey Higgins claims in several of his books, that after Asoka's subtle mandate of Buddhist worship, the Brahmins soon chased the Buddhists out of India where they established themselves with the European outposts of Asoka's missionaries. During the life of Jesus Christ and the period in which texts like the Gospel of Thomas were composed, Buddhist missionaries lived in Alexandria, Egypt. Historians believe that in the fourth century, Christian monasticism developed in Egypt, and it emerged with a corresponding structure comparable to the Buddhist monasticism of its time and place.

In the thirteenth century, international travelers, such as Giovanni de Piano Carpini and William of Ruysbroeck, sent back reports of Buddhism as a religion whose scriptures, doctrine, saints, monastic life, meditation practices, and rituals were comparable to those of Christianity. When European Christians made more direct contact with Buddhism in the early 16th century many Catholic missionaries (f.e. Francis Xavier) sent home idyllic accounts of Buddhism. At the same time, however, Portuguese colonizers of Sri Lanka confiscated Buddhist properties across the country, with the full cooperation of the Christian missionaries.

This repression of Buddhism in Sri Lanka continued during the rule of subsequently the Dutch and the English. Portuguese historian Diego De Conto reminded the Vatican that their Christian Saint Josaephat was actually the Buddha. With the arrival of Sanskrit studies in European universities in the late eighteenth century, and the subsequent availability of Buddhist texts, a discussion began of a proper encounter with Buddhism. The esteem for its teachings and practices grew, and at the end of the 19th century the first Westerners converted to Buddhism, and in the beginning of the 20th century the first westerners entered the Buddhist monastic life.

In the 20th century Christian monastics such as Thomas Merton, Wayne Teasdale, David Steindl-Rast and Karen Armstrong, and Buddhist monastics such as Ajahn Buddhadasa, Thich Nhat Hanh and the Dalai Lama have put energy into Buddhist/Christian dialogue. They each see in the otherwise disparate teachings of Jesus and the Buddha a basic commonality of insight and purpose which offers the possibility of profound remedy to an ailing world. The historian of world culture Arnold Toynbee has speculated that in centuries to come the encounter between Christianity and Buddhism may come to be seen as the momentous event of the 20th century.

BUDDHIST CULTURE AND PRE-CHRISTIAN GREECE

By the time of Jesus, the teachings of the Buddha had already spread through much of India and penetrated into Sri Lanka, Central Asia and China. They display certain similarities to Christian moral precepts of more than five centuries later; the sanctity of life, compassion for others, rejection of violence, confession and emphasis on charity and the practice of virtue. Will Durant, noting that the Emperor Ashoka sent missionaries, not only to elsewhere in India and to Sri Lanka, but to Syria, Egypt and Greece, speculated by Will Durant in the 1930s that they may have helped prepare the ground for Christian teaching.

Ashoka ascended the throne of India around 270 B.C.E. After his conversion to Buddhism he dispatched missionaries to the four points of the compass. Archeological finds indicate these missions had been "favorably received" in lands to the West. Ptolemy II Philadelphus, one of the monarchs Ashoka mentions in his edicts, is recorded by Pliny the Elder as having sent an ambassador named Dionysius to the Mauryan court at Pataliputra: "India has been treated of by several other Greek writers who resided at the courts of Indian kings, such, for instance, as Megasthenes, and by Dionysius, who was sent thither by Philadelphus, expressly for the purpose: all of whom have enlarged upon the power and vast resources of these nations."

The role of Greek Buddhist monks in the development of the Buddhist faith under the patronage of emperor Ashoka around 260 BCE, and then during the reign of Menander is described in the Mahavamsa, an important non-canonical Theravada Buddhist historical text compiled in Sri Lanka in the 6th century CE, in the Pali language. The *Mahavamsa* (Pali: "Great Chronicle") covers the history of Buddhism from the 6th century BCE to the 4th century CE. It was written in the 6th century CE by the monk Mahanama, brother of the Sri Lankan King Dhatusena, and heavily relied on the *Dipavamsa,* written five centuries earlier.

Emperor Ashoka convened the third Buddhist council around 250 BCE at Pataliputra (today's Patna). It was held by the monk Moggaliputta. The Pali canon (Tipitaka, or Tripitaka in Sanskrit, lit. the "Three Baskets"), which are the texts of reference of traditional Buddhism and considered to be directly transmitted from the Buddha, was formalized at that time. They consist of the doctrine (the Sutra Pitaka), the monastic discipline (Vinaya Pitaka) and an additional new body of subtle philosophy (the Abhidharma Pitaka).

Another objective of the council was to reconcile the different schools of Buddhism, and to purify the Buddhist movement, particularly from opportunistic factions which had been attracted by the royal patronage. Finally, the council also reported on the proselytizing efforts of Emperor Ashoka, who sought to expand the Buddhist faith throughout Asia and as far as the Mediterranean. The contemporary stone inscriptions of the Edicts of Ashoka also relate this activity in detail. Following these efforts, the Buddhist faith seems to have expanded among Greek communities under the rule of Ashoka, and tens of thousands were converted. About 50 years laters, the Greco-Bactrians invaded northern India as far as Pataliputra and founded the Indo-Greek Kingdom.

Buddhism flourished under the Indo-Greek kings, and it has been suggested that their invasion of India was intended to show their support for the Mauryan empire, and to protect the Buddhist faith from the religious persecutions of the new dynasty of the Sungas (185–73 BCE). Greek Buddhist monks continued to play a key role during the time of Menander, as far as Sri Lanka. According to Edicts of Ashoka, Greek populations generally described in ancient times throughout the Classical world as Yona, Yojanas or Yavanas, lit. "Ionians" were under his rule in northwestern India. Here in the king's domain among the Greeks, the Kambojas, the Nabhakas, the Nabhapamkits, the Bhojas, the Pitinikas, the Andhras and the Palidas, everywhere people are following Beloved-of-the-Gods' instructions in Dhamma.

-S. Dhammika, Edicts of Ashoka, Rock Edict No. 13

Far from just being on the receiving end of conversion to Buddhism, the Mahavamsa indicates that Greeks took an active role in spreading the Buddhist faith as emissaries of Ashoka.

These Greek missionaries appear in the list of the "elders" (Pali: "thera") sent far and wide by Emperor Ashoka:

"When the thera Moggaliputta, the illuminator of the religion of the Conqueror, had brought the (third) council to an end he sent forth theras, one here and one there:

- The thera Mahyantika he sent to Kasmira and Gandhara.
- The thera, MaMdeva he sent to Mahisamandala.
- To Vanavasa be sent the thera named Rakkhita, and

- To Aparantaka (he sent) the Yona named Dhammara-kkhita.
- To Maharattha (he sent) the thera named Mahadhammara-kkhita.
- But the thera Maharakkhita he sent into the country of the Yona.
- He sent the thera Majjhima to the Himalaya country, and
- To Suvambhurni he sent the two theras Sona and Uttara.
- The great thera Mahinda, the theras Utthiya, Uttiya, Sambala and Bhaddasala his disciples, these five theras he sent forth with the charge: 'Ye shall found in the lovely island of Lanka the lovely religion of the Conqueror.'" (Mahavamsa, XII)

Dhammarakkhita (Dharmaraksita in Sanskrit) was the Yona (Lit. "Ionian" or "Greek") leader of the mission to Aparantaka. The country of Aparantaka has been identified as the northwestern part of the Indian subcontinent, and comprises Northern Gujarat, Kathiawar, Kachch, and Sindh, the area where Greek communities were probably concentrated. To this day, a city in Gujarat is named Junagadh, originally "Yonagadh", lit. "City of the Greeks".

Dharmarashita is said to have preached the Aggikkhando-pama Sutra, so that 37,000 people were converted in Aparantaka and that thousands of men and women entered the Order (Mahavimsa XII). According to the Milinda Panha (I 32-35), the monk Nagasena, who famously dialogued with the Greek king Menander I to convert him to Buddhism, was a student of Dharmaraksita, and he reached enlightenment as an arhat under his guidance.

The thera ("elder") Mahyantika was sent to Kashmir and Gandhara, also areas with strong Hellenic presence. Although he is not identified as Greek in the Mahavamsa, his name probably means Maha (great) + Antika (Antiochos), a common Greek first name. The thera ("elder") Maharakkhita (Mahara-ksita in Sanskrit) is said to have been sent to the country of the Greeks. He would probably have been Greek as well due to the nature of his mission, but this is unconfirmed. The Indo-Greek king Menander I (reigned 160- 135 BCE) had his capital in Sagala, in today's northern Punjab, and is described by Strabo as one of the most powerful Greek kings of the period, even greater than Alexander the Great.

Menander probably converted to Buddhism, and seems to have encouraged the spread of the faith within the Indian subcontinent, and possibly into Central Asia as well. A documented example of the influence of a Greek Buddhist monk is found in the Mahavamsa again:

During the time of Menander I, the Yona (Ionian) Mahadhammarakkhita (Sanskrit: Mahadharmaraksita) is said to have come from "Alasandra" (thought to be Alexandria-of-the-Caucasus, the city founded by Alexander the Great, near today's Kabul) with 30,000 monks for the foundation ceremony of the Maha Thupa ("Great stupa") at Anuradhapura in Sri Lanka, during the 2nd century BCE.

"From Alasanda the city of the Yonas came the thera Yona Mahadhammarakkhita with thirty thousand bhikkhus." (*Mahavamsa*, XXIX)

These elements tend to indicate the importance of Buddhism within Greek communities in northwestern India, and the prominent role Greek Buddhist monks played in them, as well as throughout the Indian subcontinent and possibly as far as the Mediterranean, during the last centuries before the current era.

EXPANSION OF BUDDHIST CULTURE WESTWARD

Meanwhile, the Buddha's teachings had spread north-west, into Parthian territory. Buddhist stupa remains have been identified as distant as the Silk Road city of Merv.

Soviet archeological teams in Giaur Kala, near Merv, have uncovered a Buddhist monastery, complete with huge buddharupa. Parthian nobles such as An Shih Kao are known to have adopted Buddhism and were among those responsible for its further spread towards China.

Archaeologist Donald Mackenzie believed that Buddhist missionaries had a good footing in pre-Christian Britain. He quotes the early Church father Saint Origen as saying, "The island (Britain) has long been predisposed to it (Christianity) through the doctrines of the Druids and Buddhists, who had already inculcated the doctrine of the unity of the Godhead" - Origen. The Silk Road transmission of Buddhism to China started in the 1st century CE with a semi-legendary or quasi-historical account of an embassy sent to the West by the Chinese Emperor Ming (58 – 75 CE).

Extensive contacts however started in the 2nd century CE, probably as a consequence of the expansion of the Kushan Empire into the Chinese territory of the Tarim Basin, with the missionary efforts of a great number of Central Asian Buddhist monks to Chinese lands.

The first missionaries and translators of Buddhist scriptures into Chinese were Parthian, Kushan, Sogdian or Kuchean. From the 4th century onward, Chinese pilgrims also started to travel to India, the origin of Buddhism, by themselves in order to get improved access to the original scriptures, with Fa-hsien's pilgrimage to India (395-414), and later Xuan Zang (629-644). The Silk Road transmission of Buddhism essentially ended around the 7th century with the rise of Islam in Central Asia.

The first contacts between China and Central Asia occurred with the opening of the Silk Road in the 2nd century BCE. The 1st century BCE "Records of the Great Historian" tells of the travels of the Chinese explorer Zhang Qian to Central Asia around 130 BCE, who reports about a country named Shendu (India), whose peaceful Buddhist ways are mentioned in writing in the 1st century CE Han history, the Hanshu. After 130 BCE, numerous embassies to the West followed Zhang Qian's travels, and there may have been some contacts with Buddhism around that time. Chinese murals in the Tarim Basin city of Dunhuang describe Han Wudi (156-87 BCE) worshiping Buddhist statues, "golden men brought in 120 BCE by a great Han general in his campaigns against the nomads".

However, there is no such mention of Han Wudi worshiping the Buddha in Chinese historical literature. The Hou Hanshu also records the visit of Yuezhi envoys to the Chinese capital in 2 BCE, who gave oral teachings on Buddhist sutras to a student, suggesting that some Yuezhi had already started to disseminate the Buddhist faith in eastern Asia during the 1st century BCE. The *Hou Hanshu* then describes the questionable legend about the encouragement of Buddhism around 70 CE by Emperor Ming (58-75 CE):

"There is a current tradition that Emperor Ming dreamed that he saw a tall golden man the top of whose head was glowing. He questioned his group of advisors and one of them said: "In the West there is a god called Buddha. His body is sixteen chi high (3.7 metres or 12 feet), and is the colour of true gold." The Emperor, to discover the true doctrine, sent an envoy to Tianzhu (Northwestern India) to inquire about the Buddha's doctrine, after which paintings and statues of the Buddha appeared in the Middle Kingdom."

This encounter is further described in a 6th century CE account by Yang Xuanzhi:

"The establishment of the Baima Temple (Temple of the White Horse) by Emperor Ming (58-75 CE) of the Han marked the introduction of Buddhism into China. The temple was located on the south side of the Imperial Drive, three leagues (li) outside the Xiyang Gate. The Emperor dreamt of the golden man sixteen Chinese feet tall, with the aureole of sun and moon radiating from his head and his neck. A "golden god", he was known as Buddha. The emperor dispatched envoys to the Western Regions in search of the god, and, as a result, acquired Buddhist scriptures and images. At the time, because the scriptures were carried into China on the backs of white horses, White Horse was adopted as the name of the temple." (Translation: Ulrich Theobald).

M. H. Maspero established in 1901 that this story had no real basis in fact, but was almost certainly just a pious legend dating from the 2nd century CE. He also pointed out that the 3rd century *Weilüe* has a very different account of the introduction of Buddhism to China, with no mention at all of Emperor Ming. The military expansion of China into Central Asia under the rule of Emperor Ming at that time was very real, in particular with the campaign of the general Ban Chao, who managed to repel the Xiongnu from the Tarim Basin and control most of the area by around 75 CE. These contacts necessarily prompted some level of cultural exchange, and may indeed correspond to the first time Buddhist ideas were transmitted to China.

The first documented transmission of Buddhist scriptures to China occurs in 148 CE, with the arrival of the Parthian missionary An Shih Kao in China, probably on the heels of the Kushan expansion into the Tarim Basin. An Shi Kao established Buddhist temples in Loyang and organized the translation of Buddhist scriptures into Chinese, testifying to the beginning of a wave of Central Asian Buddhist proselytism that was to last several centuries. In the middle of the 2nd century CE, the Kushan Empire under king Kanishka expanded into Central Asia and went as far as taking control of Kashgar, Khotan and Yarkand, which were Chinese dependencies in the Tarim Basin, modern Xinjiang.

As a consequence, cultural exchanges greatly increased, and Central-Asian Buddhist missionaries became active shortly after in the Chinese capital cities of Loyang and sometimes Nanjing, where they particularly distinguished themselves by their translation work. They promoted both Hinayana and Mahayana scriptures. Thirty-seven of these early translators of Buddhist texts are known.

- An Shih Kao, a Parthian prince who made the first known translations of Hinayana Buddhist texts into Chinese (148-170).
- Lokaksema, a Kushan and the first to translate Mahayana scriptures into Chinese (167-186).
- An Hsuan, a Parthian merchant who became a monk in China 181.
- Zhi Yao (c. 185), a Kushan monk, second generation of translators after Lokaksema.

- Kang Meng-hsiang (194-207), first translator from Kangju.
- Zhi Qian (220-252), a Kushan monk whose grandfather had settled in China during 168-190.
- Zhi Yueh (c.230), a Kushan monk who worked at Nanjing.
- Kang Sengkai (247-280), born in Chiao-chih in the extreme south of the Chinese empire, and son of Sogdian merchant.
- Tan-ti (c.254), a Parthian monk.
- Po Yen (c.259), a Kuchean prince.
- Dharmaraksa (265-313), a Kushan whose family had lived for generations at Dunhuang.
- An Fachiin (281-306), a monk of Parthian origins.
- Po Srimitra (317-322), a Kuchean prince.
- Kumarajiva (c. 401), a Kuchean monk, and one of the most important translators.
- Fo T'u-teng (4th century), Central Asian monk who became a counselor to the Chinese court.
- Bodhidharma (440-528), was, according to Yang Xuanzhi, a monk of Central Asian origin whom he met around 520 at Loyang. Bodhidharma was the founder of the Chan (Zen) school of Buddhism.
- Five monks from Gandhara traveled in 485 CE to the country of Fusang ("The country of the extreme East" beyond the sea, probably Japan, although some historians suggest the American continent), where they introduced Buddhism:

"In former times, the people of Fusang knew nothing of the Buddhist religion, but in the second year of Da Ming of the Song dynasty (485 CE), five monks from Kipin (Kabul region of Gandhara) traveled by ship to that country. They propagated Buddhist doctrine, circulated scriptures and drawings, and advised the people to relinquish worldly attachments. As a result the customs of Fusang changed".

- Jnanagupta (561-592), a monk and translator from Gandhara.
- Shikshananda (652-710 CE), a monk and translator from Udyana, Gandhara.

- *Prajna* (c. 810). A monk and translator from Kabul, who educated the Japanese Kûkai in Sanskrit texts.

Central Asian missionnary efforts along the Silk Road were accompanied by a flux of artistic influences, visible in the development of Serindian art from the 2nd through the 11th century CE in the Tarim Basin, modern Xinjiang. Serindian art often derives from the art of the Greco-Buddhist art of the Gandhara district of what is now Pakistan, combining Indian, Greek and Roman influences. Highly sinicized forms of this syncretism can also be found on the eastern portions of the Tarim Basin, such as in Dunhuang.

Silk Road artistic influences can be found as far as Japan to this day, in architectural motifs or representations of Japanese gods.

According to Chinese sources, the first Chinese to be ordained was Zhu Zixing, after he went to Central Asia in 260 to seek out Buddhism. It is only from the 4th century CE that Chinese Buddhist monks started to travel to India to discover Buddhism first-hand. Fa-hsien's pilgrimage to India (395-414) is said to have been the first significant one. He left along the Silk Road, stayed 6 years in India, and then returned by the sea route.

Tens of Chinese monks, possibly hundreds of them, visited India during that period. The most famous of the Chinese pilgrims is Xuan Zang (629-644), whose large and precise translation work defines a "new translation period", in contrast with older Central Asian works.

He also left a detailed account of his travels in Central Asia and India. Buddhism in Central Asia began to decline in the 7th century following the incursion of the Muslim Caliphate. The vigorous Chinese culture progressively absorbed Buddhist teachings until a strongly Chinese particularism developed. Central Asian Buddhist monks from the Tarim Basin and East Asian Buddhist monks appear to have maintained strong exchanges until around the 10th century, as shown by frescos from the Tarim Basin.

CHRISTIAN AWARENESS OF BUDDHISM

Some have suggested the Church Fathers were acquainted with Buddhist beliefs and practices. The Christian theologian Clement of Alexandria states in the 2nd century CE:

"Thus philosophy, a thing of the highest utility, flourished in antiquity among the barbarians, shedding its light over the nations. And afterwards it came to Greece. First in its ranks were the prophets of the Egyptians; and the Chaldeans among the Assyrians; and the Druids among the Gauls; and the Sarmanas among the Bactrians ("Óáñìáíáßïé ÂÜêôñùí"); and the philosophers of the Celts; and the Magi of the Persians, who foretold the Saviour's birth, and came into the land of Judaea guided by a star. The Indian gymnosophists are also in the number, and the other barbarian philosophers. And of these there are two classes, some of them called Sramanas ("ÓáñìÜíáé"), and others Brahmins (*Âñáöìáíáé*)."

-Clement of Alexandria "The Stromata, or Miscellanies" Book I, Chapter XV[21]

Clement writes of the Buddha:

"Among the Indians are those philosophers also who follow the precepts of Boutta, whom they honour as a god on account of his extraordinary sanctity."

- *Clement of Alexandria, Stromata (Miscellanies), Book I, Chapter XV*

Early 3rd-4th century Christian writers such as Hippolytus and Epiphanius write of one Scythianus who visited India around 50 CE, whence he brought the "doctrine of the Two Principles". Scythianus' pupil Terebinthus supposedly presented himself as a "Buddha" ("he called himself Buddas" Cyril of Jerusalem) and became well known in Judaea. The same author says his books and knowledge were taken over by Mani, and became the foundation of the Manichean doctrine.

"Terebinthus, his disciple in this wicked error, inherited his money and books and heresy, and came to Palestine and becoming known and condemned in Judaea he resolved to pass into Persia: but lest he should be recognised there also by his name he changed it and called himself Buddas."

-Cyril of Jerusalem, Sixth Catechetical Lecture Chapter 22-24

Hippolytus, a Greek-speaking Christian in Rome, around 235 includes Indian ascetics among sources of heresy:

There is... among the Indians a heresy of those who philosophize among the Brahmins, who live a self-sufficient life, abstaining from (eating) living creatures and all cooked food... They say that God is light, not like the light one sees, nor like the sun nor fire, but to them God is discourse, not that which finds expression in articulate sounds, but that of knowledge (gnosis) through which the secret mysteries of nature are perceived by the wise.

The Syrian gnostic theologian Bar Daisan describes in the third century his exchanges with missions of holy men from India, passing through Syria on their way to Elagabalus or another Severan dynasty Roman Emperor. His accounts are quoted by Porphyry and Stobaeus. Roman historical accounts describe an embassy sent by the "Indian king Pandion (Pandya?), also named Porus," to Caesar Augustus around 13 CE. The embassy was travelling with a diplomatic letter in Greek, and one of its members was a sramana who burned himself alive in Athens to demonstrate his faith. The event made a sensation and was described by Nicolaus of Damascus, who met the embassy at Antioch, and related by Strabo (XV, 1, 73) and Dio Cassius (liv, 9). A tomb was made to the sramana, still visible in the time of Plutarch, which bore the mention:

"ΖΑΡΜΑΝΟΧΗΓΑΣ ΙΝΔΟΣ ΑΠΟ ΒΑΡΓΟΣΗΣ"

("The sramana master from Barygaza in India")

These accounts at least indicate that Indian religious men (Sramanas, to which the Buddhists belonged, as opposed to Hindu Brahmanas) were circulating in the Levant during the time of Jesus. By the time of Jesus, the teachings of the Buddha had already spread through much of India and penetrated into

Sri Lanka, Central Asia and China. They display certain similarities to Christian moral precepts of more than five centuries later; the sanctity of life, compassion for others, rejection of violence, confession and emphasis on charity and the practice of virtue.

Will Durant, noting that the Emperor Ashoka sent missionaries, not only to elsewhere in India and to Sri Lanka, but to Syria, Egypt and Greece, speculated by Will Durant in the 1930s that they may have helped prepare the ground for Christian teaching. Ashoka ascended the throne of India around 270 B.C.E. After his conversion to Buddhism he dispatched missionaries to the four points of the compass. Archeological finds indicate these missions had been "favorably received" in lands to the West.

Ptolemy II Philadelphus, one of the monarchs Ashoka mentions in his edicts, is recorded by Pliny the Elder as having sent an ambassador named Dionysius to the Mauryan court at Pataliputra: "India has been treated of by several other Greek writers who resided at the courts of Indian kings, such, for instance, as Megasthenes, and by Dionysius, who was sent thither by Philadelphus, expressly for the purpose: all of whom have enlarged upon the power and vast resources of these nations."

Records from Alexandria, long a crossroads of commerce and ideas, indicate that itinerant monks from the Indian subcontinent may have influenced philosophical currents of the time. Roman accounts centuries later speak of monks traveling to the middle east, and there is mention of an embassy sent by the Indian king Pandion, or Porus (possibly Pandya), to Caesar Augustus around 13 CE. The embassy was traveling with a diplomatic letter in Greek, and one of its members was a *sramana* who burned himself alive in Athens to demonstrate his faith. The event caused a sensation. It was described by Nicolaus of Damascus, who met the embassy at Antioch and by Strabo (XV, 1, 73) and Dio Cassius (liv, 9). A tomb, still visible in the time of Plutarch, bore mention of:

"ΖΑΡΜΑΝΟΧΗΓΑΣ ΙΝΔΟΣ ΑΠΟ ΒΑΡΓΟΣΗΣ"

("The sramana master from Barygaza in India")

Meanwhile, the Buddha's teachings had spread northwest, into Parthian territory. Buddhist stupa remains have een identified as distant as the Silk Road city of Merv. Soviet archeological teams in Giaur Kala, near Merv, have uncovered a Buddhist monastery, complete with huge buddharupa. Parthian nobles such as An Shih Kao are known to have adopted Buddhism and were among those responsible for its further spread towards China.

Archaeologist Donald Mackenzie believed that Buddhist missionaries had a good footing in pre-Christian Britain. He quotes the early Church father Saint Origen as saying, "The island (Britain) has long been predisposed to it (Christianity) through the doctrines of the Druids and Buddhists, who had already inculcated the doctrine of the unity of the Godhead" - Origen.

Some knowledge of Buddhism existed quite early in the West. In the 2nd century CE, Clement of Alexandria, the father of Christian dogmatism, wrote about the Buddha:

"Among the Indians are those philosophers also who follow the precepts of Boutta, whom they honour as a god on account of his extraordinary sanctity."

- Clement of Alexandria, Stromata (Miscellanies), Book I, Chapter XV

He also recognized Bactrian Buddhists (Sramanas) and Indian Gymnosophists for their influence on Greek thought:

"Thus philosophy, a thing of the highest utility, flourished in antiquity among the barbarians, shedding its light over the nations. And afterwards it came to Greece. First in its ranks were the prophets of the Egyptians; and the Chaldeans among the Assyrians; and the Druids among the Gauls; and the Sramanas among the Bactrians ("Óáñìáíáßïé ÂÜêôñùí"); and the philosophers of the Celts; and the Magi of the Persians, who foretold the Saviour's birth, and came into the land of Judaea guided by a star. The Indian gymnosophists are also in the number, and the other barbarian philosophers. And of these there are two classes, some of them called Sramanas, and others Brahmins ("Âñáöìáíáé")."

- *Clement of Alexandria, Stromata (Miscellanies)*

The story of the birth of the Buddha was also known: a fragment of Archelaos of Carrha (278 CE) mentions the Buddha's virgin-birth and Saint Jerome (4th century CE) mentions the birth of the Buddha, who he says "was born from the side of a virgin". Queen Maya came to bear the Buddha after receiving a prophetic dream in which she foresaw the descent of the *Bodhisattva* (Buddha-to-be) from the Tusita heaven into her womb. This story has some parallels with the story of Jesus being conceived in connection with the visitation of the Holy Spirit to the Virgin Mary.

Early 3rd century–4th century Christian writers such as Hippolytus and Epiphanius write about a Scythianus, who visited India around 50 CE from where he brought "the doctrine of the Two Principles". According to Cyril of Jerusalem, Scythianus' pupil Terebinthus presented himself as a "Buddha" ("He called himself Buddas"). Terebinthus went to Palestine and Judaea ("becoming known and condemned"), and ultimately settled in Babylon, where he transmitted his teachings to Mani, thereby creating the foundation of Manichaeism:

"But Terebinthus, his disciple in this wicked error, inherited his money and books and heresy, and came to Palestine and becoming known and condemned in Judaea he resolved to pass into Persia: but lest he should be recognised there also by his name he changed it and called himself Buddas."

BARLAAM AND JOSAPHAT

The Greek legend of Barlaam and Ioasaph, sometimes mistakenly attributed to the seventh century John of Damascus but first recorded by the Georgian monk Euthymius of Athos in the eleventh century, was ultimately derived, via Arabic and Georgian versions, from the life story of the Buddha. The king-turned-monk Ioasaph (Georgian *Iodasaph,* Arabic *Yûdhasaf* or *Bûdhasaf*) also gets his name from the Sanskrit *Bodhisattva,* the term traditionally used to refer to Gautama before he becomes a Buddha.

Barlaam and Ioasaph were placed in the Orthodox calendar of saints on 26 August, and in the Roman martyrology they were canonized (as "Barlaam and Josaphat") and assigned 27 November. The story was translated into Hebrew in the middle Ages as "Ben-Hamelekh Vehanazir" ("The Prince and the Nazirite"). Thus the Buddhist story was turned into a Christian and Jewish legend. Barlaam and Josaphat are said to have lived and died in the 3rd century or 4th century in India. In the middle ages, they were often considered to be Christian saints, but Josaphat's story appears to be in many respects a Christianized version of the story of Gautama Buddha, the founder of Buddhism.

The Greek legend of "Barlaam and Ioasaph", sometimes mistakenly attributed to the 7th century John of Damascus but actually written by the Georgian monk Euthymios in the 11th century, was ultimately derived, through a variety of intermediate versions (Arabic and Georgian) from the life story of the Buddha. The king-turned-monk Ioasaph (Georgian *Iodasaph*, Arabic *Yûdhasaf* or *Bûdhasaf*) ultimately derives his name from the Sanskrit *Bodhisattva*, the name used in Buddhist accounts for Gautama before he became a Buddha. Barlaam and Ioasaph were placed in the Greek Orthodox calendar of saints on 26 August, and in the West they were entered as "Barlaam and Josaphat" in the Roman Martyrology on the date of 27 November.

According to legend, a King Abenner or Avenier in India persecuted the Christian Church in his realm, founded by the Apostle Thomas. When astrologers predicted that his own son would some day become a Christian, Abenner had the young prince Josaphat isolated from external contact. Despite the imprisonment, Josaphat met the hermit Saint Barlaam and converted to Christianity. Josaphat kept his faith even in the face of his father's anger and persuasion.

Eventually, Abenner himself converted, turned over his throne to Josaphat, and retired to the desert to become a hermit. Josaphat himself later abdicated and went into reclusion with his old teacher Barlaam. The story of Barlaam and Josaphat was popular in the middle Ages, appearing in such works as the *Golden Legend.* Although Barlaam and Josaphat were never formally canonized, they were included in earlier editions of the Roman Martyrology (feast day 27 November) - though not in the Roman Missal - and in the Eastern Orthodox Church liturgical calendar (26 August).

It seems that St. Josaphat is actually a Christianized version of the Buddha. Wilfred Cantwell Smith traced the story from a 2nd to 4th century Sanskrit Mahayana Buddhist text, to a Manichee version, which then found its way into Muslim culture as the Arabic *Kitab Bilawhar wa-Yudasaf,* which was current in Baghdad in the 8th century. The first Christianized adaptation was the Georgian epic *Balavariani* dating back to the 10th century. A Georgian monk Euthymius of Athos translated the story into Greek, some time before he was killed while visiting Constantinople in 1028.

There the Greek adaptation was translated into Latin in 1048 and soon became well known in Western Europe as *Barlaam and Josaphat.* Recent linguistic and geographic research of the spread of Buddha's tale across Asia and Europe also points toward the saint's name and tale originating with Buddha. Josaphat's name may be traced to the Sanskrit term *Bodhisattva* via the Middle Persian *bodasif.* Investigation by researchers at the Korean Seoul National University indicates that the name *Buddha* or *Bodhisatta* in Sanskrit changed to *Bodisav* in Persian texts in the sixth or seventh century, then to *Budhasaf* or *Yudasaf* in an eighth-century Arabic document, and *Iodasaph* in Georgia in the 10th century. That name was then adapted to *Ioasaph* in Greece in the 11th century, and *Iosaphat* or *Josaphat* in Latin since then.

Besides their names, the stories of the two individuals are strikingly similar. Author Holger Kersten proposes an alternate explanation: that "Josaphat" is derived from the Arabic "Judasaf" or "Budasaf", as written in an Urdu version of the tale. He ties this name to that of a sage 'Yuz Asaf' entombed in Kashmir, the name being thus understood as Kashmiri for "Son of Yuz," i.e. Joseph, and which Kersten (following an old story) interprets as evidence that Jesus lived and died in India.

However, "Yuz Asaf" is simply the Persian and Urdu pronunciation of the Arabic Yûdhasaf, and does not go back any farther than the Arabic story, which is itself demonstrably derived from Buddhist stories. The story of Josaphat was retold as an exploration on free will against fate in the 17th century Spanish play *La vida es sueño* (*Life is a dream*) by Pedro Calderón de la Barca. In *The Romantic School,* Heinrich Heine called it the "blood of the holy poetic arts in the German Middle Ages."

POSSIBLE BUDDHIST INFLUENCE

Some scholars have suggested that the semi-apocryphal Gospel of Thomas and the Nag Hammadi texts display Buddhist influence. Elaine Pagels in her widely noted *The Gnostic Gospels* (1979), and in *Beyond Belief* (2003), makes mention of such theories. As far back as 1816 the historian George Faber in his book, The Origin of Pagan Idolatry Ascertained from Historical Testimony, stated, "There is so strong a resemblance between the characters of Jesus and of Buddha, that it cannot have been purely accidental."

In 1883 Max Müller, the pioneering scholar of comparative religion, asserted in his *India: What it Can Teach Us*: "That there are startling coincidences between Buddhism and Christianity cannot be denied, and it must likewise be admitted that Buddhism existed at least 400 years before Christianity. I go even further, and should feel extremely grateful if anybody would point out to me the historical channels through which Buddhism had influenced early Christianity." It is interesting to note that Muller himself, before examining the Buddhist/ Christian copycat claims, stated that he intended to prove the priority of the Jesus gospels over the Buddhist texts.

In *The Gospel of Jesus in relation to the Buddha Legend,* and again, in 1897, in *The Buddha Legend and the Life of Jesus,* Professor Rudolf Seydel of the University of Leipzig noted around fifty similarities between Buddhist and Christian parables and teachings. In 1918, in his *History of Religions,* Professor E. Washburn Hopkins of Yale goes so far as to say,

"Finally, the life, temptation, miracles, parables, and even the disciples of Jesus have been derived directly from Buddhism."

Much more recently, the historian Jerry H. Bentley notes "the possibility that Buddhism influenced the early development of Christianity" and that scholars "have drawn attention to many parallels concerning the births, lives, doctrines, and deaths of the Buddha and Jesus". In his *Buddhism Omnibus* Iqbal Singh similarly acknowledges the possibility of early interaction and, thus, influence of Buddhist teachings upon the Christian tradition in its formative period.

In 1992 Zacharias P. Thundy, Professor of Literature, wrote a book titled, Buddha and Christ, Nativity stories from the Indian traditions in which Thundy concludes that there was a substantial amount of borrowing by Christianity from Buddhism. He prefers not to label Jesus a Jew, Buddhist or a Buddhist-Jew, claiming that such distinctions are "fuzzy". Thundy further claims a long tradition of interchange between east and west and shows that western fables, such as those in Aesop's fables, and the story of Susans attached to the Book of Daniel, were originally Buddhist Jatakas.

In 2007 Doctor of Asian Studies Christian Lindtner published a book titled Geheimnisse um Jesus Christus. Dr. Lindtner compares the Pali and Sanskrit Buddhist texts with the Greek gospels and determines that the four gospels were reformulated from older Buddhist texts based on gematria values, puns, and syllabic equivalences. Those who have scrutinized his work claim that his gematria values and syllabic equivalences are coincidental and that his puns exist because the Greek and Sanskrit are from the same language family. Those in support of his work claim that is findings are unique and that similar finds could not be made in regard to any other seemingly non-connected literature.

Also, in 2007 the author Daniel Hopkins wrote a book named Father and Son, East is West, the Buddhist sources to Christianity and their influence on medieval myths, in which he claims that the Jesus gospels were highly allegorical and mysterious in order to hide the name of Jesus' father, which he claims was the Buddha's name. Burkhard Scherer, Professor of Indo-Tibetan Studies at England's Canterbury Christ Church University has stated: "...it is very important to draw attention to the fact that there is massive Buddhist influence in the Gospels....Since more than a hundred years, Buddhist influence in the Gospels has been known and acknowledged by scholars from both sides." He adds: "Just recently, Duncan McDerret published his excellent *The Bible and the Buddhist* (Sardini, Bornato [Italy] 2001). With McDerret, I am convinced that there are many Buddhist narratives in the Gospels."

Thomas Tweed, Professor of Religious Studies at University of North Carolina at Chapel Hill, notes that between 1879 and 1907 there were a "number of impassioned discussions about parallels and possible historical influence between Buddhism and Christianity in... a variety of periodicals". By 1906 interest waned somewhat. In the end, Albert Schweitzer's conclusion appears to have been favored: that, although some indirect influence through the wider culture was "not inherently impossible", the hypothesis that Jesus' novel ideas were borrowed directly from Buddhism was "unproved, unprovable and unthinkable."

BUDDHISM AND GNOSTICISM

Edward Conze and Elaine Pagels have suggested that Gnosticism blends teachings like those attributed to Jesus Christ with teachings found in Eastern traditions. The word gnosis (knowledge) as used by the Gnostics is equivalent to the Buddhist word *prajna*. Both traditions of Buddhism and Gnosticism held that only direct knowledge was liberating. Some basic parallels held in common with the Buddhist and the Gnostic, and canonical gospels, is that the Buddhists believed that the Buddha was like a great father with sons of light (*Bodhisattvas*), while all Christians held that Jesus was the light and the son of a great father.

While it is true that some Gnostics demonized the "Father", this concept could be the Buddhist concept of 'killing the Buddha', or leaving the raft (religion) behind. Scattered throughout the Gnostic gospels there can be found many exclusively Buddhist themes, such as within The Gospel of Mary can be found the stressing of matter as impermanent, within The Infancy of James those who chew, yet do not chew can be compared to the *Bodhisattvas* in the Surangama sutra who Taste, but do not taste, within the book Thomas the Contender, Jesus is recorded as saying, "woe to you, because the wheel that turns in your mind" which might reference the Buddhist wheel of dependent origination, within the Gospel of Thomas when Jesus is questioned about how disciples should prove that they were from God, Jesus says the proof of God in them was "motion, and rest" which again could reference the Buddhist belief that the easiest path to enlightenment was through contemplation on the ear organ and the understanding of its two defiling attributes of motion and stillness, the gospel of Phillip mentions that Jesus was martyred many times just as the Buddhist Jatakas and Pali texts mention of the Buddha in his former births.

Philip Jenkins writes that, since the mid-nineteenth century, new and fringe religious movements have often created images of Jesus, presenting him as a sage, philosopher and occult teacher, whose teachings are very similar to those of Asian religions. He asserts that the images generated by these religious movements share much in common with the images that increasingly dominate the mainstream critical scholarship of the New Testament, especially following the rediscovery of the Gnostic Gospels found at Nag Hammadi in Egypt in 1945. He alleges that, in modern scholarly writing, Jesus has become more of a Gnostic, Cynic or even a crypto-Buddhist than the traditional notion of the reformist Jewish rabbi.

Jenkins acknowledges that "the Jesus of the hidden gospels has many points of contact with the great spiritual traditions of Asia." Pagels has written that "one need only listen to the words of the Gospel of Thomas to hear how it resonates with the Buddhist tradition... these ancient gospels tend to point beyond faith toward a path of solitary searching to find understanding, or gnosis." She suggests that there is an explicitly Indian influence in the Gospel of Thomas, perhaps via the Christian communities in southern India, the so-called Thomas Christians. It is believed by some that of all of the Nag Hammadi texts, the Gospel of Thomas has the most similarities with Pure Land Buddhism within it. Edward Conze has suggested that Hindu or Buddhist tradition may well have influenced Gnosticism.

He points out that Buddhists were in contact with the Thomas Christians. Elaine Pagels notes that the similarities between Gnosticism and Buddhism have prompted some scholars to question their interdependence and to wonder whether "...if the names were changed, the 'living Buddha' appropriately could say what the Gospel of Thomas attributes to the living Jesus. " However, she concludes that, although intriguing, the evidence is inconclusive, and she further concludes that these parallels might be coincidental since parallel traditions may emerge in different cultures without direct influence.

THERAPEUTAE INFLUENCE

According to the Gospel of Matthew, Jesus spent his early childhood in Egypt which was at the end of the Silk Road. As a result of its role in trade with the East, Egypt was prosperous and enriched with religious diversity. The Therapeutae (known only from Philo) were mystics and ascetics who lived especially in the area around Alexandria, Philo described the Therapeutae in the beginning of the 1st century CE in *De vita contemplativa* ("On the contemplative life"), written ca. 10 CE. By that time, the origins of the Therapeutae were already lost in the past, and Philo was even unsure about the etymology of their name.

Philonian monachism has been seen as the forerunner of and the model for the Christian ascetic life. It has even been considered as the earliest description of Christian monasticism. This view was first espoused by Eusebius of Caesarea in his *Ecclesiastical History*. According to the linguist Zacharias P. Thundy the name "Therapeutae" is simply a Hellenisation of the Pali term for the traditional Buddhist faith, "Theravada".

The similarities between the monastic practices of the Therapeutae and Buddhist monastic practices have led to suggestions that the Therapeutae were in fact Buddhist monks who had reached Alexandria, descendants of Ashoka's emissaries to the West, and who influenced the early formation of Christianity.

The evidence for this argument rests solely on the similarity of practices and the purported derivation of the name. There is no evidence from antiquity that supports this argument. In their book *The Jesus Mysteries*, Timothy Freke and Peter Gandy argue that the Therapeutae are possible candidates for the origin of what they characterize as "the legend of Jesus Christ".

Elmar R. Gruber, a psychologist, and Holger Kersten, a specialist in religious history argue that Buddhism had a substantial influence on the life and teachings of Jesus. Gruber and Kersten claim that Jesus was brought up by the Therapeutae, teachers of the Buddhist Theravada School then living in the Bible lands. They assert that Jesus lived the life of a Buddhist and taught Buddhist ideals to his disciples; their work follows in the footsteps of the Oxford New Testament scholar Barnett Hillman Streeter, who established as early as the 1930s that the moral teaching of the Buddha has four remarkable resemblances to the Sermon on the Mount.

Asceticism can be seen as a common point between Buddhism and Christianity, and is in contrast to the absence of asceticism in Judaism:

"Asceticism is indigenous to the religions which posit as fundamental the wickedness of this life and the corruption under sin of the flesh. Buddhism, therefore, as well as Christianity, leads to ascetic practices. Monasteries are institutions of Buddhism no less than of Catholic Christianity. The assumption, found in the views of the Montanists and others that concessions made to the natural appetites may be pardoned in those that are of a lower degree of holiness, while the perfectly holy will refuse to yield in the least to carnal needs and desires, is easily detected also in some of the teachings of

Gautama Buddha. The ideal of holiness of both the Buddhist and the Christian saint culminates in poverty and chastity; i.e., celibacy. Fasting and other disciplinary methods are resorted to to curb the flesh" -*The Jewish Encyclopedia*

THE LOST YEARS OF JESUS AND NEW AGE THEORIES

One tradition claims that Jesus traveled to India and Tibet during the "Lost years of Jesus" before the beginning of his public ministry. In 1887 a Russian war correspondent, Nicolas Notovitch, visited India and Tibet. He claimed that, at the lamasery or monastery of Hemis in Ladakh, he learned of the "Life of Saint Issa, Best of the Sons of Men." His story, with a translated text of the "Life of Saint Issa," was published in French in 1894 as *La vie inconnue de Jesus Christ*. It was subsequently translated into English, German, Spanish, and Italian.

The "Life of Saint Issa, Best of the Sons of Men" purportedly recounts the travels of one known in the East as Saint Issa, whom Notovitch identified as Jesus. After initially doubting Notovitch, a disciple of Sri Ramakrishna, Swami Abhedananda, journeyed to Tibet, investigated his claim, helped translate part of the document, and later championed his views. Notovitch's writings were immediately controversial. The German orientalist Max Müller corresponded with the Hemis monastery that Notovitch claimed to have visited and Archibald Douglas visited Hemis Monastery. Neither found any evidence that Notovich (much less Jesus) had even been there himself, so they rejected his claims.

The head of the Hemis community signed a document that denounced Notovitch as a liar. Despite this contradictory evidence, a number of New Age or spiritualist authors have taken this information and have incorporated it into their own works. For example, in her book *The Lost Years of Jesus: Documentary Evidence of Jesus' 17-Year Journey to the East*, Elizabeth Clare Prophet asserts that Buddhist manuscripts provide evidence that Jesus traveled to India, Nepal, Ladakh and Tibet.

PARALLELS

According to Jerry Bentley, "Scholars have often considered the possibility that Buddhism influenced the early development of Christianity. They have drawn attention to many parallels concerning the births, lives, doctrines, and deaths of the Buddha and Jesus".

BIRTHDAY OF THE BUDDHA AND THE CHRIST

Although the Buddha's birthday is celebrated in most traditions in May, which relates to the Buddha's mother Maya Devi, there is no early textual evidence to validate this birthday. Others, such as the author of The Angel-Messiah of the Buddhist, Essenes, and Christians, claim, that based on the ancient Indian calendar in use around 600 b.c. the new year of the Indians was November 17, and so he concludes that since the Buddha was said to be born on the eighth day of the second month that the Buddha's birthday was December 25.

This belief held by Buddhists is validated by certain ancient birth accounts of the Buddha, such as in the Asvaghosha-Kirita the Buddha is described as a descendent of solar kings, who was born when the sun retired; "There the sun, even although he had retired, was unable to scorn the moon-like faces of its women which put the lotuses to shame, and as if from the access of passion, hurried towards the western ocean to enter the (cooling) water". This Buddhist text also compares the birth of the Buddha to the constellation of the seven Rishis, which some have compared to the early Christian art depicting "seven-rays" coming out of a white dove. Others have linked this to the Pali text titled Seven Suns.

Administrative Structures

The administrative structures formed by Buddhism share the following similarities with those formed by Christianity:

- Initiation into a holy trinity.
- Monasticism and communal living for spiritual adherents which adhered to principles of practicing poverty and chastity.

- Early Christian Councils reminiscent in organization to the Buddhist councils.
- Missionaries and missions which were first organized and established by Buddhists, all predate the early Christian organizations in the same areas where Christianity was first established (Antioch, etc.).

It has been asserted that the story of the birth of the Buddha was well known in the West, and possibly influenced the story of the birth of Jesus. Saint Jerome (4th century CE) mentions the birth of the Buddha, who he says "was born from the side of a virgin" (the Buddha was, according to Buddhist tradition, born from the hip of his mother). The story of the birth of the Buddha was also known: a fragment of *Archelaos of Carrha* (278 CE) mentions the Buddha's virgin-birth.

In the 1893 book, *Influence of Buddhism on Primitive Christianity*, Arthur Lillie argues that the birth accounts of the Buddha were copied into the gospels listing the following infancy parallels:

1. The palm-tree bends down to Mary as the Asoka tree to Yashodara.
2. The story of Simeon, the accounts of the bright light being almost word for word the same.
3. The idol bending down to the infant Jesus.
4. The miracle of the sparrows restored to life.
5. Judas Iscariot in early life attacked Jesus, just as Devadetta, the Judas of Buddhism, attacked Buddha. A violent blow that Jesus received in the left side made a mark that was destined to be the exact spot that received the mortal spear-thrust at the Crucifixion. [199]
6. The whole story of the disputation with the doctors seems copied servilely from the "Lalita Vistara."
7. Buddhism had invaded Persia, and Maitreya, the coming Buddha, was expected 500 years after Buddha's death. The Persian Buddhists called him Sosiosh. The Gospel of the Infancy explains the presence of the Magi, which in the Canonical Gospels is quite unintelligible. Why should

Persians come with hysterical enthusiasm to greet a Messiah whose chief exploit was to be the slaughter of all Persians and all the other nations except Jews? The "Gospel of the Infancy" announces that Zoroaster had sent them. The Persians mixed up Sakyamuni Buddha, Mithras and Zoroaster and were expecting Sosiosh at the time.

Of course many of these traditions derive from Mahayana Buddhism developing many centuries after early Christianity suggesting Christian influence. Queen Maya came to bear the Buddha after receiving a prophetic dream in which she saw the descent of the *Bodhisattva* (Buddha-to-be) from the Tucita heaven into her womb, in the shape of a small white elephant. This story has some parallels with the story of Jesus being conceived in connection with the visitation of the Holy Spirit to the Virgin Mary.

The classical scene of the Virgin Mary being supported by two attendants at her side may have been influenced by earlier iconography, such as the rather similar Buddhist theme of Queen Maya giving birth. The iconography of Mary breastfeeding the child Jesus, unknown in the West until the 5-6th century (probable date of a frieze excavated in Saqqara), has also been connected to the much more ancient iconography of the goddess Hariti, also breastfeeding her child, and wearing Hellenistic clothes in the Greco-Buddhist art of Gandhara.

Parallel lives

Scholars see strong parallels in both the myth and life of Buddha and Jesus. Buddha and his disciples traveling preachers going into homes and preaching gospels to those who hear, is one obvious parallel of a literary motif not found in other traditions. Jesus too pursues this form of preaching and teaching. Jesus speaks of himself as the 'the light' and the son of a great father while the Buddha proclaims himself to be a great father with sons of light (*Bodhisattva*). Jesus proclaims to come to convert the wicked while the Buddha proclaims that his main goal is to save those of noble character or 'those with little dust in their eyes' although in the Lotus sutra the

Buddha claims to create an illusionary 'half-way point' for those who are wicked.

Ernest De Bunsen states, "With the remarkable exception of the death of Jesus on the cross, and of the doctrine of atonement by vicarious suffering, which is absolutely excluded by Buddhism, the most ancient of the Buddhistic records known to us contain statements about the life and the doctrines of Gautama Buddha which correspond in a remarkable manner, *and impossibly by mere chance*, with the traditions recorded in the Gospels about the life and doctrines of Jesus Christ...." Although other scholars, like Zacharias P. Thundy and Dr. Christian Lindtner claim that the ancient Buddhist play *Mricchakatika* was the Buddhist source for the Christian passion narative because of the numerous parallels.

Religious symbolism

T.W. Rhys Davids, son of a Congregationalist minister who was affectionately referred to as "the Bishop of Essex," was the earliest most energetic promoter of the Theravada tradition in the West. In 1878 he wrote of its northern counterpart: "Lamaism with its shaven priests, its bells and rosaries, its images and holy water, its popes and bishops, its abbots and monks of many grades, its processions and feast days, its confessional and purgatory, and its worship of the double Virgin, so strongly resembles Romanism that the first Catholic missionaries thought it must be an imitation by the devil of the religion of Christ."

The Buddhist symbol of the eight spoked wheel is also found in Saint Peter's Plaza in Vatican. It is believed use of rosaries spread from India to Western Europe during the Crusades via its Muslim version, the tasbih. Some, however, suggest an alternative route. A form of prayer rope appears to have been used in Eastern Christendom much earlier; so, it is argued, the Muslim tasbih may in fact originate at a Christian source. Both, it is pointed out, have 33 beads, corresponding to the years of Christ's life. Prayer with the palms touching one another, the Añjali Mudrâ, is a common form of greeting and prayer gesture in all Indian spiritual traditions, including the Buddhist. It is absent in Jewish traditions, whose scriptures specify raised or clasped hands. Prayer with the palms touching one another is, however, depicted in Christian art from the middle Ages onwards. In 1921, Sir Charles Eliot, writing of apparent similarities between Christian practices and their counterparts in Buddhist tradition, expressed the view that: " When all allowance is made for similar causes and coincidences, it is hard to believe that a collection of such practices as clerical celibacy, confession, the veneration of relics, the use of the rosary and bells can have originated independently in both religions."

CRITICISM

There is some historical basis for the assertion that Buddhist influence was a factor in the formation of Christianity and of the Christian Gospels. The rock-inscriptions of Asoka may bear witness to the spread of Buddhism over the Greek-speaking world as early as the third century BCE, since they mention the flourishing existence of Buddhism among the Greeks within the dominion of Antiochus. But although Greek rulers as far as the Mediterranean are mentioned as having received Buddhist missionaries, only in Bactria and the Kabul valley did Buddhism really take root.

Also, the statement in the late Buddhist chronicle of the Mahavamsa, that among the Buddhists who came to the dedication of a great Stupa in Sri Lanka in the second century BCE, "were over thirty thousand monks from the vicinity of Alassada, the capital of the Yona country" is sometimes taken to suggest that long before the time of Christ, Alexandria in Egypt was the centre of flourishing Buddhist communities. Although it is true that Alassada is the Pali for Alexandria; but it is usually thought that the city meant here is not the ancient capital of Egypt, but as the text indicates, the chief city of the Yona country, the Yavana country of the rock-inscriptions: Bactria and vicinity. And so, the city referred to is most likely Alexandria of the Caucasus.

Also, there are various views on the origins of the oldest Buddhist teachings of the Pali Canon and the origin of the later teachings of Mahayana Buddhism is especially obscure. It is believed that most of the Mahayana sutras only appeared after 100 BCE, and most did not reach their final form until much later (11th century AD). The earlier teachings of the Pali Canon and the Agamas however, are clearly up to four centuries older than Christianity.

Although Buddhism is older than Christianity, and some Buddhist influence, such as Barlaam and Josaphat, is clearly evident, it is difficult to tell whether the similarities between Buddhism and Christianity are a result of the Buddhist influence on Christianity, another influence which acted on both religions, and coincidence.

BUDDHIST VIEWS OF JESUS

Buddhist views of Jesus differ, since Jesus is not mentioned in any Buddhist text. Some Buddhists, including Tenzin Gyatso, the 14th Dalai Lama regard Jesus as a *Bodhisattva* who dedicated his life to the welfare of human beings. Both Jesus and Buddha advocated radical alterations in the common religious practices of the day. There are occasional similarities in language, such as the use of the common metaphor of a line of blind men to refer to religious authorities with whom they disagreed. Some believe there is a particularly close affinity between Buddhism (or Eastern spiritual thought generally) and the doctrine of Gnostic texts such as The Gospel of Thomas.

The 14th century Zen master Gasan Joseki indicated that the Gospels were written by an enlightened being:

"And why take ye thought for raiment? Consider the lilies of the field, how they grow. They toil not, neither do they spin, and yet I say unto you that even Solomon in all his glory was not arrayed like one of these...Take therefore no thought for the morrow, for the morrow shall take thought for the things of itself." Gasan said: "Whoever uttered those words I consider an enlightened man."

GUANYIN AND THE VIRGIN MARY

Some have commented on the similarity between the Blessed Virgin Mary and Guan Yin. The Tzu-Chi Foundation, a Taiwanese Buddhist organization, also noticing the similarity, commissioned a portrait of Guan Yin and a baby that resembles the typical Madonna and Child painting. Some Chinese of the overwhelmingly Roman Catholic Philippines, in an act of syncretism, have identified Guan Yin with the Virgin Mary. During the Edo Period in Japan, when Christianity was banned and punishable by death, some underground Christian groups venerated the Virgin Mary disguised as a statue of Kannon; such statues are known as *Maria Kannon*. Many had a cross hidden in an inconspicuous location.

CHRISTIAN ATTEMPTS AT CONVERSION OF BUDDHISTS

In several Asian countries, Christian missionaries over the centuries have converted in many traditionally Buddhist communities. Buddhism in Sri Lanka was for several centuries heavily affected by Christian efforts to convert the population under subsequent Portuguese, Dutch and English colonizers. In the late 19th century a national Buddhist movement started, inspired by the American Buddhist Henry Steel Olcott, and empowered by the results of the Panadura debate between a Christian priest and the Buddhist monk Migettuwatte Gunananda Thera. Significant Christian populations exist in South Korea, Thailand and Japan. In countries like Thailand and Japan, Christianity is a small minority among other beliefs.

H.G. Wells in his *Outline of History* draws parallels between what he sees as the essentially similar messages of the Buddha and of Jesus, and contends that in each case followers and priests distorted the original teachings. Will Durant in *The Story of Philosophy* suggests that *Jesus-Buddha* corresponds to a "feminine ideology," Nietzsche to a masculine, and that *Plato-Socrates* fall somewhere in between. Paul Carus's *The Gospel of Buddha*, published in 1894, was modeled on the New Testament and told the story of Buddha through parables. Christopher Moore published in 2002 *Lamb: The Gospel According to Biff, Christ's Childhood Pal*, a novel which seeks to fill in the "lost" years of Jesus from the point of view of Jesus' childhood pal, "Levi bar Alphaeus who is called Biff".

They journey to the east, where they study Hindu, Taoist and Buddhist teachings. Other writers on Buddhisms relation to Christianity include the authors Arthur Lillie, Godfrey Higgins, Edward Washburn Hopkins, Zacharias P. Thundy, Christian Lindtner, Gene Matlock, Daniel Hopkins and Alexander Harris.

5

The Buddhas Teaching

ABHIDHAMMA

According to the Theravada tradition the Buddha dwelt in the celestial domain of the thirty-three divine beings (Tavatimsa-loka) to teach the doctrine of Abhidhamma to his mother for three months. Then he descended to the lake Anottata; where he instructed the same to his most illustrious disciple Sariputta in the form of mnemonic verses, who in turn taught it to the five hundred distinguished monks acknowledged as the *arahatas*. Thus Abhidhamma by way of the oral tradition of transmission (through *acharya*-disciple tradition) beginning with the Buddha was passed on to Sariputta and in the like manner through Bhaddaji, Sobhita, Piyajali, Piyapala, Piyadassi, Kosiyaputta, Siggava, Sandeha, Moggalliputta, Sudatta, Dhammiya, Dasaka, Sonaka and Revata; and then through Mahinda, Ittiya, Sambala, Pandita, and Bhaddanama it reached Sri Lanka. Interestingly, this tradition is still alive in Sri Lanka, Myanmar, and Thailand; though withered away in India, Pakistan, Bangladesh and Cambodia.

MEANING OF ABHIDHAMMA

Etymologically, Abhidhamma may be analysed as the compound of *abhi* ("to"; "toward"; "into") and *dhamma* (root: *dhr*, which means "to hold" or "bear"). However, in the context it is interpreted as "leading-to-that-which-contains-the-advanced or specialised-teachings" [of-the-Buddha]" when we examine the observations of the best known Pali commentator Buddhaghosa. The expert critic interprets the term 'Abhidhamma' as the *most advanced (atireka) or specialised (visesa) doctrine* to differentiate it from the doctrine of the *Sutta-Pitaka,* which is not so analytical; and which employs the common and conventional terms and approach.

It is noteworthy that every term of Abhidhamma has a specific connotation or well-defined meaning for the advanced monks or trainees. The above interpretation of Abhidhamma is further corroborated by the definition of 'Abhidharma' made by Vasubandhu in his Sanskrit treatise - the *Abhidharmakosa.* There he states that "Abhidharma is the undefiled wisdom and its concomitants. Further, whatever is instrumental to achieve that; or the corpus [which is an aid to that]" is Abhidharma. Asanga's interpretation of Abhidharma also extends to the understanding of the above meaning. Prefixing *abhi* in four ways with the *dhamma,* he interprets that

The dhamma which is *Nibbana-encountering;*

The dhamma which is *analytical;*

The dhamma which is *refutative* of the converse views;

The dhamma which is *progressive.*

The term Abhidharma (a-p'i-ta-mo) in the Chinese records interpret it as *ta fa* (great dhamma because of the greatness of the knowledge to the realisation of Four Noble Truths etc.); *wu-pi-fa* (peerless dhamma because of the eight forms of intelligence etc); sheng-fa (excellent dhamma as it is wisdom-realising); *tuei-fa* (facing dhamma) and *hsiang-fa* (proceeding dhamma as the cause-effect theory that proceeds from cause to effect). The modern scholars, namely, W.Geiger, T.W. and C.A.F.Rhys Davids, Oldenberg, I.B.Horner, E.J.Thomas, Kogen Mizuno, Ken Sakurabe, Taiken Kimura and Bhikkhu Jagdish Kashyap have made some serious studies to understand the meaning of this term.

Yet, no modern linguistic interpretation of the term throws any fresh light to the comprehension of the original meaning of the term because the study of Abhidhamma is not a *barren* linguistic exercise. It may be reiterated that every term of Abhidhamma is assigned a definite connotation; and is often interpreted by way of its characteristic (*lakkhana*), function (*rasa*), manifestation (*paccupatthana*) and proximate cause (*padatthan*). So, the linguistic interpretation of the term has often been misleading; and its variant renditions create more complications to a reader rather than to extend his understanding.

It is believed that Abhidhamma is a way of life; and is meant for the chosen few, particularly for the erudite monks or scholars with specialised training. It may be emphatically pointed out that the study demands no less seriousness than the study of the *Rg Veda* or *Quran*. The scholars interested in Abhidhamma may also turn to the living Burmese (or Myanmari) traditions for its purest comprehension; or the volumes of the commentaries on the canonical Abhidhammic literature.

The Seven Books of Abhidhamma are

1. *Dhammasangani;*
2. *Vibhanga;*
3. *Dhatukatha;*
4. *Puggalapannatti;*
5. *Kathavatthu;*
6. *Yamaka;* and
7. *Patthana.*

The Sarvastivadin tradition of Buddhism, however, does not accept the above text as the original composition, because they have somewhat similar texts on the *Vinaya Pitaka* and *Sutta Pitaka* in juxtaposition with the Pali versions; but are missing in the case of the Abhidhamma. Yet, the Sarvastivadins have equal number of the Abhidharmic texts:

1. *Sangitipariyayapada;*
2. *Dharmaskandha;*
3. *Dhatukaya-patha;*

4. *Prajnaptipada;*
5. *Vijnanapada;*
6. *Prakaranapada;*
7. *Jnanaprasthana.*

The Buddhist canons are classified into three; and the common and popular designation for each of these classifications is *pitaka* (literally, "basket"). These *pitakas* were first compiled in the first Buddhist council, which was held in Rajgir after the *parininbbana* (or the demise) of the Buddha (483 B.C) during the reign of Ajatasattu (Sanskritised Ajatasatru), the king of the Magadha *janapada* (or kingdom).

The first of these corpuses is called the *Vinaya Pitaka;* and the other two are called the *Sutta-Pitaka* and the *Abhidhamma-Pitaka.* The *Vinaya Pitaka* deals with the Buddhist codes and conducts and may be regarded as the Corpus of the Discipline. It supposedly records the recitations made by the thera Upali in the council. The latter two pitakas, collectively called the 'Dhamma' (or the doctrine), are the collection of the recitations given by Ananda (the closest disciple of the Buddha) in the same council. The recitations of the aforementioned two monks, as a matter of fact, are the answers by way of the explanations and elucidations to the questions posed by the President of the council - Mahathera Mahakassapa.

Many scholars believe that the Tipitaka was compiled in the third Buddhist council. But such claims are unfounded when we look at the *Mahavamsa* (one of the most reliable sources of the Buddhist history; and a principal source for the construction of the history of ancient India) it is explicitly stated that even before the convention of the third Buddhist council (which took place in Pataliputta [Sanskritised: Pataliputra or modern Patna during the reign of the Emperor Asoka] one thousand erudite monks "*well versed in the Tipitaka ...*" (or the three canons) were chosen for the re-compilation of the original and purest teachings of the Buddha to eliminate the interpolations crept therein in the original corpuses.

The above statement corroborates to the fact that the Tipitaka definitely existed before the third Buddhist council, however, its form could have been somewhat different from what was compiled in the third council; or what is handed down to us by the tradition in its current form. The *Abhidhamma Pitaka* primarily deals with the philosophy and psychology of the Theravada school of Buddhism.

The "*theravada*", however, refers to that school of Buddhism which, supposedly "adhere to the most original and purest form of the Buddhist teachings", advocated by those *theras* (monks) who obtained the erudition directly through the Master. Further, they used the *bhasa Magadhika* or the *mula bhasa* (the original language) to record the original text or the *pariyaya*, (the text of the canons). The term *pariyaya*, however, when abbreviated became 'pari' or 'pali'; and in course of time was applied to denote the language of the entire gamut of the canons; and the exegeses and other compositions on those texts having the same language.

The virtue of *mudita*, i.e., finding joy in the happiness and success of others, has not received sufficient attention either in expositions of Buddhist ethics, or in the meditative development of the four sublime states *(brahma-vihara)*, of which *mudita* is one. It was, therefore, thought desirable to compile this little book of essays and texts and to mention in this introduction a few supplementary features of this rather neglected subject. It has been rightly stated that it is relatively easier for man to feel compassion or friendliness in situations which demand them, than to cherish a spontaneous feeling of shared joy, outside a narrow circle of one's family and friends.

It mostly requires a deliberate effort to identify oneself with the joys and successes of others. Yet the capacity of doing so has psychological roots in man's nature which may be even deeper that his compassionate responses. There is firstly the fact that people *do* like to feel happy (with - or without - good reason) and would prefer it to the shared sadness of compassion. Man's gregarious nature (his "sociability") already gives him some familiarity with shared emotions and shared pleasure, though mostly on a much lower level than that of our present concern. There is also in man (and in some animals) not only an aggressive impulse, but also a natural bent towards mutual aid and co-operative action.

Furthermore, there is the fact that happiness is infectious and an unselfish joy can easily grow out of it. Children readily respond by their own smiles and happy mood to smiling faces and happiness around them. Though children can be quite jealous and envious at times, they also can visibly enjoy it when they have made a playmate happy by a little gift and they are then quite pleased with themselves. Let parents and educators wisely encourage this potential in the child. Then this seed will quite naturally grow into a strong plant in the adolescent and the adult, maturing from impulsive and simple manifestations into the sublime state of unselfish joy (*mudita*-brahmavihara). Thus, here too, the child may become "the father of a man."

Such education towards joy with others should, of course, not be given in a dry didactic manner, but chiefly in a practical way by gently making the child observe, appreciate, and enjoy the happiness and success of others and by trying himself to create a little joy in others. This can be aided by acquainting the child with examples of selfless lives and actions for his joyful admiration of them (and these, of course, should not be limited to Buddhist history). This feature should not be absent in Buddhist youth literature and schoolbooks, throughout all age groups. And this theme should be continued in Buddhist magazines and literature for adults.

Admittedly, the negative impulses in man, like aggression, envy, jealousy, etc., are much more in evidence than his positive tendencies towards communal service, mutual aid, unselfish joy, generous appreciation of the good qualities of his fellow-men, etc. Yet, as all these positive features are definitely found in man (though rarely developed), it is quite realistic to appeal to them, and activate and develop that potential by whatever means we can, in our personal relationships, in education, etc. "If it were impossible to cultivate the Good, I would not tell you to do so," said the Buddha.

This is, indeed, a positive, optimistic assurance. If this potential for unselfish joy is widely and methodically encouraged and developed, starting with the Buddhist child (or, for that matter, with any child) and continued with adults (individuals and Buddhist groups, including the *Sangha*), the seed of *mudita* can grow into a strong plant which will blossom forth and find fruition in many other virtues, as a kind of beneficial "chain reaction": magnanimity, tolerance, generosity (of both heart and purse), friendliness, and compassion. When unselfish joy grows, many noxious weeds in the human heart will die a natural death (or will, at least, shrink): jealousy and envy, ill will in various degrees and manifestations, cold-heartedness, miserliness (also in one's concern for others), and so forth.

Unselfish joy can, indeed, act as a powerful agent in releasing dormant forces of the Good in the human heart. We know very well how envy and jealousy (the chief opponents of unselfish joy) can poison a man's character as well as the social relationships on many levels of his life. They can paralyze the productivity of society, on governmental, professional, industrial, and commercial levels. Should not, therefore, all effort be made to cultivate their antidote, that is *mudita*? *Mudita* will also vitalize and ennoble charitable and social work. While compassion *(karuna)* is, or should be, the inspiration for it, unselfish joy should be its boon companion.

Mudita will prevent compassionate action from being marred by a condescending and patronizing attitude which often repels or hurts the recipient. Also, when active compassion and unselfish joy go together, it will be less likely that works of service turn into dead routine performed indifferently. Indifference, listlessness, boredom (all nuances of the Pali term *arati)* are said to be the 'distant enemies' of *mudita*. They can be vanquished by an alliance of compassion and unselfish joy. In him who gives and helps, the joy he finds in such action will enhance the blessings imparted by these wholesome deeds: unselfishness will become more and more natural to him, and such ethical unselfishness will help him towards a better appreciation and the final realization of the Buddha's central doctrine of No-self *(anatta)*.

He will also find it confirmed that he who is joyful in his heart will gain easier the serenity of a concentrated mind. These are, indeed, great blessings which the cultivation of joy with others' happiness can bestow! Nowadays, moral exhortations fall increasingly on deaf ears, whether they are motivated theologically or otherwise. Preaching morals with an admonishing finger is now widely resented and rejected. This fact worries greatly the churches and educators in the West. But there are ample indications that this may, more or less, happen also in the Buddhist countries of the East where ethics is still taught and preached in the old hortatory style and mostly in a rather stereotype and unimaginative way, with little reference to present-day moral and social problems.

Hence modern youth will increasingly feel that such "moralizings" are not their concern. In fact within the frame of the Buddhist teachings which do not rely on the authoritarian commandments of God and church, but on man's innate capacity for self-purification, such conventionalized presentation of ethics which chiefly relies on over-worked scriptural references, must appear quite incongruous and will prove increasingly ineffective for young and old alike. The need for reform in this field is urgent and of vital importance. It was also with this situation in view, that the preceding observations have stressed the fact that a virtue like unselfish and altruistic joy has its natural roots in the human heart and can be of immediate benefit to the individual and society.

In other words, the approach to a modern presentation of Buddhist ethics should be pragmatic and contemporary, enlivened by a genuine and warm-hearted human concern. In this troubled world of ours, there are plenty of opportunities for thoughts and deeds of compassion; but there seem to be all too few for sharing in others' joy. Hence it is necessary for us to create new opportunities for unselfish joy, by the active practice of loving-kindness (*metta*) and compassion (*karuna*), in deeds, words, and meditative thought. Yet, in a world that can never be without disappointments and failures, we must also arm ourselves with the equanimity (*upekkha*) to protect us from discouragement and feelings of frustration, should we encounter difficulties in our efforts to expand the realm of unselfish joy.

A NEGLECTED VIRTUE

Mudita - unselfish or sympathetic joy - is one of the most neglected topics within the whole range of the Buddha Dhamma, probably because of its subtlety and of the wealth of nuances latent within it. Besides getting honorable mention within the context of The Four Divine Abidings *(brahma-vihara),* few commentators have had much more to say about it apart from explaining that it means "sympathetic joy at the good fortune or success of others." Only one notable writer, Conze (in *Buddhist Thought in India),* has had the insight to suggest that *mudita,* i.e. sympathy, is a pre-requisite of *metta* (loving-kindness) and of *karuna* (compassion).

He thus names appreciation as one of the components of *mudita.* How right he is! For one cannot appreciate another person without seeing some good in him. If one does not appreciate the other person in the slightest degree, one would be hard put to experience joy at any stroke of good fortune or success that may befall him. To stimulate feelings of pleasure when, in fact, one feels none, would be the grossest of hypocrisy. Thus, *mudita* tacitly implies looking for the good in others and learning to recognize and admire what good there is.

Likewise, if one has a misanthropic view of mankind, regarding people as essentially evil and not worth being concerned about, one cannot, on the face of it, make much headway with any of The Four Divine Abidings. To have a sympathetic attitude towards human beings does not betoken an idealization of man, but rather a realistic appraisal: that, though often in error and grievously at fault, man has, nevertheless, the potential to rise above his darkness and ignorance into the light of knowledge and even to undreamed of heights of Nirvana.

Unless one has that measure of faith and confidence in mankind which the Buddha himself had, the practice of *metta* and *karuna* is impossible. Thus, the broadest and most simple aspect of *mudita* as sympathy towards mankind is also the most basic and important. To regard *mudita* as being relevant only on certain relatively rare occasions when our friends and acquaintances come into a bonanza of some kind, is to fragment it and render it trivial, thereby missing the essential matrix. It should not be regarded as a matter of turning on a tap from which *mudita* will gush forth.

There should be, in a certain sense, a quiet stream of sympathy and understanding flowing within the individual all the time. Though, to be sure, it does also mean developing the capacity to participate in another person's finest hour and doing so spontaneously and sincerely. It is indeed a depressing fact that people are much more ready to sympathize with the misfortunes of others than to rejoice with them, a psychological quirk in people which wrung from Montaigne the ironic statement:

> There is something altogether not too displeasing in the misfortunes of our friends.

Turning back to the essential matrix of *mudita* as sympathy towards mankind, faith in its potential for good and acceptance of its worthwhileness, this is precisely what is lacking in the world today. There is abroad a kind of cosmic gloom and, among some large sections of people, a feeling of defeatism. Probably the scene is largely colored by the shadow of the hydrogen bomb and the various other horrible weapons of destruction which we know the nations are so busy in manufacturing. All in all, too much has happened in too short a time.

More scientific and technological discoveries have been telescoped into the last fifty (or is it thirty?) years than in the previous five hundred, and the total result is, at the moment, of dubious benefit to humanity as a whole, though of inestimable worth to the new millionaires who have managed to muscle in on the expanding economy. Electric and nuclear power, the spectacular forging ahead of communication, transport and industry have brought in their wake such negative by-products as over-population, more and more urbanization into colossal, concentrated centers, such as Tokyo, New York, and London (and even Sydney and Melbourne), which, in turn, has given rise to other unfortunate results, both physical, and psychological: pollution from industrial waste, destruction of natural resources; individual de-socialization, alienation, stress, as evidenced by the delinquency figures, the drift to drugs, character disorders, feelings of the meaninglessness of life, rise in crime, wanton destructiveness (a sure symptom of frustration and an unlived life), despair, suicide.

We know that such ills have always existed in society, and that probably they always will to some degree, but the frightening thing about the present situation is that they are insidiously increasing, in spite of the fact that many people, and especially the youth, have never had it so good. As it is, man feels more insecure than ever, more uncertain and lost. Viewing these symptoms, many people throughout the world have drawn the conclusion that man has arrived at the period of moral decline and disintegration and that humanity has become so depraved as to be hopelessly beyond redemption or recall. Such a view has always been characteristic of old age. We can, with a certain degree of amusement read the lines:

To whom do I speak today? Brothers are evil; Friends today are not of love. To whom do I speak today? Hearts are thievish; every man seizes his neighbor's goods. To whom do I speak today? The gentle man perishes, the bold-faced goes everywhere... To whom do I speak today? When a man should arouse wrath by his evil conduct, He stirs all men to mirth, although his iniquity is wicked...

The above admonition was composed in ancient Egypt during the Middle Kingdom, thousands of years ago, but the words are those which every generation hears. There is proneness in periods of crisis and transition, to conjure up in the mind a fantasy of a previous golden age, when people were of sterling worth and life was lived in accordance with the noble virtues. But, we may well ask, when was there such an age, and where? If people who harbor such quaint notions were to read history, they would realize that such a belief is just about as valid as that there ever was a time "when flowers bloomed for ever and sweethearts were always true," in the words of the old song.

Ancient history and the middle Ages are definitely OUT as far as morality is concerned. Without going so far back, merely a couple of hundred years, Smollett wrote this of eighteenth century England:

Commerce and manufacture flourished to such a degree of increase as has never been known in this island; but this advantage was attended with an irresistible tide of luxury and excess which flowed through all degrees of people, breaking down all the bounds of civil policy, and opening a way for licentiousness and immorality. The highways were infested with rapine and assassination; the cities teemed with the brutal votaries of lewdness, intemperance, and profligacy.

In the nineteenth century (relatively recently), Wordsworth wrote:

The wealthiest man among us is the best: No grandeur now in nature or in book Delight us. Rapine, avarice, expense, this is idolatry; and these we adore. Plain living and high thinking are no more; the homely beauty of the good old cause is gone, our fearful innocence, and pure religion breathing household laws.

And James Hemming, a modern writer in his book *Individual Morality:*

Nineteenth-century London was frequently shaken by the destructive antics of informally organized hooligan gangs of young aristocrats. Those young roughs, having idled away their days, spent their nights beating people up, smashing up coffee stalls, alarming women and such like - the Bucks, the Corinthians, and all their imitators and hangers-on. Such bands were following, somewhat less cruelly, in the tradition of the nefarious Mohocks, who terrorized eighteenth-century London.

Sexual propriety? Quoting again from Hemming:

Brothels in the nineteenth century were big business, and, laws to forbid living on the immoral earnings of women, after several rebuffs in Parliament, did not reach the statute books till 1885.

But this was in England, the most progressive country in Europe. There is no evidence for believing that conditions were better on the Continent. Understandably, twenty-five years after World War II, we are still appalled by the memory of the Nazi gas-chambers and the genocide which was their aim. This is by no means an isolated instance of genocide. History bears witness to similar incidents of destructive hate, culminating in mass murder.

The Albigenses were wiped out to a man, and in 1572, at the Massacre of St. Bartholomew's Eve, thousands of Huguenots were slaughtered, Pope Gregory XIII commanding bonfires to be lit and a medal to be struck in celebration! The idea that the mass destruction of one's ideological enemies is justified was already old in the days of the Old Testament. Saul was commanded:

Now go and smite Amalek, and utterly destroy all that they have and spare them not; but slay man and woman, infant and suckling, ox and sheep, camel and ass.

All of the foregoing is not intended as apologetics justifying violence, bloodbaths, or individual or collective acts of immorality but merely to dispel the myth that there was ever a previous idyllic phase, when man could have said with some semblance of truth:

God's in His Heaven and all's right with the world.

So, let us lay to rest forever the belief that in the past men were truer, kinder, more upright, and generally more worthy than they are today. Let us give that piece of romantic fiction the respectable funeral that it deserves. Our ancestors and predecessors were no better than we are, and we are certainly not worse than they were. In many respects we have improved considerably on the ways of our forbears. Actually, there has been a great deal of progress, considering that slavery hung on in England until 1772, in America till 1863, and serfdom in Russia till 1861.

And, in spite of the injustices and lack of moral scruples that still exist, there is more awareness, kindliness, and sensitivity in many human societies than there has ever been before. Today when a national disaster of great magnitude occurs in a country, quite often the rest of the world rallies around and helps - perhaps not to the extent that it should, but nonetheless, to *some* extent. Such a broadening expansion of the human conscience would have been deemed a Utopian ideal in former times and impossible. When acts of genocide were perpetrated in the past, people just accepted it: that was that, and there was nothing to be done about it.

In our time, the whole world was revolted by the Nazi gas-chambers, eventually rose against the loathsome disease of Fascism and smashed it even thought it took the combined might of the allied force five years of bitter conflict to do so. However, in the past, without exception, whatever was inflicted upon a people, they mostly took.

Today they don't - they protest, they demonstrate, they kick up a fuss. They have become articulate because they have realized that the greatest evil of all is not poverty, racialism, or war but powerlessness.

Naturally, such an unexpected show of interest in public affairs is embarrassing to governments accustomed to an inert and docile population and there is some wistful talk by diehards of "the silent majority," but the present indications are that "the silent majority" is likely to become a silent minority in the face of such urgent problems as over-population, and destruction of natural resources, which, if left unchecked, will make the earth uninhabitable within a foreseeable future. However, against this general tendency is the lamentable fact that nothing was done about the rape of Tibet, and even now there are no large-scale or forceful protests being made about the genocide that is being practiced in that country by the Chinese?

So, far from feeling dejected and dispirited about mankind, we should be hopeful and buoyant. There would be infinitely more cause for alarm and despair if people were as easy to manipulate as sheep or merely apathetic. The arguing and the restlessness throughout the world is about the principles on which we should run our lives, a struggle for values other than the profit motive, for ways and means to make possible greater co-operation between individuals and nations, and for moral maturity in coping with man's new powers and responsibilities.

People discuss, argue, petition, protest, demonstrate because of their sympathy, compassion, and love for mankind. It is very difficult to differentiate between the three or to recognize precisely the line of demarcation where one ends and the other begins, because they are illimitable. There are, of course, others who see in these conflicts only hatred but this view is hardly tenable because it is much easier and much more comfortable to remain uninvolved, drifting with the current, nor swimming against it.

The Ven. Nyanaponika has summed up the interdependence of the Four Divine Abidings in the following quotation:

Love imparts to equanimity its selflessness, its boundless nature and even its fervor...

Compassion guards equanimity from falling into cold indifference and keeps it from indolent or selfish isolation. Until equanimity has reached perfection, compassion urges it to enter again and again into the battlefields of the world. Sympathetic joy gives to equanimity the mild serenity that softens its stern appearance. It is the divine smile on the face of the Enlightened One.

MUDITA

A feature of the Buddha-Dhamma is cognizance of the pairs of opposites in the training to get beyond them. The Buddha's method of mental training and development was to teach by first defining unwholesome or unskillful thoughts, words, and deeds, or practices which characterize many of man's proclivities, and then to propound their opposites of a wholesome or skillful nature as an achievement to be sought after for the abolition of them both, eventually, when even the good must be left behind as well as the evil; when even the Raft of Dhamma is to be abandoned - after crossing the flood of *samsara*.

The trouble with so many of the unwise is their desire to abandon the Raft of Dhamma before reaching the further shore. The Buddha's method of expounding the negative and the positive, the passive, and the dynamic aspects of behavior, in both abstract and concrete terms, is obviously to create awareness of what is to be sought after and nurtured. The basic ignorance featured in Buddhism is not so much a rejection of the truth as it is a failure to perceive it. It is, as it were, a "blind spot" in our perception akin to the physical damage of a section of the brain or the nervous system which results in impaired vision or locomotion.

In other words, the depth of our ignorance may be measured by our lack of consciousness of it. This is why it is so necessary that we should see and recognize our failings and shortcomings if we are to eradicate them. It is also important that we should be mindful of "the good that has arisen," and to foster and develop it to the point of perfection. To realize our imperfections is the beginning of wisdom - the first light to shine on the darkness of our ignorance. While we are blissfully unaware of unwholesome states of mind within ourselves, such states will continue to flourish, and their roots will dig deeper into our very being.

Just so too, in our relationships with our fellow men, the unperceived evils will be repeated unconsciously and unrecognized, building up a cumulative unhappy future for us under the retributive causal law of karma. In dealing with *mudita* or altruistic joy, we are once more to some extent frustrated with the inadequacy of translations for *brahma-vihara* or *appamañña* - the former as "sublime or divine abode," and the latter as "boundless state." To reduce either of these terms to modern idiom is difficult. The four characteristics grouped under these terms are: loving-kindness, compassion, altruistic joy, and equanimity, extended to universal application. In their perfection they are "sublime" and "boundless," and to be "dwelt in" as one speaks of "dwelling in Peace," so we will leave it at that.

As with all perfections, these four desirable characteristics are the antidotes to the poisons of their opposite imperfections, and here is where the recognition of their opposites is apposite. Less has been said or written of *mudita* than of the other three of these four characteristics, perhaps, again, because of its somewhat clumsy translation. While loving-kindness and compassion are objective, reaching out to all sentient beings, *mudita* and equanimity are subjective, or personal in their application. It may seem strange at first, until we critically examine the source, to speak of either selfish or unselfish joy. Joy is an emotional ecstasy arising from pleasure. It is something intensely personal.

While we can and do share our pleasures to some extent with others, the resultant impact of them on various personalities will vary as widely as the personalities. At times what may give rise to rapturous joy in us, when shared, may give rise to positive aversion in another. A pertinent example of this would be the reactionary effect of certain music on people of differing tastes. While it is not uncommon for some of the modern generation to literally swoon in ecstasy under the influence of the combination of discordant and dissonant notes and chords, others find them anything but entertaining or pleasurable.

Here we have what might be termed "selfish joy" on the part of the participants, by those who have to suffer most unwilling participation. For all that, within the group enjoying it, there is reciprocity of delight, happiness, and rapture between the entertainers and the entertained. Superficially, then, we could say it is not the phenomenon of joy itself, that is either selfish or altruistic by nature, but that time, place, and circumstance must all be considered in relation one to the others. However, to bring *mudita* within the ambit of the Buddha-Dhamma we need to go deeper into the necessity for cultivating this perfection. What are the opposites to be eliminated by its cultivation?

We never tire of asserting the interdependence of every aspect of the Buddha-Dhamma, no matter which particular facet is being discussed. We have already stated that ignorance is failure of perception, and it is true that greed and hatred do arise through the non-perception of their source and subsequent results; that basically craving born of ignorance is the culprit, and that the purpose of the Buddha-Dhamma is to eliminate craving. It is craving that gives rise to jealousy, envy, covetousness, avarice, and greed in all of its manifestations. Here it is that *mudita* when practiced and developed becomes a "sublime" and "boundless" state of mind to be "dwelt in" as a corrective characteristic for their removal.

One of the most frequently used similes by the Buddha was that of fire. At times it was the destructive quality of fire that was likened to the destructive nature of the passions. At other times it was the ardent nature of fire that was to be emulated in the pursuance of the path to holiness. In its uncontrolled existence fire is a destructive danger. Under control it is one of man's greatest boons and blessings. In either case it was a motivating force to be reckoned with, at all times active, potent, and energetic. The three roots of evil - greed, hatred, and delusion - are also known as "the three fires."

On one occasion the Buddha and his band of monks were for the time staying on Gaya Head, a mountain near the city of Gaya. From their elevated position they watched one of the great fires that from time to time ravaged the countryside. This inspired what is known as "The Fire Sermon," which the third recorded discourse is delivered by the Buddha subsequent to his Enlightenment, and at the beginning of his long ministry. To the Buddha, the world of *Samsara* was like the flaming plains below, "Everything is burning," said the Buddha, "burning with the fire of passion, with the fired of hatred, with the fire of stupidity." (Vin. 21)

It is these three fires that give rise to jealousy, envy, covetousness, avarice, and greed. The craving for possessions, the craving for sensual pleasures, the begrudged success of others, the hatred that is begotten by the gains of others, the odious comparison of greater status compared with our humble circumstances, these are the "fires" that burn within us to our undoing. It is now evident why *mudita* is such an important characteristic to be cultivated. When we can view the success of others with the same equanimity, and to the same extent, as we would extend *metta* and *karuna* - loving-kindness and compassion - to those who suffer grief and distress, sadness and tribulation, sorrow and mourning, then we are beginning to exercise *mudita,* and are in the process of eradicating greed and craving.

Developed still further, we can reach the stage of sharing with others their joy of possession, their financial or social successes, their elevation to positions of civic or national importance, or their receipt of titles and honorifics. In such a manner *mudita* is counteractive to conceits of all kinds, and its growth and development checks craving's grip. Until we have developed this subjective characteristic within ourselves how can we develop the objective characteristics of *metta* and *karuna?* The accumulated possessions, results of our greed, may give us the pleasure and the happiness of the miser gloating over his hoard of gold. The happiness born of shared pleasures, shared love, shared possessions, shared delights in another's success, will surpass the meager selfish happiness of the miser.

Unselfish joy multiplies in ratio to the extension of its application, quite apart from its purifying effect on our own lives. In Ñanamoli's translation of Buddhaghosa's *Visuddhimagga* he uses "gladness" for *mudita,* with the footnote: "*Mudita* - gladness - as one of the divine abidings is always used in the sense of gladness at others' success." Buddhaghosa illustrates this by saying: "On seeing or hearing about a dear person being happy cheerful and glad, gladness can be aroused thus: 'This being is indeed glad. How good! How excellent!'

Just as he would be glad on seeing a dear and beloved person, so he pervades all being with gladness."

In "The Analysis of the Sixfold Sense-Field" the Buddha speaks of the six joys connected with renunciation. While such joys are subjective by nature, they are devoid of any taint of egoistic craving that could give rise to the cankers of jealousy, envy, covetousness, or greed. These joys arise on the realization of the impermanence of material shapes, sounds, smells, flavors, touches, and mental states, and the renunciation of attachment to them.

THE NATURE AND IMPLICATIONS OF MUDITA

Altruistic joy is one of the four "sublime states" of mind - friendliness, compassion, altruistic joy, and equanimity - which together form one related group among the various spiritual or physical exercises generally described as meditation or contemplation. These all have as their common aim the attainment of mental calm or equanimity, which is intended in turn to foster the development of liberating insight. "A still mind, like still water, yields a clear reflection of what is before it." This is why this particular series ends with equanimity, but the route by which it is attained in this case is different from that traversed for the most of the other themes used as a focus for concentration.

The others, such as meditation on the breath, on death, on visual objects *(kasina)*, or on the Buddha, the Doctrine, and the Order of the Enlightened One, are entirely concerned with the self-cultivation of the meditator. Most of these themes are abstract or inanimate, while the Buddha and the Order (in the strict sense applicable here) have transcended any power of ours to help or hinder them. So the only person concerned or affected in these forms of training is the meditator. It was doubtless to encourage those wrestling by these means with their own inner weakness or conflicts that the following verse of the *Dhammapada* was uttered:

Let no one neglect his own task for the sake of another's however great; let him, after he has discerned his own task, devote himself to his task. – *Dhammapada*, 166

But if this were the whole story it would be difficult for such self-cultivation to serve in turn as a basis for the freedom from bondage to the self-concept, which is the main characteristic of the development of insight. Indeed, it was the recognition of the dangers of self-preoccupation, or self-righteousness, liable to arise in these often acute struggles for self-discipline, that impelled the more extreme exponents of the Pure Land school of Buddhism to abandon self-cultivation in favor of the less exacting path of reliance on the Buddha's transforming grace.

But the cultivation of the "sublime states" represents a less radical form of compensation which, while compatible with other practices, can help to broaden the meditator's perspective in order to achieve a mode of equanimity which does not imply withdrawal into oneself or indifference to others. The starting point here, of course, is on the ethical plane in the practice of generosity in practical ways *(dana)* which, in order to become interiorized and thereby go beyond mere outward form, must be grounded in an attitude of friendliness *(metta)* for all beings without distinction.

Since this outlook implies the recognition that all beings are subject to joys and sorrows just as we are, it finds a natural development in sympathy - that is to say, compassion - for their sorrows and joy in their blessings. The former of these seems much the easier to achieve, since it is possible to feel compassion for suffering even in the absence of any positive friendliness for the sufferer, whereas it is only possible to share genuinely in another's joy if there is some element of true affection or friendliness present.

This is perhaps why, on a much lower level of sensitivity, the reporting of news seems so heavily concentrated on the side of crimes and disasters, which are perhaps felt more likely to arouse interest than happier events and deeds. If the latter arouse any interest at all, it is likely to be spiced with envy or cynicism. Not only does genuine joy in the prosperity of others require some element of affection; it requires this to be of a quite high order. A great deal of what passes for love is really aimed at mere emotional gratification on the part of the lover, for whom the "beloved" is little more than a prop for acting out some drama satisfying a purely subjective need - the beloved's own needs being treated less seriously.

Indeed, even apart from outright commercialization, a certain habit of bargaining with affections seems remarkably widespread, when one begins to take notice of it. In the light of this, the ability to feel a genuine joy in another's happiness, equal to one's satisfaction with one's own, represents a truly "sublime state." So it is not surprising that in the history of Buddhism, which cultivated this attitude systematically, there arose an aspiration to share with others not only one's material resources, but the spiritual resources described as merit.

This aspiration follows naturally enough from the basic theory as to what merit is. Merit is the accumulation of tendencies resulting from enlightened deeds which, according to the law of moral causation (the law of karma), conduce to the future happiness of the doer.

Here he is joyful, hereafter he is joyful, and in both worlds the well-doer is joyful. "I have done good" is the thought that make him happy. Still greater is his joy when he goes to states of bliss. If the doer is still in a state where only purely personal forms of satisfaction are possible, the fruits of merit can only take this form. But suppose he loves even one being so much that, if that being is in some state of deprivation, he can only be made happy by the improvement of that being's lot, then the merit which is due to him can only take effect by benefiting him through that other's welfare.

The wider his altruism expands, so that purely personal gratifications no longer adequately satisfy him, the wider must be the range of the benefit which his own merit would need to bring to others if it is to fulfill its defined function of bringing happiness to him. At the same time, his altruistic tendencies will ensure that he will have vastly more merit due to him, so his resources will tend to become commensurate with the aspirations, for example, of Santideva, when he says:

May I be an alleviator of the sorrows of all beings and a divine medicine to those afflicted by disease? May I be the benefactor and bringer of peace to them until all their bodily ailments and mental tribulations are at the end.

The principle of the sharing or transference of merit, so much stressed in Mahayana Buddhism (though not unknown in Theravadan practices) is sometimes objected to by Western Buddhists because of a superficial resemblance to the Christian doctrine of atonement, which they have rejected. But the principles entailed are not really identical, since the Christian doctrine is based on an essential distinction between the roles of the Creator and the created, while the Buddhist sharing of merit arises from a combination of the definition of merit and of the nature of altruistic joy.

It has a further importance too, in that it anticipates the emancipation to be derived from insight into the emptiness of the self-concept, that is to say, awakening to the emptiness of the concepts "I" and "mine" in terms of ultimate truth. On this level, the description "mine" as applied to merit will finally be seen to be as inapplicable as in the case of any other assumed possession. This was already explicitly set out in one of the Buddha's earliest discourses, "The Marks of the Not-self," in which he taught his first five disciples to contemplate each of the five components of personality in the terms: "This is not mine; this I am not; this is not my self."

The fourth of these components is the aggregate of mental tendencies or activities, which include merit and demerit. Even on a lower plane than that of perfect insight, it can be seen that our deeds are not exclusively ours, because no one acts in absolute isolation, so that every act involves some stimulus or opportunity arising from activity of others. On the other hand, a too persistent insistence on the individual nature of merit can only impede the ultimate awakening to the Not-self.

This has some bearing, too, on the reason why friendliness, compassion, and altruistic joy are regarded as leading to an equanimity which does not imply an indifference to the joys and sorrows of others. In the absence of such a conclusion, the alternate sharing of joys and sorrows, like these emotions arising on one's own account, would be as endless as the world-cycles which it is the Buddhist aspiration to transcend. The goal of the "divine states" is that the aspirant, who in process achieves the role of a *Bodhisattva* in a two-way empathy with others by his perfect sharing of their joys and sorrows, is in a position to radiate to them stability, which in turn will help them to be less subject to their own emotional vicissitudes. In this way, he and they are liberated together, each sustaining the other.

THE MEDITATIVE DEVELOPMENT OF UNSELFISH JOY

One who begins the development of unselfish joy should not start with dearly beloved person, a neutral person or hostile person. For it is not the mere fact that a person is dearly beloved, which makes him an immediate cause of developing unselfish joy, and still less so neutral or hostile person. Persons of the opposite sex and those who are dead are not suitable subjects for this meditation. A very close friend, however, can be a suitable subject. One who is called in the commentaries an affectionate companion; for he is always in a joyous mood: he laughs first and speaks afterwards. He should be the first to be pervaded with unselfish joy.

Or on seeing or hearing about a dear person being happy, cheerful, and joyous, unselfish joy can be aroused thus: "This being, verily, is happy! How good, how excellent!" For this is what is referred to in the Vibhanga: "And how does a bhikkhu dwell pervading one direction with his heart imbued with unselfish joy? Just as he would be joyful on seeing a dear and beloved person, so he pervades all being with unselfish joy". But if his affectionate friend or the dear person was happy in the past but is now unlucky and unfortunate, then unselfish joy can still be aroused by remembering his past happiness; or by anticipating that he will be happy and successful again in the future.

Having thus aroused unselfish joy with respect to a dear person, the meditator can then direct it towards a neutral one, and after that towards a hostile one. But if resentment towards the hostile one arises in him, he should make it subside in the same way as described under the exposition of loving-kindness. He should then break down the barriers by means of impartiality towards the four that is, towards these three and himself. And by cultivating the sign (or after-image, obtained in concentration), developing and repeatedly practicing it, he should increase the absorption to triple or (according to the Abhidhamma division) quadruple *jhana*.

Next, the versatility (in this meditation) should be understood in the same way as stated under loving-kindness. It consists in:

a. Unspecified pervasion in these five ways:

"May all beings... all breathing things... all creatures... all persons... all those who have a personality be free from enmity, affliction, and anxiety, and live happily!"

b. Specified pervasion in these seven ways:

"May all women... all men... all Noble Ones... all not Noble Ones... all deities... all human beings... all in states of misery (in lower worlds) be free from enmity, etc."

c. Directional pervasion in these ten ways:

"May all beings (all breathing things, etc.; all women, etc.) in the eastern direction... in the western direction... northern... southern direction... in the intermediate eastern, western, northern, and southern direction... in the downward direction... in the upward direction be free from enmity, etc."

This versatility is successful only in one whose mind has reached absorption (*jhana*). When this meditator develops the mind-deliverance of unselfish joy through any of these kinds of absorption he obtains these eleven advantages: he sleeps in comfort, wakes in comfort, and dreams no evil dreams, he is dear to human beings, dear to non-human beings, deities guard him, fire and poison and weapons do not affect him, his mind is easily concentrated, the expression of his face is serene, he dies unconfused, if he penetrates no higher he will be reborn in the Brahma World.

THE BUDDHA'S TEACHING AND THE ORIGIN OF LIFE

Daya Sirisena, President, Board of Trustees, Sirisena Dharma Mandiraya, Meditation Centre, Moratuwa Pepiliyana Sunethradevi Pirivena. The Gautama Buddha did not give any specific teaching regarding the origin of the universe or of life, the question was said to be unanswerable from the level of ordinary mundane, intelligence. The Buddha explains "The origin of beings revolving in *Samsara* (Life Cycle) being cloaked by *Avijja* (ignorance) is undiscoverable.

At the same time it is laid down as a natural consequence of the law of Dependant Origination, (paticca-samuppada) that in the ceaseless cycle of cause and effect there cannot be any link in the sequence that can be designated a first cause. Each effect in its turn becomes a cause and beginning is nowhere apparent, it is a closed circle of related conditions, each factor being dependant on the presiding ones.

When it is said the world cycles or world periods known in Buddhism as Kappas are of immeasurable duration, it must be remembered that all time concepts are relative, we measure them from our own stand point in an immeasurably, vaster space context, the time context is correspondingly enlarged, so that events covering millions of years by our calculations can be measurable in terms of seconds.

The brain may reel at the concept of infinity of space time constructions fitting into impregnating one another endlessly in all directions. But it is not entirely outside the scope of human imagination. It figures quite largely in Buddhist thought these are infinite number (conventionally expressed as "ten thousand" or "in calculable") of world-systems and thirty one planes of existence having vast differences in time measurement, what is unthinkable is a state of non causality where neither space, time nor events have any existence.

This has to be understood by direct perception, which means bursting the bonds of relativity, and its concepts and processes.

"Na Hethu deva Brahma va
Samsara Atathikarako
Suddhamma pavanthanthi
Hethu sambhara appaccayati"

"There is no God or Brahma
Who is the Creator of this world
Empty Phenomena roll on all
Subject to causality"

When we understand the truth there could never have been a beginning an origin out of nothingness of the universe or the life process. It is true that the universe as we know it evolved out of the dispersed matter of previous universe, and when it passes away it remains in the form of active forces will in time give rise to another universe in exactly the same way. The process is cyclic and continuous. This is why it is said in Buddhist-texts the origin of Phenomena is not discoverable and the beginning of beings obstructed by ignorance and enslave by craving is not to be found.

The same one universe gives rise to another through the residual energy which is continuously renewing itself that is through the principal of the indestructibility of matter. So the life of a being gives rise to another being which is not the same in identity and without involving an unchanging permanent self that which links them is called in Buddhism "Kamma" or volitioned activity; the continuation of the causal process is called "*Samsara*" or the cycles of rebirths: the actuality of rebirth and existence without any unchanging principal of identity or self is called "anatta".

"Nasacho Nassa Anno" from the craddle to the grave man's personality changes from infant, child, young person, old then the death. All link, same but not the same in actual sense, but accumulated tendencies or habit formations continue with the new life and continue, that is why the Buddha explains that the *Samsara* is long and hazardous. 2551 years ago Gauthama Sammaasambuddha discovered a incomparable doctrine to mankind all who could benefit by his teachings for 45 years from the re-sermon in Migadaya Baranesa to the five ascetic to the last exoration before the parinirvana it is one them, them of liberation to mankind.

Today signifies the Birth, Enlightenment, and *Parinirvana* of Gauthama Sammasambuddha. His voice speaks to us clearly today as ever did 2551 years ago not only through his teachings preserved over centuries, but through the discoveries of Modern Science. May all living beings be happy and content?

THE BUDDHAS UNIQUE METHODOLOGY

The Dhamma, the truth taught by the Buddha, unfolds gradually. The Buddha made clear many times that Awakening does not occur like a bolt out of the blue to the untrained and unprepared mind. Rather, it culminates a long journey of many stages:

Just as the ocean has a gradual shelf, a gradual slope, a gradual inclination, with a sudden drop-off only after a long stretch, in the same way this Doctrine and Discipline (dhamma-vinaya) has a gradual training, a gradual performance, a gradual progression, with a penetration to gnosis only after a long stretch.

Monks, I do not say that the attainment of gnosis is all at once. Rather, the attainment of gnosis is after gradual training, gradual action, and gradual practice. And how is there the attainment of gnosis after gradual training, gradual action, and gradual practice? There is the case where, when conviction has arisen, one visits [a teacher]. Having visited, one grows close. Having grown close, one lends ear. Having lent ear, one hears the Dhamma. Having heard the Dhamma, one remembers it. Remembering, one penetrates the meaning of the teachings.

Penetrating the meaning, one comes to an agreement through pondering the teachings. There being an agreement through pondering the teachings, desire arises. When desire has arisen, one is willing. When one is willing, one contemplates.

Having contemplated, one makes an exertion. Having made an exertion, one realizes with the body the ultimate truth and, having penetrated it with discernment, sees it. In more practical terms, the Buddha taught this "gradual training" (*anupubbi-katha*) as a process that unfolds in six stages, guiding newcomers from first principles through progressively more advanced teachings, all the way to the fulfillment of the Four Noble Truths and the full realization of *nibbana*:

Then the Blessed One, having encompassed the awareness of the entire assembly with his awareness, asked himself, "Now who here is capable of understanding the Dhamma?" He saw Suppabuddha the leper sitting in the assembly, and on seeing him the thought occurred to him, "This person here is capable of understanding the Dhamma." So, aiming at Suppabuddha the leper, he gave a step-by-step talk, i.e., a talk on giving, a talk on virtue, a talk on heaven; he declared the drawbacks, degradation, and corruption of sensual passions, and the rewards of renunciation. Then when he saw that Suppabuddha the leper's mind was ready, malleable, free from hindrances, elated, & bright, he then gave the Dhamma-talk peculiar to Awakened Ones, i.e., stress, origination, cessation, & path. And just as a clean cloth, free of stains, would properly absorb a dye, in the same way, as Suppabuddha the leper was sitting in that very seat, the dustless, stainless Dhamma eye arose within him, "Whatever is subject to origination is all subject to cessation."

At each stage of the training the practitioner discovers a new and important dimension of the law of cause-and-effect - kamma, the cornerstone of Right View. It is thus a very useful organizing framework with which to view the entirety of the Buddha's teachings. The gradual training begins with the practice of generosity, which helps begin the long process of weakening the unawakened practitioner's habitual tendencies to cling - to views, to sensuality, and to unskillful modes of thought and behavior. This is followed by the development of virtue, the basic level of sense-restraint that helps the practitioner develop a healthy and trustworthy sense of self. The peace of mind born from this level of self-respect provides the foundation for all further progress along the path.

The practitioner now understands that some kinds of happiness are deeper and more dependable than anything that sense-gratification can ever provide; the happiness born of generosity and virtue can even lead to rebirth in heaven - either literal or metaphorical. But eventually the practitioner begins to recognize the intrinsic drawbacks of even this kind of happiness: as good as rebirth in wholesome states may be, the happiness it brings is not a true and lasting one, for it relies on conditions over which he or she ultimately has no control.

This marks a crucial turning point in the training, when the practitioner begins to grasp that true happiness will never be found in the realm of the physical and sensual world. The only possible route to an unconditioned happiness lies in renunciation, in turning away from the sensual realm, by trading the familiar, lower forms of happiness for something far more rewarding and noble. Now, at last, the practitioner is ripe to receive the teachings on the Four Noble Truths, which spell out the course of mental training required to realize the highest happiness: *nibbana.*

Many Westerners first encounter the Buddha's teachings on meditation retreats, which typically begin with instructions in how to develop the skillful qualities of right mindfulness and right concentration. It is worth noting that, as important as these qualities are, the Buddha placed them towards the very end of his gradual course of training. The meaning is clear: to reap the most benefit from meditation practice, to bring to full maturity all the qualities needed for Awakening, the fundamental groundwork must not be overlooked. There is no short-cutting this process.

BUDDHA'S TEACHINGS OF MODERATION AND PEACE

As Buddha's appearing in the world is for one major reason: to save himself and others. Through the Mahayana texts, we can see his compassionate teachings to save all sentient beings, was propagated and implanted in China. But in ancient times, the seed of morality was planted into people as "a fortress aimed at protecting the Dharma against false ideologies, and to receive and maintain the essence of the doctrines." But in the 21st century, the problem has enlarged its scope and we have the heavy responsibility of propagating the Dharma.

This is worth our effort to think and be of concern with while we are trying to educate the modern *Sangha*. Our founder, Shakaymuni, our most venerable, is an unbiased reformer. He was open-minded to hear the opinions of various schools in the age of chaotic thoughts. In his time, in India there were well over 90 heretical thoughts, and with the advent of Buddhism, it started a revolution that had a huge impact on the society and religion as a whole. Nevertheless, Buddha's avocation emphasizes on both wisdom and morality.

It also strikes a balance between ideals and realities with the mind ever focusing on compassion and peace. On the social level, it broke the caste system and its teachings for all were based on equality and compassion. On the personal level, he opposed extreme hedonism and solely austere practices, by focusing on liberality and humanity to realize the truth with wisdom, philosophy and ability of human introspection and so on.

In other words, with reference to Buddha's ideals found in Mahayana Buddhist Education, the analysis of the scriptures has shown that the Buddha advocated compassion, good deeds, keeping of the precepts, tolerance, etc the whole life to attain a state of harmony in life and in the society. It is unavoidable that any schools developing to a certain degree will have divisive disagreements based on differentiation of views. The "Arya-Sthavira-Nikaya" and "Mahasanghika" confrontation existed in Buddhism and later on, this became the disputes evolving into "Mahayana" and "Theravada".

This is a natural phenomenon, part of the process of propagation of Buddhism. But with the moving times, we should completely and in overall context sort, accept, eliminate and purify all ideas and systems from cultural abuses of the past while we discuss the contemporary issues dealt to Buddhist education. Moreover, we should adopt a broad view towards the different means of Buddhism with a mind focused on tolerance and peace. In face of the vicissitudes of humanity's Buddhism, we must propagate Buddhism to all sentient beings and to help promote the universality of Buddha's teachings to the whole world.

THE ESTABLISHMENT OF MAHAYANA BUDDHIST SCHOOLS IN CHINA

The word "school" implies if one belongs to that school of Buddhism; it must follow the teachings, ideology, ceremonies and activities of that school. In China, about 13 schools prevailed during the Sui and T'ang Dynasties I will highlight some of the important schools to show the school's establishment and its scriptures and teachings bases.

The Three Treatise School

This school was established according to the teachings of these three discourses: the "Mâdhyamika-sâstra", the "Dvâdasânikâya-sâstra", and the "Asta-sâstra" which are based on the concept of wisdom (prajòa). The origin of this school comes in line with the "Wisdom Sutra." Seven hundred years after Buddha entered into nirvana, the *Bodhisattva* Nâgârjuna formulated the "Treatise on the Perfection of Great Wisdom" which was dependent on the "Wisdom Sutra".

He then went on expounding it in the "Mâdhyamika-sâstra", and the "Asta-sâstra". Thus the "Theory of Mediation" was formed in India and the *Bodhisattva* Nâgârjuna was considered as the founder of the Three Treatise School in China. In the third year of Hung Shih of Yao Chin Country in the Eastern Jin Dynasty, Kumârajïva came to Changan and translated the "Treatise on the Perfection of Wisdom", the "Mâdhyamika-sâstra", the "Dvàdaâanikâya-sâstra", and the "Asta-sâstra", establishing the teachings of the Three Treatise School in China.

The school actively engages to counter heresies, extol the positive aspects and to eliminate confusion of humanity by returning to the meaning of emptiness, which is the middle path. The methodology of this school is to allow in-depth comprehension of the dependent origination and the nature that is void of all things being the real nature; the truth of being empty or real emptiness.

This eliminates all confusion by focusing on getting nothing and thus emptiness. Therefore, its main purpose is to get practitioners to realize the real teachings of dependent origination and the void nature in the process of eliminating the suffering and claiming the positive aspects of emptiness to achieve equanimity. Equanimity means that all false perception by wisdom is removed to transform the sentient beings, and to then carry out the goal of saving the world with middle path by means of great wisdom. This is the system that was developed by the Three Treatise School.

The Tiantai School

This school is named after the mountain that Venerable Master Chih Yu established his monastery in the Sui Dynasty (538-597 AD). He was known as the "Master of the Wisdom" in Tiantai and was referred to as the Little Swakyamuni of the Eastern land. The main scripture is the "Lotus Sutra", while references are made to the "Pari- nirvana Sutra", the "Mahâprajâpâramita Sutra" and the "Treatise on the Perfection of Great Wisdom".

The teachings was divided into five periods corresponding to the Lotus Sutra accounts of the methods that the Buddha used to explain the dharma from the time he attained enlightenment to the time he entered nirvana. These five periods are:

1. The Huayan Period-After the Buddha's enlightenment, he expounded the "Lotus Sutra" to the *Bodhisattvas.*
2. The Agama Period-when the Buddha delivered the four noble truths in the "Agamas" to the ordinary people with undeveloped faculties.

3. The Vaipulaya Period (Elementary Mahayana) - when the Buddha delivered the Mahayana Sutra in addition to the Hinayana Sutras.
4. The Perfection of Wisdom Period-when the Buddha further taught the *Prajna*paramita Sutras in order to awaken people by enlightening their mind with persistence and reflection on the meaning of emptiness.
5. The Lotus and Nirvana Period-for those who have developed their faculty of wisdom, the Buddha taught the "Lotus Sutra" which made the three vehicles subsume into a single vehicle to make beings achieve the path to Buddhahood.

These are "Master of the Wisdom" divisions for the Tathagata's teachings. He adopted this method to teach according to the level of intellect and their ability to grasp the sublime truths, from the mundane to the highest state of the Buddha's vehicle. The Tiantai School's comprehension of the Buddha's teachings and its position within the Mahayana are thus obvious.

The Pure Land

This school promotes the rebirth to the Pure Land of Ultimate Bliss. This so-called "Pure Land", which means the land accomplished by the pure merits, is different from the "impure merits". The idea of the "Pure Land in the Western Paradise" is grounded on the Sukhavativyuha Sutra", the "Vipašyana Sukhâvatïvyoha Sutra" and the "Amitâbha Sura" as well as the main scripture, the "Treatise of Reincarnation in the Pure Land" created by *Bodhisattva* Vasubandhu.

This school was founded by Master Hui Yuan (334-416 AD) in China's Mt. Lu. He was a scholar specializing in the "nature void of *Prajna*". He chanted the name of the Buddha in 90-day intervals as promoted by the "Pratyutpanna*Samadhi* Sutra". The practice includes: the taking of no rest, correction of body karma, verbally chanting the Buddha's name, and contemplating the Buddha's form with the three karmic interactions.

To practice this is to practices the deeds stated in the "Pratyutpanna *Samadhi* Sutra." An accomplished individual, who have attained *Samadhi* by Chanting the Buddha's name, could see the Buddhas from the ten directions before his eyes. Into the 1st year of Yung Ping of Northern Wei Dynasty (508 AD), Bodhiruci came to China and taught the "Vipasyana Sukavativyuha Sutra" compiled by Tan Juan and passed on the complete scriptures of the Pure Land. Again, during the T'ang Dynasty, Master Tao Cho and Master Shan Tao, inherited the teachings of Tan Juan and made every effort to extol the Buddha's power of Purvapranidhana.

They proposed that in the age of final dharma, all sentient beings' intellect would be shallow and that the only way is to chant the name of the Buddha. This subsequently established the ideas and teachings of the Mahayana Pure Land in China. An observation made is that Buddhist schools in China revealed a changing and diverging feature in circulation through the times.

The Ch'an or Zen School

This school is also named as the "Buddha Heart" or "Tamo" school. Tamo came to China to propagate the teachings of the "Lankavatara School" and started the practice of Ch'an in China, so he is regarded as the forerunner of Ch'an in China. This school of Mahayana explores the origin of the immutable mind by "Beholding the Buddha nature within oneself. Tamo handed down the lineage to Hui Kuo (Deva-light), who is Ch'an's second patriarch.

Hui Kuo then handed down the leadership to Seng Tsan who passed it on to Tao Hsin and then to Hung Jeng, our 5th Partiarch. The fifth Patriarch had two disciples: Shen Hsiu and Hui Neng, and soon after Hung Jeng entered his nirvana, Shen Hsiu whose practices advocated the practical spirit taught in the northern regions of China and become to be known as the Northern Ch'an. Since Hui Neng received the 5th Partriach robe because of his gatha to show his enlightened mind, he succeeded as the 6th Patriarch of Zen and taught mainly in the south, was known as the Southern Ch'an.

From Hui Neng, who was succeeded by more than 40 disciples, Zen has since spread widely in China. Among them was Shen Hui, in Heze Monastery, he intiated the "Heze School," sparing no efforts to promote the method of sudden enlightenment with "no arising thought" as "sit" and "realization of the true nature" as "meditation". The sudden enlightenment in Ch'an was popular as it teaches that one can be suddenly enlightened when one directly enters into the original bodhi.

This style of Ch'an taught that Mahayana Buddhist practitioners got their enlightenment solely by the heart. In Taiwan today, there are still people devoting to the research on the doctrines of each of these schools; however, concerning the advocating of practical methods to practice, only the Ch'an and Pure Land schools do. We will next give you a brief sketch of the features of education found in Mahayana Pure Land School in accordance to the methods promoted in Taiwan.

FEATURES OF THE PURE LAND'S EDUCATION

System Pure Land implies pure and clean land, where the Buddha resides, practices Bodhi and develop a resolute heart. In regards to the teachings of the Pure Land prevailing in China, the practitioners think highly of the Pure Land of Ultimate Bliss, where is commonly referred to as the Pure Land of Western Paradise, as stated in the "Sukhâvativyûha Sûtra". In China, the practitioners are taught and prepared for reincarnation into the pure land-which consists of right views, keeping of commandments, chanting the name of the Buddha, attaining concentration (*Samadhi*), compassion (mercy), and wisdom.

Thus the first thing a practitioner must have is the correct views regarding the Buddha-Dharma, and have their faith or belief built on the Buddha's compassionate heart and vows. To establish the correct views, one has to take on the power of vow of the Amitabha, i.e. to chant the Buddha's name in accordance with the Dharma, realizing the incredible powers of Amitabha's vow, having the wish to make the same vows and walk with Amitabha, wishing for the self to be like

Amitabha with the power of commandment keeping and save all sinful and suffering sentient beings that are countless and boundless to have pure world, it is important that as a Mahayana Practitioner, one should learn more about the Pure Land methods.

Today, people in Taiwan only chant the Buddha's name with vow aiming to be reincarnated into the pure land, but we realize that is not for the practitioners who are practicing the Pure Land methods of Amitabha, to be only reincarnated in the Pure Land of Ultimate Bliss for onself and abandoning the suffering of other beings, of which if one holds on to such an attitude, it is to fall into the practices of the Hinayana.

To chant the name of the Buddha is to take on vow of the Buddha as it is the pattern of acquiring through chanting the Buddha's wisdom, his compassion that all the Buddha's take compassion as their main path; they will not abandon any of the sentient beings suffering. When one who chants the name of the Buddha, the more compassionate the heart gets, the broader the capacity of the mind is and the deeper the merciful wisdom is. Correspondingly true to the fact that true wisdom and the emptiness (*sunyatâ*) of wisdom (*prajna*) in the Buddha-Dharma will be brought out.

Hence, with the realization of *sunyatâ* of *prajnâ*, with deep conviction that all phenomena are impermanent, all things are no-self and the eternity is Nirvana. Fully possessing all correct views, correct beliefs, correct wisdom, and correct deeds, one has to make efforts to purify the Buddha's land and to benefit all sentient beings. In a complicated society like ours filled with unitarianism and human's selfishness, cheating of others, taking advantage of each other and not believing in one another but for the individual's benefits. This happens no matter where we are, between countries, races, societies, families and people.

For humanity is living under a huge and invisible pressure that harms civilizations making people feel uneasy at heart and at a loss, it is an urgent need to pray for a peaceful, easy and happy world without the abuse of drugs, the slaughter, persecution and wars. In my opinion, the only way to purify the world is to promote pure land on earth. In the world we live now, the darkness could be seen everywhere and in any country. The education of Mahayana Pure Land teachings is to work hard toward the goal of an ideal environment suitable for humanity to dwell in.

Yet, it is not the easiest to promote for in the way is human ignorance and foolishness. Taking Taiwan as an example, advocating of pure land on earth must be implemented by the individual's faith on a mutual basis and to practice the purification of his or her own three karmas - body, speech and mind - to eliminate the three poisons - desire, aversion and ignorance - which is to keep purifying the heart, to abide by the law and precepts (vinaya), to build mutual trust and respect, and to direct the human mind to enter in sublimation of the spiritual sphere from the moral ethics of respecting the lives of all sentient beings and not to oppress others for the sake of one's own benefits.

At the present moment, all around the world, national boundaries are disappearing gradually. However, each one has its own cultural connections and as people learns to get along with others, with the complexities of racialism constantly arising, causing racial massacres or as pagans who were persecuted due to the differences in religious perceptions. Buddhism enlightens and guides all sentient beings with compassion and wisdom to face the global village and hopes that there will be no international disputes forever and ever and to coexist peacefully with the idea of purifying the world. This is the central ideal world that the Chinese Mahayana Pure Land system yearns to bring to humanity.

The Chinese Schools were established through the process of absorption and elimination of unique and creative viewpoints. Though Buddhism is divided into the Southern and Northern Buddhists, the beliefs for Buddhism is the same, and so is the keeping of our precepts. One has to know that the responsibilities of being the disciples of the Buddha is that the "benefiting sentient beings is the career, and disseminating the Dharma is the domestic chore."

However, as keeping to this great vow, one has to start with the education as the source of preserving the *Sangha* to propagate the Dharma. Buddhism comes with education. Consequently, education is the light in Buddha Dharma's existence! Its successes or failures have direct consequence with the wax or wane in Buddhism. The world nowadays exists in the age of diminishing, and "it is in the duty of every one of us to do good deeds in the world." We hope that all will do the good and be able to get along with others as well.

Buddhist's thought on education is that we have the goal of creating the pure land on earth together with a perfectly calm mind! Push and move the world forward into creating a living space that is more suitable for humanity, by bringing the teachings of the Pure Land in Mahayana Buddhism to effect; contemplate the future direction of Buddhist education with broad and healthy views. Hoping that we as Buddha's disciples pursue multinational cooperation without any ill will but to be on a very intimate terms and to respect one another.

Like a saying we have circulating through the ages: "A bosom friend from afar brings the distant land near." And this is to say nothing of being "in the same family as Buddha's children". Being his disciples, we hope to be united, progressing with the times and with the "unity comes the power" to eliminate the ills and extol the virtues and enhance the holy mission of Buddhism.

THE FOUR NOBLE TRUTHS

1. LIFE MEANS SUFFERING

To live means to suffer, because the human nature is not perfect and neither is the world we live in. During our lifetime, we inevitably have to endure physical suffering such as pain, sickness, injury, tiredness, old age, and eventually death; and we have to endure psychological suffering like sadness, fear, frustration, disappointment, and depression. Although there are different degrees of suffering and there are also positive experiences in life that we perceive as the opposite of suffering, such as ease, comfort and happiness, life in its totality is imperfect and incomplete, because our world is subject to impermanence. This means we are never able to keep permanently what we strive for, and just as happy moments pass by, we ourselves and our loved ones will pass away one day, too.

2. THE ORIGIN OF SUFFERING IS ATTACHMENT

The origin of suffering is attachment to transient things and the ignorance thereof. Transient things do not only include the physical objects that surround us, but also ideas, and -in a greater sense- all objects of our perception. Ignorance is the lack of understanding of how our mind is attached to impermanent things. The reasons for suffering are desire, passion, ardour, pursuit of wealth and prestige, striving for fame and popularity, or in short: *craving* and *clinging*. Because the objects of our attachment are transient, their loss is inevitable, thus suffering will necessarily follow. Objects of attachment also include the idea of a "self" which is a delusion, because there is no abiding self. What we call "self" is just an imagined entity, and we are merely a part of the ceaseless becoming of the universe.

3. THE CESSATION OF SUFFERING IS ATTAINABLE

The cessation of suffering can be attained through *nirodha*. Nirodha means the unmaking of sensual craving and conceptual attachment. The third noble truth expresses the idea that suffering can be ended by attaining dispassion. Nirodha extinguishes all forms of clinging and attachment. This means that suffering can be overcome through human activity, simply by removing the cause of suffering. Attaining and perfecting dispassion is a process of many levels that ultimately results in the state of *Nirvana*. Nirvana means freedom from all worries, troubles, complexes, fabrications and ideas. Nirvana is not comprehensible for those who have not attained it.

4. THE PATH TO THE CESSATION OF SUFFERING

There is a path to the end of suffering - a gradual path of self-improvement, which is described more detailed in the

Eightfold Path. It is the middle way between the two extremes of excessive self-indulgence (hedonism) and excessive self-mortification (asceticism); and it leads to the end of the cycle of rebirth. The latter quality discerns it from other paths which are merely "wandering on the wheel of becoming", because these do not have a final object. The path to the end of suffering can extend over many lifetimes, throughout which every individual rebirth is subject to karmic conditioning. Craving, ignorance, delusions, and its effects will disappear gradually, as progress is made on the path.

THE NOBLE EIGHTFOLD PATH

The Noble Eightfold Path is one of the principal teachings of the Buddha, who described it as the way leading to the cessation of suffering (*dukkha*) and the achievement of self-awakening. It is used in Buddhist practice as a technique to develop insight into the true nature of phenomena (or reality) and to eradicate greed, hatred, and delusion. The Noble Eightfold Path is the fourth of the Buddha's Four Noble Truths; the first element of the Noble Eightfold Path is, in turn, an understanding of the Four Noble Truths. It is also known as the *Middle Path* or *Middle Way*.

All eight elements of the Path begin with the word "right", which translates the word *samyakaa* (in Sanskrit) or *sammâ* (in Pâli). These denote completion, togetherness, and coherence, and can also suggest the senses of "perfect" or "ideal". In Buddhist symbolism, the Noble Eightfold Path is often represented by means of the dharma wheel, whose eight spokes represent the eight elements of the path?

According to discourses found in both the Theravada school's Pali canon and the Agamas (a class of early Buddhist school sutras that were preserved in the Chinese Mahayana tradition), the Noble Eightfold Path was rediscovered by Gautama Buddha during his quest for enlightenment. The scriptures describe an ancient path which has been followed and practised by all the previous Buddhas. The Noble Eightfold Path is a practice said to lead its practitioner toward self-awakening and liberation. The path was taught by the Buddha to his disciples so that they, too, could follow it.

> In the same way I saw an ancient path, an ancient road, traveled by the Rightly Self-awakened Ones of former times. And what is that ancient path, that ancient road, traveled by the Rightly Self-awakened Ones of former times? Just this noble eightfold path: right view, right aspiration, right speech, right action, right livelihood, right effort, right mindfulness, right concentration...I followed that path. Following it, I came to direct knowledge of aging & death, direct knowledge of the origination of aging & death, direct knowledge of the cessation of aging & death, direct knowledge of the path leading to the cessation of aging & death...Knowing that directly, I have revealed it to monks, nuns, male lay followers & female lay followers...-*Nagara Sutta*

The practice of the Noble Eightfold Path varies from one Buddhist school to another. Depending on the school, it may be practiced as a whole, only in part, or it may have been modified. Each Buddhist lineage claims the ability to implement the path in the manner most conducive to the development of its students.

THE THREEFOLD DIVISION OF THE PATH

The Noble Eightfold Path is sometimes divided into three basic divisions, as follows:

Division	*Eightfold Path factors*	*Acquired factors*
Wisdom (Sanskrit: *prajñā*, Pāli: *paññā*)	1. Right view	9. Right knowledge
	2. Right intention	10. Right liberation
Ethical conduct (Sanskrit: *śīla*, Pāli: *sīla*)	3. Right speech	
	4. Right action	
	5. Right livelihood	
Concentration (Sanskrit and Pāli: *samādhi*)	6. Right effort	
	7. Right mindfulness	
	8. Right concentration	

This presentation is called the 'Three Higher Trainings' in Mahayana Buddhism; higher moral discipline, higher concentration and higher wisdom. 'Higher' here refers to the fact that these trainings that lead to liberation and enlightenment are engaged in with the motivation of renunciation or bodhichitta.

THE PRACTICE

According to the *bhikkhu* (monk) and scholar Walpola Rahula, the divisions of the noble eightfold path "are to be developed more or less simultaneously, as far as possible according to the capacity of each individual. They are all linked together and each helps the cultivation of the others." Bhikkhu Bodhi explains that "with a certain degree of progress all eight factors can be present simultaneously, each supporting the others. However, until that point is reached, some sequence in the unfolding of the path is inevitable".

According to the discourses in the Pali and Chinese canons, right view, right resolve, right speech, right action, right livelihood, right effort, and right mindfulness are used as the support and requisite conditions for the practice of right concentration. Understanding of the right view is the preliminary role, and is also the forerunner of the entire Noble Eightfold Path. The practitioner should first try to understand the concepts of right view. Once right view has been understood, it will inspire and encourage the arising of right intention within the practitioner.

Right intention will lead to the arising of right speech. Right speech will lead to the arising of right action. Right action will lead to the arising of right livelihood. Right livelihood will lead to the arising of right effort. Right effort will lead to the arising of right mindfulness. The practitioner must make the right effort to abandon the wrong view and to enter into the right view. Right mindfulness is used to constantly remain in the right view. This will help the practitioner restrain greed, hatred and delusion.

Once these support and requisite conditions have been established, a practitioner can then practice right concentration more easily. During the practice of right concentration, one will need to use right effort and right mindfulness to aid concentration practice. In the state of concentration, one will need to investigate and verify his or her understanding of right view. This will then result in the arising of right knowledge, which will eliminate greed, hatred and delusion. The last and final factor to arise is right liberation.

WISDOM

"Wisdom", sometimes translated as "discernment" at its preparatory role, provides the sense of direction with its conceptual understanding of reality. It is designed to awaken the faculty of penetrative understanding to see things as they really are. At a later stage, when the mind has been refined by training in moral discipline and concentration, and with the gradual arising of right knowledge, it will arrive at a superior right view and right intention.

RIGHT VIEW

Right view can also be translated as "right perspective", "right vision" or "right understanding". It is the right way of looking at life, nature, and the world as they really are. It is to understand how reality works. It acts as the reasoning for the practitioner to start practicing the path. It explains the reasons for human existence, suffering, sickness, aging, and death, the existence of greed, hatred, and delusion. It gives direction and efficacy to the other seven path factors.

Right view begins with concepts and propositional knowledge, but through the practice of right concentration, it gradually becomes transmuted into wisdom, which can eradicate the fetters of the mind. Understanding of right view will inspire the person to lead a virtuous life in line with right view. In the Pali and Chinese canons, it is explained thus:

And what is right view? Knowledge with reference to stress (dukkha can also be translated as suffering), knowledge with reference to the origination of stress (or suffering), knowledge with reference to the cessation of stress (or suffering), knowledge with reference to the way of practice leading to the cessation of stress (or suffering): This is called right view.

There are two types of right view:

1. View with taints: this view is mundane. Having this type of view will bring merit and will support the favourable existence of the sentient being in the realm of *samsara*.
2. View without taints: this view is supramundane. It is a factor of the path and will lead the holder of this view toward self-awakening and liberation from the realm of *samsara*.

Right view has many facets; its elementary form is suitable for lay followers, while the other form, which requires deeper understanding, is suitable for monastics. Usually, it involves understanding the following reality:

1. Moral law of karma: Every action (by way of body, speech, and mind) will have karmic results (a.k.a. reaction). Wholesome and unwholesome actions will produce results and effects that correspond with the nature of that action. It is the right view about the moral process of the world.
2. The three characteristics: everything that arises will cease (impermanence). Mental and body phenomena are impermanent, source of suffering and not-self.
3. Suffering: Birth, aging, sickness, death, sorrow, lamentation, pain, grief, distress, and despair are suffering. Not being able to obtain what one wants is also suffering. The arising of craving is the root cause of the arising of suffering and the cessation of craving is the root cause of the cessation of the suffering. The way leading to the cessation of suffering is the noble eightfold path. This type of right view is explained in terms of Four Noble Truths.

Right view for monastics is explained in detail in the *Sammâdittthi Sutta* ("Right View Discourse"), in which Ven. Sariputta instructs that right view can alternately be attained by the thorough understanding of the unwholesome and the wholesome, the four nutriments, the twelve *nidanas* or the three taints. "Wrong view" arising from ignorance (*avijja*), is the precondition for wrong intention, wrong speech, wrong action, wrong livelihood, wrong effort, wrong mindfulness and wrong concentration. The practitioner should use right effort to abandon the wrong view and to enter into right view. Right mindfulness is used to constantly remain in right view.

The purpose of right view is to clear one's path of the majority of confusion, misunderstanding, and deluded thinking. It is a means to gain right understanding of reality. Right view should be held with a flexible, open mind, without clinging to that view as a dogmatic position. In this way, right view becomes a route to liberation rather than an obstacle.

RIGHT INTENTION

Right intention can also be known as "right thought", "right resolve", "right conception", "right aspiration" or "the exertion of our own will to change". In this factor, the practitioner should constantly aspire to rid themselves of whatever qualities they know to be wrong and immoral. Correct understanding of right view will help the practitioner to discern the differences between right intention and wrong intention. In the Chinese and Pali Canon, it is explained thus:

And what is right resolve? Being resolved on renunciation, on freedom from ill will, on harmlessness: This is called right resolve. It means the renunciation of the worldly things and an accordant greater commitment to the spiritual path; good will; and a commitment to non-violence, or harmlessness, towards other living beings.

ETHICAL CONDUCT

For the mind to be unified in concentration, it is necessary to restrain from unwholesome deeds of body and speech to prevent the faculties of bodily action and speech from becoming tools of the defilements. Ethical conduct is used primarily as aids for mental purification.

RIGHT SPEECH

Right speech, deals with the way in which a Buddhist practitioner would best make use of their words. In the Pali Canon, it is explained thus:

And what is right speech? Abstaining from lying, from divisive speech, from abusive speech, and from idle chatter: This is called right speech.

The *Samaññaphala Sutta, Kevatta Sutta* and *Cunda Kammaraputta Sutta* elaborate:

Abandoning false speech...He speaks the truth, holds to the truth, is firm, reliable, no deceiver of the world...

Abandoning divisive speech...What he has heard here he does not tell there to break those people apart from these people here...Thus reconciling those who have broken apart or cementing those who are united, he loves concord, delights in concord, enjoys concord, and speaks things that create concord...

Abandoning abusive speech...He speaks words that are soothing to the ear, that are affectionate, that go to the heart, that are polite, appealing and pleasing to people at large...

Abandoning idle chatter...He speaks in season, speaks what is factual, what is in accordance with the goal, the Dhamma, and the Vinaya. He speaks words worth treasuring, seasonable, reasonable, circumscribed, and connected with the goal...

The *Abhaya Sutta* elaborates:

In the case of words that the Tathagata knows to be unfactual, untrue, unbeneficial (or: not connected with the goal), unendearing and disagreeable to others, he does not say them. In the case of words that the Tathagata knows to be factual, true, unbeneficial, unendearing and disagreeable to others, he does not say them.

In the case of words that the Tathagata knows to be factual, true, beneficial, but unendearing and disagreeable to others, he has a sense of the proper time for saying them. In the case of words that the Tathagata knows to be unfactual, untrue, unbeneficial, but endearing and agreeable to others, he does not say them.

In the case of words that the Tathagata knows to be factual, true, unbeneficial, but endearing and agreeable to others, he does not say them. In the case of words that the Tathagata knows to be factual, true, beneficial, and endearing and agreeable to others, he has a sense of the proper time for saying them. Why is that? Because the Tathagata has sympathy for living beings.

RIGHT ACTION

Right action (*samyaka-karmânta / sammâ-kammanta*) can also be translated as "right conduct". As such, the practitioner should train oneself to be morally upright in one's activities, not acting in ways that would be corrupt or bring harm to oneself or to others. In the Chinese and Pali Canon, it is explained as:

And what is right action? Abstaining from taking life, from stealing, and from illicit sex [or sexual misconduct]. This is called right action. -*Saccavibhanga Sutta*

And what, monks, is right action? Abstaining from taking life, abstaining from stealing, abstaining from unchastity: This, monks, is called right action. -*Magga-vibhanga Sutta*

For the lay follower, the *Cunda Kammaraputta Sutta* elaborates: And how is one made pure in three ways by bodily action? There is the case where a certain person, abandoning the taking of life, abstains from the taking of life.

He dwells with his...knife laid down, scrupulous, merciful, and compassionate for the welfare of all living beings. Abandoning the taking of what is not given, he abstains from taking what is not given.

He does not take, in the manner of a thief, things in a village or a wilderness that belong to others and have not been given by them. Abandoning sensual misconduct, he abstains from sensual misconduct.

He does not get sexually involved with those who are protected by their mothers, their fathers, their brothers, their sisters, their relatives, or their Dhamma; those with husbands, those who entail punishments, or even those crowned with flowers by another man. This is how one is made pure in three ways by bodily action.

For the monastic, the *Samaññaphala Sutta* adds: Abandoning uncelibacy, he lives a celibate life, aloof, refraining from the sexual act that is the villager's way.

RIGHT LIVELIHOOD

Right livelihood (*samyakaa-âjîva* / *sammâ-âjîva*) means that practitioners ought not to engage in trades or occupations which, either directly or indirectly, result in harm for other living beings. In the Chinese and Pali Canon, it is explained thus:

And what is right livelihood? There is the case where a disciple of the noble ones, having abandoned dishonest livelihood, keeps his life going with right livelihood: This is called right livelihood.

The five types of businesses that are harmful to undertake are:

1. Business in weapons: trading in all kinds of weapons and instruments for killing.
2. Business in human beings: slave trading, prostitution, or the buying and selling of children or adults.
3. Business in meat: "meat" refers to the bodies of beings after they are killed. This includes breeding animals for slaughter.
4. Business in intoxicants: manufacturing or selling intoxicating drinks or addictive drugs.
5. Business in poison: producing or trading in any kind of toxic product designed to kill.

SAMÂDHI: MENTAL DISCIPLINE, CONCENTRATION, MEDITATION

Samadhi is literally translated as "concentration", it is achieved through training in the higher consciousness, which brings the calm and collectedness needed to develop true wisdom by direct experience.

RIGHT EFFORT

Right effort (*samyakaa-vyâyâma* • *sammâ-vâyâma*) can also be translated as "right endeavor". In this factor, the practitioners should make a persisting effort to abandon all the wrong and harmful thoughts, words, and deeds. The practitioner should instead be persisting in giving rise to what would be good and useful to them and others in their thoughts, words, and deeds, without a thought for the difficulty or weariness involved. In the Chinese and Pali Canon, it is explained thus:

And what, monks, is right effort?

i. There is the case where a monk generates desire, endeavors, activates persistence, upholds and exerts his intent for the sake of the non-arising of evil, unskillful qualities that have not yet arisen.
ii. He generates desire, endeavors, activates persistence, upholds and exerts his intent for the sake of the abandonment of evil, unskillful qualities that have arisen.
iii. He generates desire, endeavors, activates persistence, upholds and exerts his intent for the sake of the arising of skillful qualities that have not yet arisen.
iv. He generates desire, endeavors, activates persistence, upholds and exerts his intent for the maintenance, non-confusion, increase, plenitude, development, and culmination of skillful qualities that have arisen.

This, monks, is called right effort. Although the above instruction is given to the male monastic order, it is also meant for the female monastic order and can be practiced by lay followers from both genders.

The above four phases of right effort mean to:

1. Prevent the unwholesome that has not yet arisen in oneself.
2. Let go of the unwholesome that has arisen in oneself.
3. Bring up the wholesome that has not yet arisen in oneself.
4. Maintain the wholesome that has arisen in oneself.

RIGHT MINDFULNESS

Right mindfulness (*samyaka-smrti / sammâ-sati*) also translated as "right memory", "right awareness" or "right attention".

Here, practitioners should constantly keep their minds alert to phenomena that affect the body and mind. They should be mindful and deliberate, making sure not to act or speak due to inattention or forgetfulness. In the Pali Canon, it is explained thus:

> And what, monks, is right mindfulness?
>
> i. There is the case where a monk remains focused on the body in and of itself-ardent, aware, and mindful-putting away greed and distress with reference to the world.
>
> ii. He remains focused on feelings in and of themselves-ardent, aware, and mindful-putting away greed and distress with reference to the world.
>
> iii. He remains focused on the mind in and of itself-ardent, aware, and mindful-putting away greed and distress with reference to the world.
>
> iv. He remains focused on mental qualities in and of themselves-ardent, aware, and mindful-putting away greed and distress with reference to the world.
>
> This, monks, is called right mindfulness.

Although the above instruction is given to the male monastic order, it is also meant for the female monastic order and can be practiced by lay followers from both genders. Bhikkhu Bodhi, a monk of the Theravada tradition, further explains the concept of mindfulness as follows:

> The mind is deliberately kept at the level of bare attention, a detached observation of what is happening within us and around us in the present moment. In the practice of right mindfulness the mind is trained to remain in the present, open, quiet, and alert, contemplating the present event. All judgments and interpretations have to be suspended, or if they occur, just registered and dropped.

The Maha Satipatthana Sutta also teaches that by mindfully observing these phenomena, we begin to discern its arising and subsiding and the Three Characteristics of Dharma in direct experience, which leads to the arising of insight and the qualities of dispassion, non-clinging, and release.

RIGHT CONCENTRATION

Right concentration (*samyaka-samâdhi* • *sammâ-samâdhi*), as its Pali and Sanskrit names indicate, is the practice of concentration (*Samadhi*). As such, the practitioner concentrates on an object of attention until reaching full concentration and a state of meditative absorption (*jhana*). Traditionally, the practice of *Samadhi* can be developed through mindfulness of breathing (*anapanasati*), through visual objects (*kasina*), and through repetition of phrases. *Samadhi* is used to suppress the five hindrances in order to enter into *jhana*. *Jhana* is an instrument used for developing wisdom by cultivating insight and using it to examine true nature of phenomena with direct cognition.

This leads to cutting off the defilements, realizing the dhamma and, finally, self-awakening. During the practice of right concentration, the practitioner will need to investigate and verify their right view. In the process right knowledge will arise, followed by right liberation. In the Pali Canon, it is explained thus:

And what is right concentration?

i. Herein a monk aloof from sense desires, aloof from unwholesome thoughts, attains to and abides in the first meditative absorption [*jhana*], which is detachment-born and accompanied by applied thought, sustained thought, joy, and bliss.

ii. By allaying applied and sustained thought he attains to, and abides in the second *jhana*, which is inner tranquillity, which is unification (of the mind), devoid of applied and sustained thought, and which has joy and bliss.

iii. By detachment from joy he dwells in equanimity, mindful, and with clear comprehension and enjoys bliss in body, and attains to and abides in the third *jhana*, which the noble ones [ariyas] call "dwelling in equanimity, mindfulness, and bliss".

iv. By giving up of bliss and suffering, by the disappearance already of joy and sorrow, he attains to, and abides in the fourth *jhana*, which is neither suffering nor bliss, and which is the purity of equanimity - mindfulness.

This is called right concentration. Although this instruction is given to the male monastic order, it is also meant for the female monastic order and can be practiced by lay followers from both genders. According to the Pali and Chinese canon, right concentration is dependent on the development of preceding path factors:

The Blessed One said: "Now what, monks, is noble right concentration with its supports and requisite conditions? Any singleness of mind equipped with these seven factors - right view, right resolve, right speech, right action, right livelihood, right effort, and right mindfulness - is called noble right concentration with its supports and requisite conditions. - *Maha-cattarisaka Sutta*

THE ACQUIRED FACTORS

In the *Mahâcattârîsaka Sutta* which appears in the Chinese and Pali canons, the Buddha explains that cultivation of the noble eightfold path leads to the development of two further factors, which are right knowledge/insight (*sammâ-ñana*) and right liberation/release (*sammâ-vimutti*). These two factors fall under the category of wisdom (*paññâ*).

RIGHT KNOWLEDGE AND RIGHT LIBERATION

Right knowledge is seeing things as they really are by direct experience, not as they appear to be, nor as the practitioner wants them to be, but as they truly are. A result of Right Knowledge is the tenth factor - Right liberation.

These two factors are the end result of correctly practicing the noble eightfold path, which arise during the practice of right concentration. The first to arise is right knowledge: this is where deep insight into the ultimate reality arises. The last to arise is right liberation: this is where self-awakening occurs and the practitioner has reached the pinnacle of their practice.

THE NOBLE EIGHTFOLD PATH AND COGNITIVE PSYCHOLOGY

In the essay "Buddhism Meets Western Science", Gay Watson explains:

Buddhism has always been concerned with feelings, emotions, sensations, and cognition. The Buddha points both to cognitive and emotional causes of suffering. The emotional cause is desire and its negative opposite, aversion. The cognitive cause is ignorance of the way things truly occur, or of three marks of existence: that all things are unsatisfactory, impermanent, and without essential self.

The noble eightfold path is, from this psychological viewpoint, an attempt to change patterns of thought and behavior. It is for this reason that the first element of the path is right understanding (*sammâ-ditthi*), which is how one's mind views the world. Under the wisdom (*paññâ*) subdivision of the noble eightfold path, this worldview is intimately connected with the second element, right thought (*sammâ-samkappa*), which concerns the patterns of thought and intention that controls one's actions. These elements can be seen at work, for example, in the opening verses of the *Dhammapada*:

Preceded by perception are mental states,

For them is perception supreme,

From perception have they sprung.

If, with perception polluted, one speaks or acts,

Thence suffering follows

As a wheel the draught ox's foot.

Preceded by perception are mental states,

For them is perception supreme,

From perception have they sprung.

If, with tranquil perception, one speaks or acts,

Thence ease follows

As a shadow that never departs.

Thus, by altering one's distorted worldview, bringing out "tranquil perception" in the place of "perception polluted", one is able to ease suffering. Watson points this out from a psychological standpoint:

Research has shown that repeated action, learning, and memory can actually change the nervous system physically, altering both synaptic strength and connections. Such changes may be brought about by cultivated change in emotion and action; they will, in turn, change subsequent experience.

THE PANCHA SILA

The five precepts are the basis of Buddhist morality. To take *Pancha Sila*, that is, to vow to live according to the following rules of conduct, is a set of vows a lay-person may take on, to try and live by, to the best of their understanding. So here goes: *Pancha* (five) *Sila* (discipline), the Five Precepts:

1. Do not take life.
2. Do not take what is not given.
3. Do not distort facts.
4. Refrain from misuse of the senses.
5. Refrain from self-intoxication through alcohol or drugs.

1. Do not take life

This obviously includes killing, both people and animals. In the extreme it would include killing plants and insects. Though it is perhaps possible to avoid killing these latter, in practice every act of eating makes us co-responsible for killing plants. This can't be avoided. Still, this rule is the basis of the vegetarianism of many Buddhists. Because although those who eat meat often don't kill animals themselves, they are helping make it financially and socially acceptable for butchers to kill animals.

2. Do not take what is not given

This rule is usually translated as: don't steal. But in fact this goes a bit further. To not take what is not given, really means only taking that where explicitly somebody says: this is yours. Taking money from a wallet that somebody left on the train is clearly not acceptable if you read this rule of conduct.

3. Do not distort fact

This one is usually translated as: don't lie. Again: it wider than that. Sometimes the use of words can make something seem acceptable, when it could also have been said very differently and be totally unacceptable. This would not be a lie, but it would be a distortion of fact.

4. Refrain from misuse of the senses

The senses in Buddhist and Hindu philosophy include not only the five generally thought of: touch, hearing, seeing, smelling and tasting, but also the mind: thinking. This means overindulgence in touching (for instance sex), hearing (overindulging in listening to music for instance), seeing (too much focuss on beauty or ugliness around us), smelling and tasting (overindulgence in food preparation for instance). Lay people aren't expected to refrain from sex, yet they are expected to refrain from overdoing it. Moderation in this respect has become highly unpopular, with kids having sex at earlier ages every year and sexual crime becoming almost usual. To be a virgin equals being ashamed, these days. Buddhist morality is old-fashioned in this respect.

The the last sense which can be overindulged is thinking or thought, or use of the mind. One often meets people who think so much, they forget to practice. Or they out-think any morality one can come up with. The mind is a highly deceptive tool and overuse makes it overly powerful over us. When thoughts start seeming real, and control ones life, beyond what is reasonable, it is perhaps time to consider whether perhaps one has overindulged in thinking.

5. Refrain from self-intoxication through alcohol or drugs

This sila is very relevant in our present day world. It has to do with the previous one, in the sense that people seem to use alcohol as a way of making life more interesting, less mundane. The sensual experiences of daily life don't seem enough and fun can only be had, social contacts can only be made (in certain circles), under the influence. Romanticizing drugs like Marijuana is highly dangerous as the brains of our youth get befuddled through the use. On the dangers of Marijuana.

Self-intoxication includes any use of substance to change a mood. Pills like Prozac, coffee or stronger measures to wake you up, chocolate to cheer you up, etc.

BEING REASONABLE

Even for those who take Pansil, or in other words: vow to live by these rules; it is up them to decide where to draw the line. Some Buddhists eat meat; others feel that should be avoided. Many Buddhists drink coffee, even though it could be construed to change consciousness and therefore fall under the heading of self-intoxication. Still, every honest Buddhist will try to live by these rules to the best of their under-standing and ability. Living by these rules is not so much something to be proud of, as it is a reminder of what hasn't yet been accomplished.

Self-righteousness exists in any religious group, but should obviously be avoided. Most people will realize the fact that these rules of conduct are only outward, and though important in their own way, don't signify inner wisdom or enlightenment. Since becoming wise (in Southern Buddhism: an Arhat, in Northern Buddhism: a Buddha), is the only object of Buddhism - anything else ought to be merely a stepping stone.

THE THREE MARKS

According to the Buddhist tradition, all phenomena other than Nirvana are marked by three characteristics, sometimes referred to as the *Dharma seals*: impermanence, suffering, and impersonality.

According to tradition, after much meditation, the Buddha concluded that everything in the physical world (and everything in the phenomenology of psychology) is marked by these three characteristics:

- *Anicca* (Sanskrit *anitya*) or "impermanence". This refers not only to the fact that all conditioned things (sankhara) eventually cease to exist, but also that all conditioned things are in a constant state of flux. (Visualize a leaf growing on a tree. It dies and falls off the tree but is soon replaced by a new leaf.)
- *Dukkha* (Sanskrit *duhkha*) or "unsatisfactoriness" (or "dis-ease"; also often translated "suffering", though this is somewhat misleading). Nothing found in the physical world or even the psychological realm can bring lasting deep satisfaction.
- *Anatta* (Sanskrit *anatman*) or "no-self" is used in the suttas both as a noun and as a predicative adjective to denote that phenomena are not, or are without, a permanent self, to describe any and all composite, consubstantial, phenomenal and temporal things, from the macrocosmic to microcosmic, be it matter pertaining to the physical body or the cosmos at large, as well as any and all mental machinations, which are impermanent.

There is often a fourth Dharma Seal mentioned:

- Nirvana is peace. Nirvana is the "other shore" from *samsara*.

Together the three characteristics of existence are called *ti-lakkhana* in Pali or *tri-laksana* in Sanskrit.

By bringing the three (or four) seals into moment-to-moment experience through concentrated awareness, we are said to achieve wisdom – the third of the three higher trainings – the way out of *samsara*. Thus the method for leaving *samsara* involves a deep-rooted change in world view.

ANICCA

All compounded phenomena (things and experiences) are inconstant, unsteady, and impermanent. Everything we can experience through our senses is made up of parts, and its existence is dependent on external conditions. Everything is in constant flux, and so conditions and the thing itself is constantly changing. Things are constantly coming into being, and ceasing to be. Nothing lasts.

The important point here is that phenomena arise and cease according to (complex) conditions and not according to our whims and fancy. While we have limited ability to effect change to our possessions and surroundings, experience tells us that our feeble attempts are no guarantee that the results of our efforts will be to our liking. More often than not, the results fall short of our expectations.

In Mahayana Buddhism, a caveat is added: one should indeed always meditate on the impermanence and transitory nature of compound structures and phenomena, but one must guard against extending this to the realm of Nirvana, where impermanence holds no sway. In this view, the ultimate nature of reality is free from the stains of dualistic thought, and should therefore not be labeled as 'one' or the 'other' (i.e. 'permanent' or 'impermanent').

Dzongsar Jamyang Khyentse Rinpoche states that in the four seals of the Mahayana, Nirvana should be viewed as "beyond extremes". Furthermore, he states that "In many philosophies or religions, the final goal is something that you can hold on to and keep. The final goal is the only thing that truly exists. But nirvana is not fabricated, so it is not something to be held on to. It is referred to as 'beyond extremes.'

We somehow think that we can go somewhere where we'll have a better sofa seat, a better shower system, a better sewer system, a nirvana where you don't even have to have a remote control, where everything is there the moment you think of it. But as I said earlier, it's not that we are adding something new that was not there before. Nirvana is achieved when you remove everything that was artificial and obscuring."

DUKKHA

Whatever is impermanent is subject to change. Whatever is subject to change is subject to suffering. -*The Buddha*

Striving for what we desire, we may experience stress and suffering - *dukkha*. Getting what we desired, we may find delight and happiness. Soon after, the novelty may wear out and we may get bored with it. Boredom is a form of dissatisfaction (or suffering) and to escape from it, we divert ourselves from such boredom by indulging in a pursuit of new forms of pleasure. Sometimes not willing to relinquish objects that we are already uninterested in, we start to collect and amass possessions instead of sharing with others who may have better uses for them than we do. Boredom is a result of change: the change of our interest in that object of desire which so captivated us in the first place.

Change may also take place in the object of our desire as opposed to change from within. Silverware may become tarnished, a new dress worn thin or a gadget gone obsolete. Or it may become broken, causing us to grieve. In some cases it may get lost or stolen. In some cases, we may worry about such losses even before they happen. Husbands and wives worry about losing their spouses even though their partners are faithful. Unfortunately, sometimes our very worry and fear drives us to act irrationally, resulting in distrust and breaking up of the very relationship that we cherished so much.

While we like changes such as becoming an adult when we are in our teens, we dislike the change called aging. While we strive for change to become rich, we fear the change of retrenchment. We are selective in our attitude towards the transient nature of our very existence. Unfortunately, this transient nature is unselective. We can try to fight it, just as many have tried since beginningless time, only to have our efforts washed away through the passages of time. As a result, we continually experience dissatisfaction or suffering due to the very impermanence of compounded phenomena.

Only in the realm of Nirvana - so Buddhism insists - can

true and lasting happiness be found. Nirvana is the opposite of the conditional, the transitory and the painful, so it does not result in disappointment or deterioration of the state of bliss. Nirvana is the refuge from the otherwise universal tyranny of change and suffering. In other schools of Buddhism, nirvana is not viewed as the goal, but merely as a projection from the state of *samsara*. According to these schools *samsara* (daily routine) and nirvana (perfection) are two sides of the same coin.

ANATTA

In Indian philosophy, the concept of a self is called âtman (that is, "soul" or metaphysical self), which refers to an unchanging, permanent essence conceived by virtue of existence. This concept and the related concept of Brahman, the Vedantic monistic ideal, which was regarded as an ultimate âtman for all beings, were indispensable for mainstream Indian metaphysics, logic, and science; for all apparent things there had to be an underlying and persisted reality, akin to a platoio form. The Buddha rejected all concepts of âtman, emphasizing not permanence, but changeability.

He taught that all concepts of a substantial personal self were incorrect, and formed in the realm of ignorance. The Buddha criticized conceiving theories even of a unitary soul or identity immanent in all things as unskillful in the Great Discourse on Causation. In fact, according to the Buddha's statement in Khandha Samyutta 47, all thoughts about self are necessarily, whether the thinker is aware of it or not, thoughts about the five aggregates or one of them.

In a number of major Mahayana sutras (e.g. the Mahaparinirvana Sutra, the *Tathagatagarbha* Sutra, the Srimala Sutra, among others), the Buddha is presented as clarifying this teaching by saying that, while the skandhas (constituents of the ordinary body and mind) are not the self, there does truly exist an eternal, unchanging, blissful Buddha-essence in all sentient beings, which is the uncreated and deathless Buddha-nature ("Buddha-dhatu") or "True Self" of the Buddha himself. The "*Tathagatagarbha*"/Buddha nature does not represent a substantial self; rather, it is a positive language expression of "sunyata" (emptiness) and represents the potentiality to realize Buddhahood through Buddhist practices; the intention of the teaching of *Tathagatagarbha* (Buddha nature) is soteriological rather than theoretical.

This immaculate Buddhic Self (atman) is in no way to be construed as a mundane, impermanent, suffering "ego", of which it is the diametrical opposite. On the other hand, this Buddha-essence or Buddha-nature is also often explained as the *potential* for achieving Buddhahood, rather than an existing phenomenon one can grasp onto as being *me* or *self*.

Anatta is discussed in the *Questions of King Milinda*, composed during the period of the Hellenistic Indo-Greek kingdom of the 2nd and 1st centuries BCE. In this text, the monk Nagasena demonstrates the concept of absolute "non-Self" by likening human beings to a chariot and challenges the Greek king "Milinda" (Menander) to find the essence of the chariot. Nagasena states that just as a chariot is made up of a number of things, none of which are the essence of the chariot in isolation, without the other pieces, similarly no one part of a person is a permanent entity; we can be broken up into five constituents - body, sensations, ideation, mental formations and consciousness - the consciousness being closest to the permanent idea of "Self", but is ever-changing with each new thought according to this viewpoint.

According to some thinkers both in the East and the West, the doctrine of "non-Self", may imply that Buddhism is a form of nihilism or something similar. However, as thinkers like Nagarjuna have clearly pointed out, Buddhism is not simply a rejection of the concept of existence or meaning, but of the hard and fast distinction between existence and non-existence, or rather between *being* and *no-thingness*. Phenomena are not independent from causes and conditions and do not exist as isolated things as we perceive them to be.

The lack of a permanent, unchanging, substantial Self in beings and things does not mean that they do not experience growth and decay on the relative level. But on the ultimate level of analysis, one cannot distinguish an object from its causes and conditions or even distinguish between object and subject (an idea appearing relatively recently in Western science). Buddhism thus has much more in common with Western empiricism, pragmatism, anti-foundationalism, and even poststructuralism than with nihilism.

In the Nikâyas, the Buddha and his disciples commonly question or declare "Is that which is impermanent, subject to change, subject to suffering fit to be considered thus: 'This I am, this is mine, this is my self'?" The question which the Buddha poses to his audience is whether compounded phenomena are fit to be considered as self, to which the audience agrees that it is unworthy to be considered so. And in relinquishing such an attachment to compounded phenomena, such a person gives up delight, desire and craving for compounded phenomena and is unbounded by its change.

When completely free from attachments, craving or desire to the five aggregates, such a person experiences then transcends the very causes of suffering. In this way, the insight wisdom or prajñâ of non-Self gives rise to cessation of suffering, and not an intellectual debate over whether a self exists or not. It is by realizing (not merely understanding intellectually, but making real in one's experience) the three marks of conditioned existence that one develops prajñâ, which is the antidote to the ignorance that lies at the root of all suffering.

INTERPRETATIONS OF THE THREE MARKS BY VARIOUS SCHOOLS

Some Buddhist traditions assert that Anatta pervades everything, and is not limited to personality, or soul. These traditions assert that Nirvana also has the quality of Anatta, but that Nirvana (by definition) is the cessation of Dukkha and Anicca.

In his Mulamadhyamakakarika (XXV: 19), Nagarjuna says: There is not the slightest difference between *Samsara* and Nirvana.

This verse points us to an interesting stress between

dukkha and nirvana, through an argument based in anatta. This specific stress can be seen to be the key to (and possibly source for the development of) the deity yogas of vajrayana. The sutra path enjoins us to identify the entire world (internally and externally) as *samsara* - a continual churning of suffering that nobody wants to be part of. Our practice is that of *leaving* the shores of *samsara*.

On the other hand, we are told that unconditioned, enlightened activity is not actually different from *samsara*. Whereas the deity yoga of vajrayana enjoins us to identify the entire world as nirvana - a continual play of enlightening activity that everyone wishes to be a part of. Our practice here is that of *arriving* at the shores of nirvana.

At this level, the distinction between Sutra and Vajrayana remain that of view (*departing* vs. *arriving*), but basically the practitioner remains involved in undergoing a transformative development to his or her Weltanschauung, and in this context, these practices remain rooted in psychological change, grounded in the development of Samatha, or training in concentration.

However, there are certain practices in Tantra which are not solely concerned with psychological change; these revolve around the basic idea that it is possible to induce deep levels of concentration through psycho-physical methods as a result of special exercises. The purpose remains the same (to achieve liberating view), but the method involves a 'short cut' for the training in Samatha.

6

Theravada Buddhism

Theravada; literally, "the Teaching of the Elders" or "the Ancient Teaching", is the oldest surviving Buddhist school. It was founded in India. It is relatively conservative, and generally closest to early Buddhism, and for many centuries has been the predominant religion of Sri Lanka (about 70% of the population) and most of continental Southeast Asia (Cambodia, Laos, Burma, Thailand).

Theravada is also practiced by minorities in parts of southwest China (by the Shan and Tai ethnic groups), Vietnam (by the Khmer Krom), Bangladesh (by the ethnic groups of Baruas, Chakma, and Magh), Malaysia and Indonesia, while recently gaining popularity in Singapore and the Western World. Today Theravada Buddhists number over 100 million worldwide, and in recent decades Theravada has begun to take root in the West and in the Buddhist revival in India.

ORIGIN OF THE SCHOOL

The Theravâda school is ultimately derived from the Vibhajjavâda (or 'doctrine of analysis') grouping which was a continuation of the older Sthavira (or 'teaching of the Elders') group at the time of the Third Buddhist Council around 250 BCE, during the reign of Emperor Asoka in India. Vibhajjavadins saw themselves as the continuation of orthodox Sthaviras and after the Third Council continued to refer to their school as the Sthaviras/Theras ('The Elders'), their doctrines were probably similar to the older Sthaviras but were not completely identical.

After the Third Council geographical distance led to the Vibhajjavâdins gradually evolving into four groups: the Mahîúâsaka, Kâúyapîya, Dharmaguptaka and the Tâmraparnîya. The Theravada is descended from the Tâmraparnîya, which means 'the Sri Lankan lineage'. Some sources claim that only the Theravada actually evolved directly from the Vibhajjavâdins. According to Buddhist scholar A.K. Warder, the Theravada "spread rapidly south from Avanti into Maharastra and Andhra and down to the Cola country (Kanchi), as well as Ceylon.

For sometime they maintained themselves in Avanti as well as in their new territories, buy gradually they tended to regroup themselves in the south, the Great Vihara (Mahavihara) in Anuradhapura, the capital of Ceylon, become the main centre of their tradition, Kanchi a secondary center and the northern regions apparently relinquished to other schools." The name of Tamraparniya was given to the Sri Lankan lineage in India but there is no indication that this referred to any change in doctrine or scripture from the Vibhajjavadins, since the name points only to geographical location.

The Theravadin accounts of its own origins mention that it received the teachings that were agreed upon during the Third Buddhist Council, and these teachings were known as the Vibhajjavada. In the 7th century, Chinese pilgrims Xuanzang and Yi Jing refer to the Buddhist school in Sri Lanka as 'Sthavira'. In ancient India, those schools that used Sanskrit as their religious language referred to this school as the 'Sthaviras', but those that use Pali as their religious language referred to this school as the 'Theras'. Both 'Sthaviras' (Sanskrit) and 'Theras' (Pali) both literally mean 'The Elders'.

The school has been using the name 'Theravada' for itself in a written forms since at least the fourth century CE when the term appears in the *Dipavamsa*. There is little information about the later history of Theravada Buddhism in India, and it is not known when it disappeared in its country of origin. The Theravada school had also reached Burma around the time it arrived in Sri Lanka and something of a synergy gradually developed. Around the end of the tenth century C.E, for example, war in Sri Lanka had extinguished the Theravadin ordination lineage, and a contingent of Burmese monks had to be imported to rekindle it.

Burmese and Sri Lankan Theravada reinforced each other sufficiently, so that by the time Buddhism died out in India in the eleventh century, it had established a stable home in these countries. Gradually the Theravada form of Buddhism spread to Thailand, Laos, and Cambodia. Royal houses in Sri Lanka and Southeast Asia associated themselves closely with Buddhism. States in those areas strictly enforced orthodoxy, and ensured that Theravada remained traditionalist. This contrasts with the relationship of Buddhism to states throughout most of Buddhism's history in India.

According to Sinhalese tradition, Buddhism was first brought to Sri Lanka by Mahinda, who is believed to have been the son of the Mauryan emperor Asoka, in the third century BCE, as a part of the missionary activities of the Asokan era. In Sri Lanka, Mahinda established the Mahavihara Monastery of Anuradhapura. Later it became divided into three subgroups, known after their monastic centers as the Mahavihara, the Abhayagirivihara, and the Jetavanavihara. In 1164, with the guidance of two monks from a forest branch of the Mahavihara, Sri Lanka King reunited all bhikkhus in Sri Lanka into the orthodox Mahavihara School.

A few years after the arrival of Sthavira Mahinda, Sanghamitta, who is also believed to be the daughter of Emperor Asoka, came to Sri Lanka. She started the first nun order in Sri Lanka, but the nun order died out in Sri Lanka in the 11th century and in Burma in the 13th. In 429 CE, by request of China's emperor, nuns from Anuradhapura were sent to China to establish the Nun Order. The order was then spread to Korea. In 1996, 11 selected Sri Lankan nuns were ordained fully as Bhikkhunis by a team of Theravada monks in concert with a team of Korean Nuns in India. There is disagreement among Theravada vinaya authorities as to whether such ordinations are valid.

In the last few years the head of the Dambulla chapter of the Siyam Nikaya in Sri Lanka has carried out ordination ceremonies for hundreds of nuns. This has been criticized by some other leading figures in the Siyam Nikaya and Amarapura Nikaya, and the governing council of Burmese Buddhism has declared that there can be no valid ordination of nuns in modern times, though some Burmese monks disagree with this. According to Mahavamsa the Sri Lanka chronical, after the conclusion of the Third Buddhist Council, a missionary was also sent to Suvannabhumi where two monks Sona and Uttara, are said to have proceeded.

Scholar opinions differ as to where exactly this land of Suvannabhumi is located, but Suvannabhumi is believed to be located somewhere in the area which now includes lower Burma, Thailand, Malay Peninsula and Sumatra Island. The Mon and Pyu were one of the earliest people to inhabit Burma. Recent archaeological findings at Pyu settlement at Samon Valley (around 100 km south-east of Bagan) have shown that they have trade links with India at around 500 BC-400 BC and with China at around 200 BC. Chinese sources which have been dated to around 240 A.D. have mentioned a Buddhist kingdom by the name of Lin-Yang, which some scholars have identified it as the ancient Pyu kingdom of Beikthano which is 300 km north of Yangon.

The Burmese slowly become Theravadin when they come into contact with the Pyu and Mon civilization. The Mon was also one of the earliest people to inhabit Thailand. The Thai slowly become Theravadin when they come into contact with the Mon civilization. Despite its success in Southeast Asia, Theravada Buddhism in China has generally been limited to areas bordering Theravada countries. In Chinese historiography, it is normally referred to as Hinayana, a term used in Mahayana texts to denigrate Buddhists who did not accept the Mahayana sutras; this usage is increasingly regarded as derogatory within the Buddhist community.

MODERN DEVELOPMENTS

The following modern trends or movements have been identified.

- Modernism: attempts to adapt to the modern world and adopt some of its ideas; includes among other things
    - green movement
    - syncretism with other Buddhist traditions
    - women's rights
    - gay rights
- Reformism: attempts to restore a supposed earlier, ideal state of Buddhism; includes in particular the adoption of Western scholars' theories of original Buddhism (in recent times the "Western scholarly interpretation of Buddhism" is the official Buddhism prevailing in Sri Lanka and Thailand.)
- Ultimatism: tendency to concentrate on advanced teachings such as the Four Noble Truths at the expense of more elementary ones
- Neotraditionalism; includes among other things
    - revival of ritualism
    - remythologization
- Insight meditation
- Social action
- Devotional religiosity
- Reaction to Buddhist nationalism
- Renewal of forest monks
- Revival of samatha meditation

Buddhist revivalism has also reacted against changes in Buddhism caused by colonialist regimes. Western colonialists and Christian missionaries deliberately imposed a particular type of Christian monasticism on Buddhist clergy in Sri Lanka and colonies in Southeast Asia, restricting monks' activities to individual purification and temple ministries. Prior to British colonial control, monks in both Sri Lanka and Burma had been responsible for the education of the children of lay people, and had produced large bodies of literature.

After the British takeover, Buddhist temples were strictly administered and were only permitted to use their funds on strictly religious activities. Christian ministers were given control of the education system and their pay became state funding for missions. Foreign, especially British rule had an enervating effect on the *sangha*.

According to Walpola Rahula, Christian missionaries displaced and appropriated the educational, social, and welfare activities of the monks, and inculcated a permanent shift in views regarding the proper position of monks in society through their institutional influence upon the elite. Many monks in post-colonial times have been dedicated to undoing this paradigm shift. Movements intending to restore Buddhism's place in society have developed in both Sri Lanka and Burma.

Theravada promotes the concept of Vibhajjavada (Pali), literally "Teaching of Analysis." This doctrine says that insight must come from the aspirant's experience, critical investigation, and reasoning instead of by blind faith; however, the scriptures of the Theravadin tradition also emphasize heeding the advice of the wise, considering such advice and evaluation of one's own experiences to be the two tests by which practices should be judged.

In Theravada, the cause of human existence and suffering (*dukkha*) is identified as craving (*tanha*), which carries with it the defilements (*kilesas*). Those defilements that bind human to the cycle of rebirth are classified into a set of ten "Fetters", while those defilements that impede concentration (*Samadhi*) are presented in a fivefold set called the "Five Hindrances". The level of defilement can be coarse, medium, and subtle. It is a phenomenon that frequently arises, remains temporarily and then vanishes. Theravadins believe defilements are not only harmful to one, but also harmful to others.

They are the driving force behind all inhumanities a human being can commit. Theravadins believe these defilements are the habits born of ignorance (*avijja*) which afflict the minds of all unenlightened beings. It is believed that unenlightened beings are under the influence of the defilements, unenlightened beings cling to them through ignorance of the truth. But in reality, those mental defilements are nothing more than taints that have afflicted the mind and create suffering and stress. It is also believed that unenlightened beings cling to the body, assuming it as their own "Self", but in reality the body is an impermanent phenomenon formed from the four basic elements.

Often characterized by earth, water, fire and air, in the early Buddhist texts these are defined to be abstractions representing the sensorial qualities solidity, fluidity, temperature, and mobility, respectively. The mental defilements' frequent instigation and manipulation of the mind is believed to have prevented the mind from seeing the true nature of reality. Unskillful behavior in turn can strengthen the defilements, but following the Noble Eightfold Path can weaken or eradicate them.

It is also believed that unenlightened beings experience the world through their imperfect six sense doors (eye, ear, nose, tongue, tactile sense, and mind) and then use the mind clouded by defilements to form their own interpretation, perception and conclusion. In such a condition the perception or conclusion made will be based on that being's own illusion of reality. In the state of *jhana* (deep concentration), the five physical sense doors will fade, the mental defilements will be suppressed, and wholesome mental traits will become strengthened. The mind can then be used to investigate and gain insight into the true nature of reality.

There are three stages of defilements. During the stage of passivity the defilements lies dormant at the base of the mental continuum as latent tendencies (*anusaya*), but through the impact of sensory stimulus it will manifest (*pariyutthana*) itself to the surface of consciousness in the form of unwholesome thoughts, emotions, and volitions. If they gather additional strength, the defilement will reach the dangerous stage of transgression (*vitikkama*), which will then involve physical or vocal actions. It is believed that in order to be free from suffering and stress these defilements need to be permanently uprooted. Initially the defilements are restrained through mindfulness to prevent them from taking over the mind and bodily action.

They are then uprooted through internal investigation, analyzing, experiencing and understanding the true nature of those defilements by using *jhana*. This process needs to be repeated for each and every defilement. The practice will then lead the meditator to realize the Four Noble Truths, Enlightenment, and Nirvana. Nirvana is the ultimate goal of Theravadins. *Nirvana* is said to be the perfect bliss and the person is liberated from the repeated cycle of birth, illness, aging and death.

Theravadins believe that every individual is personally responsible for their own self-awakening and liberation, as they are the ones that were responsible for their own actions and consequences. Simply learning or believing in the true nature of reality as expounded by the Buddha is not enough; the awakening can only be achieved through direct experience and personal realization. An individual will have to follow and practice the Noble Eightfold Path as taught by the Buddha to discover the reality for them.

In Theravada belief, Buddhas, gods or deities are incapable of giving a human being the awakening or lifting them from the state of repeated cycle of birth, illness, aging and death (*samsara*). For Theravadins, Buddha is only a Teacher of the Noble Eightfold Path, while gods or deities are still subject to anger, jealousy, hatred, vengeance, craving, greed, delusion, and death. It is believed that some people who practice with earnestness and zeal can attain Nirvana within a single lifetime, as did many of the first few generations of Buddha's disciples.

For others, the process may take multiple lifetimes, with the individual reaching higher and higher states of realization. One who has attained Nirvana is called an *Arahant*. It is believed that the Nirvana is most quickly attained as a disciple of Buddha, since Lord Buddha is believed to have possessed the ultimate knowledge on how to guide a person through the process of enlightenment. According to the early scriptures, the Nirvana attained by *Arahants* is identical to that attained by the Buddha himself, as there is only one type of Nirvana. Buddha was superior to *Arahants* because the Buddha had discovered the path all by himself, and has taught it to others (i,e., metaphorically turning the wheel of Dhamma). *Arahants,* on the other hand, attained Nirvana due in part to the Buddha's teachings.

Theravadins revere the Buddha as a single supremely gifted person but do recognize the existence of other such Buddhas in the distant past and future. Maitreya (Pali: Metteyya), for example, is mentioned very briefly in the Pali Canon as a Buddha who will come in the distant future. Traditionally Theravadins can either have the conviction (or "faith") in the Buddha's teaching or practice the minor precepts in the hope of gaining some minor benefits or they can investigate and verify by direct experience the truth of the Buddha's teaching by practicing the *jhana* which is part of the Noble Eightfold Path for their own Enlightenment.

FUNDAMENTALS OF THERAVADA

One thing that should be mentioned first and foremost is that the Theravada philosophy is a continuous analytical process of life, not a mere set of ethics and rituals. The ultimate theory of Theravada uses the Four Noble Truths, also known as the Four Sublime Truths. In the simplest form these can be described as the problem, the cause, the solution and the pathway to solution (implementation).

THE FOUR NOBLE TRUTHS

A formal description of the Four Noble Truths follows:

1. *Dukkha* (suffering) - This can be somewhat broadly classified into three categories. Inherent suffering or the suffering one undergoes in all the worldly activities, what one suffers in day-to-day life: birth, aging, diseases, death,

sadness, etc. In short, that entire one feels from separating from 'loving' attachments and/or associating with 'hating' attachments is encompassed into the term. The second class of suffering, called suffering due to Change, implies that things suffer due to attaching themselves to a momentary state which is held to be 'good'; when that state is changed, things are subjected to suffering. The third, termed 'Sankhara Dukkha', is the most subtle. Beings suffer simply by not realizing that they are mere aggregates with no definite, unchanging identity.

2. *Dukkha Samudaya* (cause of suffering) - Craving, which leads to Attachment and Bondage, is the cause of suffering. Formally, this is termed 'Tanha'. It can be classified into three instinctive drives. 'Kama Tanha' is the Craving for any pleasurable sense object (which involves sight, sound, touch, taste, smell and mental perceptives). 'Bhava Tanha' is the Craving for attachment to an ongoing process, which appears in various forms, including the longing for existence. 'Vibhava Tanha' is the Craving for detachment from a process, which includes non-existence and causes the longing for self-annihilation.
3. *Dukkha Nirodha* (cessation of suffering) - One cannot possibly adjust the whole world to one's taste in order to eliminate suffering and hope that it will remain so forever. This would violate the chief principle of Change. Instead, one adjusts one's own mind through detachment so that the Change, of whatever nature, has no effect on one's peace of mind. Briefly stated, the third Noble Truth implies that elimination of the cause (craving) eliminates the result (suffering). This is inferred in the scriptural quote by The Buddha, 'Whatever may result from a cause, shall be eliminated by the elimination of the cause'.
4. *Dukkha Nirodha Gamini Patipada* (pathway to freedom from suffering) - This is the Noble Eightfold Pathway towards freedom or Nirvana. The path can roughly be rendered into English as right view, right intention, right speech, right actions, right livelihood, right effort, right mindfulness and right concentration.

THE THREE CHARACTERISTICS

These are the three characteristics of all conditioned phenomena in Theravada thought.

1. *Anicca* (impermanence): Change is. All conditioned phenomena are subject to Change, including physical characteristics, qualities, assumptions, theories, knowledge, etc. Nothing is permanent, because, for something to be permanent there has to be an unchanging cause behind it. Since all causes are recursively bound together, there can be no ultimate unchanging cause.
2. *Dukkha* (suffering) - Craving causes suffering, since what is craved is transitory, changing, and perishing. The craving for impermanent things causes disappointment and sorrow.

   There is a tendency to label practically everything in the world, as either 'good', 'comfortable' or 'satisfying', as opposed to 'bad', 'uncomfortable', and 'unsatisfying'. Since we label things in terms of 'like' or 'dislike', we create suffering for ourselves. If one succeeds in giving up the tendency to label things and free him from the instincts that drive him towards attaining what he himself labels collectively as 'liking', he attains the ultimate freedom. The problem, the cause, the solution and the implementation, all of these are within oneself, not outside.
3. *Anatta* (not-self) - The concept 'Anatta' can be rendered as *lack of fixed, unchanging identity*; no phenomenon constitutes an individual's permanent, essential Self. A living being is a composite of the five aggregates (*khandhas*), which is the physical forms (*rupa*), feelings or sensations (*vedana*), perception (*sanna*), mental formations (*sankhara*), and consciousness (*vinnana*), none of which can be identified as Self. From the moment of conception, all entities (including all living beings) are subject to a process of continuous change. A practitioner should, on the other hand, develop and refine his or her mind to a state so as to see through this phenomenon.

Direct realization of these three characteristics leads to freedom from worldly bonds and attachments, thus leading to the state where one is completely, ultimately free, the state which is termed Nirvana, which literally means 'Freedom'.

THE THREE NOBLE DISCIPLINES

The pathway towards Nirvana or the Noble Eightfold Pathway is sometimes stated in a more concise manner, known as the Three Noble Disciplines. These are known as discipline (*sîla*), training of mind (*samâdhi*) and wisdom (*paññâ*).

MEDITATION

Meditation (Pali: *Bhavana*) means the positive reinforcement of one's mind. Broadly categorized into Samatha and Vipassana, Meditation is the key tool implemented in attaining *jhana*. Samatha literally means "to make skillful", and has other renderings also, among which are "tranquilizing, calming", "visualizing", and "achieving". Vipassana means "insight", or "abstract understanding". In this context, Samatha Meditation makes a person skillful in concentration of mind. Once the mind is sufficiently concentrated, Vipassana allows one to see through the veil of ignorance (of the Four Noble Truths).

In the Pali Canon discourses, the Buddha frequently instructs his disciples to practice *Samadhi* (concentration) in order to establish and develop *jhana* (full concentration). *Jhana* is the instrument used by the Buddha himself to penetrate the true nature of phenomena (through investigation and direct experience) and to reach Enlightenment. Right Concentration (*samma-Samadhi*) is one of the elements in the Noble Eightfold Path. *Samadhi* can be developed from mindfulness with breathing (*anapanasati*), from visual objects (*kasina*), and repetition of phrases.

The traditional list contains 40 objects of meditation (*kammatthâna*) to be used for Samatha Meditation. Every object has a specific goal; for example, meditation on the parts of the body (*kayanupassana* or *kayagathasathi*) will result in a lessening of attachment to our own bodies and those of others, resulting in a reduction of sensual desires. Mettâ (loving kindness) generates the feelings of goodwill and happiness toward us and other beings; *metta* practice serves as an antidote to ill-will, wrath and fear.

LEVELS OF ATTAINMENT

Through practice, (Theravadin) practitioners can achieve four stages of enlightenment:

1. Stream-Enterers - Those who have destroyed the first three fetters (false view of self, doubt, and clinging to rites and rituals) will be safe from falling into the states of misery (they will not be born as an animal, *peta* (ghost), or hell being). At most they will have to be reborn only seven more times before attaining Nirvana.
2. Once-Returners - Those who have destroyed the first three fetters and have lessened the fetters of lust and hatred will attain Nirvana after being born once more in the world.
3. Non-Returners - Those who have destroyed the five lower fetters, which bind beings to the world of the senses. Non-returners will never again return to the human world and after they die, they will be born in the high heavenly worlds, there to attain Nirvana. Attaining the state of non-returner is portrayed in the early texts as the ideal goal for laity.
4. Arahants - Those who have reached Enlightenment, realized Nirvana, and have reached the quality of deathlessness are free from all the fermentations of defilement. Their ignorance, craving and attachments have ended. Attaining the state of arahant is portrayed in the early texts as the ideal goal for monastics.

SCRIPTURES

The Theravada school upholds the Pali Canon or Tipitaka as the most authoritative collection of texts on the teachings of Gautama Buddha. The Sutta and Vinaya portion of the

Tipitaka shows considerable overlap in content to the Agamas, the parallel collections used by non-Theravada schools in India which are preserved in Chinese and partially in Sanskrit, Prakrit, and Tibetan, and the various non-Theravada Vinayas. On this basis, both these sets of texts are generally believed to be the oldest and most authoritative texts on Buddhism by scholars.

It is also believed that much of the Pali Canon, which is still used by Theravâda communities, was transmitted to Sri Lanka during the reign of Asoka. After being orally transmitted (as was the custom in those days for religious texts) for some centuries, were finally committed to writing in the last century BCE, at what the Theravada usually reckons as the fourth council, in Sri Lanka. Theravada is one of the first Buddhist schools to commit the whole complete set of its Buddhist canon into writing.

Much of the material in the Canon is not specifically "Theravadin", but is instead the collection of teachings that this school preserved from the early, non-sectarian body of teachings. According to Peter Harvey, it contains material which is at odds with later Theravadin orthodoxy. He states:

The Theravadins, then, may have added texts to the Canon for some time, but they do not appear to have tampered with what they already had from an earlier period.

The Pali Tipitaka consists of three parts: the Vinaya Pitaka, Sutta Pitaka and Abhidhamma Pitaka. Of these, the Abhidhamma Pitaka is believed to be a later addition to the first two pitakas, which, in the opinion of many scholars, were the only two pitakas at the time of the First Buddhist Council. The Pali Abhidhamma was not recognized outside the Theravada school.

In the 4th or 5th century CE Buddhaghosa Thera wrote the first Pali commentaries to much of the Tipitaka (which were based on much older manuscripts, mostly in old Sinhalese), and after him many other monks wrote various commentaries, which have become part of the Theravada heritage. These texts, however, do not enjoy the same authority as the Tipitaka does. The Tipitaka is composed of 45 volumes in the Thai edition, 40 in the Burmese and 58 in the Sinhalese, and a full set of the Tipitaka is usually kept in its own (medium-sized) cupboard.

The commentaries, together with the Abhidhamma, define the specific Theravada heritage. Related versions of the Sutta Pitaka and Vinaya Pitaka were common to all the early Buddhist schools, and therefore do not define only Theravada, but also the other early Buddhist schools, and perhaps the teaching of Gautama Buddha himself. Theravada Buddhists consider much of what is found in the Chinese and Tibetan scriptural collections to be apocryphal, meaning that they are not authentic words of the Buddha.

LAY AND MONASTIC LIFE

Traditionally, Theravada Buddhism has observed a distinction between the practices suitable for a lay person and the practices undertaken by ordained monks (and, in ancient times, nuns). While the possibility of significant attainment by laymen is not entirely disregarded by the Theravada, it occupies a position of significantly less prominence than in the Mahayana and Vajrayana traditions. This distinction - as well as the distinction between those practices advocated by the Pali Canon, and the folk religious elements embraced by many monks - has motivated some scholars to consider Theravada Buddhism to be composed of multiple separate traditions, overlapping though still distinct.

Most prominently, the anthropologist Melford Spiro in his work *Buddhism and Society* separated Burmese Theravada into three groups: *Apotropaic Buddhism* (concerned with providing protection from evil spirits), *Kammatic Buddhism* (concerned with making merit for a future birth), and *Nibbanic Buddhism* (concerned with attaining the liberation of Nirvana, as described in the Tipitaka). He stresses that all three are firmly rooted in the Pali Canon. These categories are not accepted by all scholars, and are usually considered non-exclusive by those who employ them.

The role of lay people has traditionally been primarily occupied with activities that are commonly termed 'merit making' (falling under Spiro's category of kammatic Buddhism). Merit making activities include offering food and other basic necessities to monks, making donations to temples and monasteries, burning incense or lighting candles before images of the Buddha, and chanting protective or merit-making verses from the Pali Canon. Some lay practitioners have always chosen to take a more active role in religious affairs, while still maintaining their lay status.

Dedicated lay men and women sometimes act as trustees or custodians for their temples, taking part in the financial planning and management of the temple. Others may volunteer significant time in tending to the mundane needs of local monks (by cooking, cleaning, maintaining temple facilities, etc.). Lay activities have traditionally not extended to study of the Pali scriptures, or the practice of meditation, though in the 20th Century these areas have become more accessible to the lay community, especially in Thailand. A number of senior monastics in the Thai Forest Tradition, including Ajahn Buddhadasa, Luang Ta Maha Bua, Ajahn Plien Panyapatipo, Ajahn Pasanno, and Ajahn Jayasaro, have begun teaching meditation retreats outside of the monastery for lay disciples.

In the UK, Ajahn Chah a disciple of Ajahn Mun, set up a monastic lineage at Chithurst in West Sussex, "Cittaviveka", with his disciple Ajahn Sumedho, and then "Amaravati" in Hertfordshire was founded which has a retreat center for lay retreats. Ajahn Sumedho extended this to Harnham in Northumberland as Aruna Ratanagiri under the present guidance of Ajahn Munindo, another disciple of Ajahn Chah. Nirvana, the highest goal of Theravada Buddhism, is attained through study and the practice of morality, meditation and wisdom (*sila, Samadhi, panna*).

The goal of Nirvana (and its associated techniques) has

traditionally been seen as the domain of the fully ordained monastic, whereas many of the same techniques can be used by laypeople to generate happiness in their lives, without focusing on Nirvana. Monastic roles in the Theravada can be broadly described as being split between the role of the (often urban) scholar monk and the (often rural or forest) meditation monk. Both types of monks serve their communities as religious teachers and officiants by presiding over religious ceremonies and providing instruction in basic Buddhist morality and teachings.

Scholar monks undertake the path of studying and preserving the Pali literature of the Theravada. They may devote little time to the practice of meditation, but may attain great respect and renown by becoming masters of a particular section of the Pali Canon or its commentaries. Masters of the Abhidhamma, called Abhidhammika, are particularly respected in the scholastic tradition. Meditation monks, often called forest monks because of their association with certain wilderness-dwelling traditions, are considered to be specialists in meditation.

While some forest monks may undertake significant study of the Pali Canon, in general meditation monks are expected to learn primarily from their meditation experiences and personal teachers, and may not know more of the Tipitaka than is necessary to participate in liturgical life and to provide a foundation for fundamental Buddhist teachings. More so than the scholastic tradition, the meditation tradition is associated with the attainment of certain supernatural powers described in both Pali sources and folk tradition.

These powers include the attainment of Nirvana, mind-reading, supernatural power over material objects and their own material bodies, seeing and conversing with gods and beings living in hell, and remembering their past lives. These powers are called abhiñña. Sometimes remain of the cremated bone fragment of an accomplished forest monk is believed able to transfom itself into crystal-like relics (*sârira-dhâtu*).

ORDINATION

The minimum age for ordaining as a Buddhist monk is 20 years, reckoned from conception. However, boys under that age are allowed to ordain as novices (*samanera*), performing a ceremony such as *Shinbyu* in Burma. Novices shave their heads, wear the yellow robes, and observe ten basic precepts. Although no specific minimum age for novices is mentioned in the scriptures, traditionally boys as young as seven are accepted. This tradition follows the story of the Lord Buddha's son, Rahula, who was allowed to become a novice at the age of seven. Monks follow 227 rules of discipline, while nuns follow 311 rules.

In most Theravada countries, it is a common practice for young men to ordain as monks for a fixed period of time. In Thailand and Burma, young men typically ordain for the 3 month Rain Retreat (*vassa*), though shorter or longer periods of ordination are not rare. Traditionally, temporary ordination was even more flexible among Laotians. Once they had undergone their initial ordination as young men, Laotian men were permitted to temporarily ordain again at any time, though married men were expected to seek their wife's permission. Throughout Southeast Asia, there is little stigma attached to leaving the monastic life. Monks regularly leave the robes after acquiring an education, or when compelled by family obligations or ill-health.

Ordaining as a monk, even for a short period, is seen as having many virtues. In many Southeast Asian cultures, it is seen as a means for a young man to 'repay' his parents for their work and effort in raising him, because the merit from his ordination accrues to them as well. Thai men who have ordained as a monk may be seen as more fit husbands by Thai women, who refer to men who have served as monks with a colloquial term meaning 'cooked' to indicate that they are more mature and ready for marriage. Particularly in rural areas, temporary ordination of boys and young men traditionally gave peasant boys an opportunity to gain an education in temple schools without committing to a permanent monastic life.

In Sri Lanka, temporary ordination is not practiced, and a monk leaving the order is frowned upon. The continuing influence of the caste system in Sri Lanka may play a role in the taboo against temporary ordination and leaving the monkhood. Though Sri Lankan monastic nikayas are often organized along caste lines, men who ordain as monks temporarily pass outside of the conventional caste system, and as such during their time as monks may act (or be treated) in a way that would not be in line with the expected duties and privileges of their caste.

Some well-known Theravadin monks are: Ajahn Mun Bhuridatta, Ajahn Chah, Ledi Sayadaw, Ajahn Plien Panyapatipo, Ajahn Sumedho, Ajahn Brahm, Bhikkhu Bodhi, Buddhadasa, Mahasi Sayadaw, Nyanaponika Thera, Preah Maha Ghosananda, Sayadaw U Pandita, Ajahn Amaro, Thanissaro Bhikkhu and Walpola Rahula.

MONASTIC PRACTICES

The practices usually vary in different sub-schools and monasteries within Theravada. But in the most orthodox forest monastery, the monk usually models his practice and lifestyle on that of the Buddha and his first generation of disciples by living close to nature in forest, mountains and caves. Forest monasteries still keep alive the ancient traditions through following the Buddhist monastic code of discipline in all its detail and developing meditation in secluded forests.

In a typical daily routine at the monastery during the 3 month vassa period, the monk will wake up before dawn and will begin the day with group chanting and meditation. At dawn the monks will go out to surrounding villages bare-footed on alms-round and will have the only meal of the day before noon by eating from the bowl by hand. Most of the time is spent on Dhamma study and meditation. Sometimes the abbot or a senior monk will give a Dhamma talk to the visitors. Laity who stays at the monastery will have to abide by the traditional eight Buddhist precepts.

After the end of the Vassa period, many of the monks

will go out far away from the monastery to find a remote place (usually in the forest) where they can hang their umbrella tents and where it is suitable for the work of self-development. When they go wandering, they walk barefoot, and go wherever they feel inclined. Only those requisites which are necessary will be carried along. These generally consist of the bowl, the three robes, a bathing cloth, an umbrella tent, a mosquito net, a kettle of water, a water filter, razor, sandals, some small candles, and a candle lantern.

The monks do not fix their times for walking and sitting meditation, for as soon as they are free they just start doing it; nor do they determine for how long they will go on to meditate. Some of them sometimes walk from dusk to dawn whereas at other times they may walk from between two to seven hours. Some may decide to fast for days or stay at dangerous places where ferocious animals live in order to aid their meditation. Those monks who have been able to achieve a high level of attainment will be able to guide the junior monks and lay Buddhists toward the four degrees of spiritual attainment.

LAY DEVOTEE

In Pali the word for a male lay devotee is *Upasaka*. *Upasika* is its female equivalent. One of the duties of the lay followers, as taught by the Buddha, is to look after the needs of the monk/nuns. They are to see that the monk/nuns do not suffer from lack of the four requisites: food, clothing, shelter and medicine. As neither monks nor nuns are allowed to have an occupation, they depend entirely on the laity for their sustenance. In return for this charity, they are expected to lead exemplary lives.

In Burma and Thailand, the monastery was and is still regarded as a seat of learning. In fact today about half of the primary schools in Thailand are located in monasteries. Religious rituals and ceremonies held in a monastery are always accompanied by social activities. In times of crisis, it is to the monks that people bring their problems for counsel. Traditionally, a ranking monk will deliver a sermon four times a month: when the moon waxes and wanes and the day before the new and full moons. The laity also has a chance to learn meditation from the monks during these times.

It is also possible for a lay disciple to become enlightened. As Bhikkhu Bodhi notes, "The Suttas and commentaries do record a few cases of lay disciples attaining the final goal of Nirvana. However, such disciples either attain Arahantship on the brink of death or enter the monastic order soon after their attainment. They do not continue to dwell at home as Arahant householders, for dwelling at home is incompatible with the state of one who has severed all craving."

INFLUENCES

According to the linguist Zacharias P. Thundy the word "Theravada" may have been Hellenized into "Therapeutae", to name a coenobitic order near Alexandria described around the 1st century CE. The similarities between the Therapeutae and Buddhist monasticism, combined with Indian evidence of Buddhist missionary activity to the Mediterranean around 250 BC (the Edicts of Asoka), have been pointed out. The Therapeutae would have been the descendants of Asoka's emissaries to the West, and would have influenced the early formation of Christianity. However, the Macmillan *Encyclopedia of Buddhism* states that theories of influences of Buddhism on early Christianity are without historical foundation.

MONASTIC ORDERS WITHIN THERAVADA

Theravada monks typically belong to a particular *nikaya*, variously referred to as monastic orders or fraternities. These different orders do not typically develop separate doctrines, but may differ in the manner in which they observe monastic rules. These monastic orders represent lineages of ordination, typically tracing their origin to a particular group of monks that established a new ordination tradition within a particular country or geographic area.

In Sri Lanka caste plays a major role in the division into

nikayas. Some Theravada Buddhist countries appoint or elect a *sangharaja*, or Supreme Patriarch of the *Sangha*, as the highest ranking or seniormost monk in a particular area, or from a particular nikaya. The demise of monarchies has resulted in the suspension of these posts in some countries, but patriarchs have continued to be appointed in Thailand. Burma and Cambodia ended the practice of appointing a *sangharaja* for some time, but the position was later restored, though in Cambodia it lapsed again.

THE NATURE OF THE BUDDHA

Buddha-nature is a doctrine important for many schools of Mahayana Buddhism. The Buddha Nature or Buddha Principle (*Buddha-dhâtu*) is taught to be a truly real, but internally hidden immortal potency or element within the purest depths of the mind, present in all sentient beings, for awakening and becoming a Buddha. There are conflicting interpretations of the idea in Mahayanic philosophy. The idea may be traced to Abhidharmic thought, and ultimately to statements of the Buddha in the Nikayas. Other terms for the Buddha-nature are *Tathâgatagarbha* and *Sugatagarbha*.

LUMINOUS MIND IN THE NIKAYAS

There is a clear reference in the Anguttara Nikaya to a "luminous mind" present within all people, be they corrupt or pure, whether or not it itself is stained or pure. When it is "unstained," it is supremely poised for Arahantship, and so could be conceived as the "womb" of the Arahant, for which a synonym is tathagata. The Lankavatara Sutra describes the *Tathagatagarbha* ("Arahant womb") as "by nature brightly shining and pure," and "originally pure," though "enveloped in the garments of the skhandhas, dhatus and ayatanas and soiled with the dirt of attachment, hatred, delusion and false imagining."

It is said to be "naturally pure," but it appears impure as it is stained by adventitious defilements. Thus the Lankavatara Sutra identifies the luminous mind of the Canon with the *Tathagatagarbha*. It also equates the *Tathagatagarbha* (and *alaya-vijnana*) with nirvana, though this is concerned with the actual attainment of nirvana as opposed to nirvana as a timeless phenomenon. The Canon does not support the identification of the "luminous mind" with nirvanic consciousness, though it plays a role in the realization of nirvana. Upon the destruction of the fetters, according to one scholar, "the shining nibbanic consciousness flashes out of the womb of arahantship, being without object or support, so transcending all limitations."

CENTRAL TENETS OF BUDDHA-NATURE DOCTRINE

The Buddha-nature doctrine centres on the possession by sentient beings of the supposedly innate, immaculate buddha-mind or buddha-element (*Buddha-dhatu*), which is, prior to the attainment of complete buddhahood, said to be not clearly seen and known in its full radiance. The Buddha Nature is equated in the Mahaparinirvana Sutra with the changeless and deathless True Self of the Buddha. In the Lankavatara Sutra, however, it is said that the *Tathagatagarbha* might be mistaken for a Self, which according to this sutra, it is not.

This Buddha-nature is described in the Mahaparinirvana Sutra to be incorruptible, uncreated, and indestructible. It is eternal bodhi ("Awake-ness") indwelling *samsara*, and thus opens up the immanent possibility of Liberation from all suffering and impermanence. No being of any kind is without the *Buddha-dhatu* (Buddha-nature). It is indicated in the Angulimaliya Sutra that if the Buddhas themselves were to try to seek for any sentient being that lacked the Buddha-nature, not one such person would be found. In fact, it is stated in that sutra that it is impossible for Buddhas not to discern the presence of the everlasting Buddha-nature in each and every being:

"Even though all Buddhas themselves were to search assiduously, they would not find a tathâgata-garbha (Buddha -nature) that is not eternal, for the eternal *dhâtu*, the *buddha-dhâtu* (Buddha Principle, Buddha Nature), the *dhâtu* adorned with infinite major and minor attributes, is present in all beings".

The eternality, unshakeability and changelessness of the Buddha-nature (often referred to as "*Tathagatagarbha*") is also frequently stressed in the sutras which expound this Buddha Element. The Srimala Sutra, for example, says:

"The *Tathagatagarbha* is not born, does not die, does not transfer [Tib: *'pho ba*], does not arise. It is beyond the sphere of the characteristics of the compounded; it is permanent, stable and changeless."

The development of the Buddha-nature doctrine is closely related to that of *Tathagatagarbha* (Sanskrit: "Buddha-matrix"). In the *Anunatva-Apurnatva-Nirdesa*, the Buddha links the *Tathagatagarbha* to the Dharmadhatu (ultimate, all-equal, uncreated essence of all phenomena) and to essential being, stating:

"What I call 'be-ing' (*sattva*) is just a different name for this permanent, stable, pure and unchanging refuge that is free from arising and cessation, the inconceivable pure Dharmadhatu."

This eternal refuge of the *Dharmadhatu / Buddha-dhatu* (transcendentally empty of all that is conditioned, afflicted, defective, and productive of suffering) is equated in the *Nirvana Sutra* with Buddhic Knowledge (*jnana*). Such Knowledge perceives both non-Self and the Self, Emptiness (*sunyata*) and non-Emptiness, wherein *"the Empty is the totality of samsara [birth-and-death] and the non-Empty is Great Nirvana."*

It is a recurrent theme of the Mahayana *Mahaparinirvana Sutra* that the Buddha-nature is indestructible and forever untarnished. Professor Jeffrey Hopkins translates several passages from the sutra in which the Buddha speaks of this topic and defines the Buddha-nature as pure, eternal, and truly real self:

'... that which has permanence, bliss, Self, and thorough purity is called the "meaning of pure truth"'.

'Permanent is the Self; the Self is thoroughly pure. The thoroughly pure is called "bliss". Permanent, blissful, Self, and thoroughly pure is the one-gone-thus [i.e. Buddha]';

'Self means the matrix-of-one-gone-thus [i.e. the *Tathagatagarbha*/ Buddha-nature]. The existence of the buddha-nature in all sentient beings is the meaning of "Self"'.

'The buddha-nature, by its own nature, cannot be made non-existent; it is not something that becomes non-existent. Just the inherent nature called "Self" is the secret matrix-of-one-gone-thus [i.e. *Tathagatagarbha* / Buddha-nature]; in this way that secret matrix cannot be destroyed and made non-existent by anything.'

In explaining what it means by sentient beings' having the Buddha nature, the 'Mahaparinirvana Sutra' distinguishes three different ways of understanding the term "to have":

Good son, there are three ways of having: first, to have in the future, Secondly, to have at present, and thirdly, to have in the past. All sentient beings will have in future ages the most perfect enlightenment, i.e., the Buddha nature. All sentient beings have at present bonds of defilements, and do not now possess the thirty-two marks and eighty noble characteristics of the Buddha. All sentient beings had in past ages deeds leading to the elimination of defilements and so can now perceive the Buddha nature as their future goal. For such reasons, I always proclaim that all sentient beings have the Buddha nature.

Thus according to Heng-Ching Shih, the teaching of the universal Buddha nature does not intend to assert the existence of substantial, entity-like self endowed with excellent features of a Buddha. Rather, Buddha nature simply represents the potentiality to be realized in the future. This type of interpretation of the Buddha-nature is not, however, universally accepted by Buddhists or scholars.

Dr. Shenpen Hookham, Oxford Buddhist scholar and Tibetan lama of the Shentong tradition, writes of the Buddha-nature or True Self as something real and permanent, and already present within the being as uncompounded

Enlightenment. She calls it 'the Buddha within', and comments:

'In scriptural terms, there can be no real objection to referring to Buddha, Buddhajnana [Buddha Awareness/ Buddha Knowledge], Nirvana and so forth as the True Self, unless the concept of Buddha and so forth being propounded can be shown to be impermanent, suffering, compounded, or imperfect in some way... in Shentong terms, the non-self is about what is *not* the case, and the Self of the Third Dharmachakra [i.e. the Buddha-nature doctrine] is about what truly IS.'

Buddhist scholar and chronicler, Dr. Merv Fowler, writes that the Buddha-nature really is present as an essence within each being. Fowler comments:

'The teaching that Buddha-nature is the hidden essence within all sentient beings is the main message of the *Tathagatagarbha* literature, the earliest of which is the *Tathagatagarbha Sutra*. This short sutra says that all living beings are in essence identical to the Buddha regardless of their defilements or their continuing transmigration from life to life... As in the earlier traditions, there is present the idea that enlightenment, or nirvana, is not something which has to be achieved, it is something which is already there... In a way, it means that everyone is really a Buddha now.'

Writer on Zen Buddhism, Peter Haskel, likewise indicates this idea of already and ever-present enlightenment (the Buddha-nature) within all beings. In his book, *Bankei Zen*, he shows how the Zen master, Bankei, taught that the Buddha Nature or Buddha Mind is inherent in each being from birth, is uncreated, unborn, and is of the same 'one substance' of past Buddhas and present beings, without any difference - just like the one water of the vast ocean.

In the Tibetan Book of the Dead, it is taught that at death there is an encounter with this true inner nature, *sugatagarbha* or *Dharmata*, when the veils of egocentricity tend briefly to drop away, and shining, unobstructed Awareness is disclosed to us. In line with Tibetan Nyingma doctrine, Tibetan lama, Chokyi Nyima Rinpoche, equates this radiant essence with the Buddha Nature. He writes:

"... all sentient beings already possess an enlightened essence, the sugatagarbha [i.e. the Buddha Nature]. This essence is present and permeates anyone who has mind, just as oil completely permeates any sesame seed... The moment our ego-clinging falls apart, then our innate wisdom, the luminosity of dharmata, will vividly, nakedly appear. This ground luminosity is not just empty; it is also luminous - aware."

An important Sanskrit treatise, entitled the *Ratnagotra-vibhaga,* on the Buddha Nature sees the *Tathagatagarbha* (Buddha Nature) as "Suchness" or "Thusness" - the abiding Reality of all things - in a state of tarnished concealment within the being.

The idea is that the ultimate consciousness of each being is spotless and pure, but surrounded by negative tendencies which are impure. Professor Paul Williams comments on how the impurity is actually not truly part of the Buddha Nature, but merely conceals the immanent true qualities of Buddha Mind (i.e. the Buddha Nature) from manifesting openly:

"The impurities that taint the mind and entail the state of unenlightenment (*samsara*) are completely adventitious... On the other hand from the point of view of the mind's pure radiant intrinsic nature, because it is like this i.e. pure and Buddhic, it is possessed of all the many qualities of a Buddha's mind. These do not need actually to be brought about but merely need to be allowed to shine forth. Because they are intrinsic to the very nature of consciousness itself they, and the very state of Buddhahood, will never cease."

Buddha nature is completely rejected by Theravada Buddhism due to the fact that the concept comes from later Mahayana sutras which it sees as inauthentic.

Though not explicitly denied in any form of Indian Mahayana, some scholars, especially those associated with Madhyamaka, did not have an active interest in this doctrine. Nevertheless, the Buddha-nature doctrine did become a cornerstone of East Asian Buddhist and Tibetan Buddhist soteriological thought and practice. Buddha-nature remains a widespread and important doctrine in much of Far Eastern Buddhism today.

DEVELOPMENT OF BUDDHA-NATURE

The Buddha-nature doctrine may be traced back in part to the abhidharmic debate over metaphysics, which arose among the Nikaya schools as they attempted to reconcile various perceived problems, including how to integrate the doctrine of anatta, which stipulates that there is no underlying self, with Buddhist psychology (i.e., what is the subject of karma, suffering, etc.; how do these processes occur) and soteriology (what is the subject of enlightenment; (how) does enlightenment occur?).

Debates between different Nikaya schools at this time provided a context for the later origination of the Mahayana and Mahayana concepts. The concept of "seeds" espoused by the Sautrântika in debate with the Sarvastivadiṇs over the metaphysical status of dharmas is a precursor to the store-consciousness of the Yogacara school and the *Tathagatagarbha*, the latter of which is closely related to Buddha-nature and the former of which is identified with it in Yogacara.

VARYING INTERPRETATIONS OF BUDDHA-NATURE

Schools and scholars of Buddhism have varying interpretations of what the Buddha Nature is. In Chinese Ch'an Buddhism the Buddha Nature tends to be seen as the essential nature of all beings. Writing from this tradition, Master Hsing Yun, forty-eighth patriarch of the Linji School of Ch'an Buddhism, equates (in line with pronouncements in key *Tathagatagarbha* sutras) the Buddha Nature with the Dharmakaya, defining these two as: "The inherent nature that exists in all beings.

In Mahayana Buddhism, enlightenment is a process of uncovering this inherent nature ... The Buddha nature is identical with transcendental reality. The unity of the Buddha with everything that exists."

In the Tibetan Kagyu tradition, Thrangu Rinpoche sees the Buddha Nature as the indivisible oneness of Wisdom and Emptiness:

"The union of wisdom and emptiness is the essence of Buddha-hood or what is called Buddha-nature (Skt. *Tathagata-garbha*) because it contains the very seed, the potential of Buddhahood. It resides in each and every being and because of this essential nature, this heart nature; there is the possibility of reaching Buddhahood."

In contrast to this, the 14th Dalai Lama, representing the Gelukpa School of Tibetan Buddhism, sees the Buddha Nature as the "original clear light of mind" but is at pains to point out that it ultimately does not really exist, as it is Emptiness:

"Once one pronounces the words emptiness and absolute, one has the impression of speaking of the same thing, in fact of the absolute. If emptiness must be explained through the use of just one of these two terms, there will be confusion. I must say this; otherwise you might think that the innate original clear light as absolute truth really exists."

In a similar vein, the Buddhist scholar, Sallie B. King, sees the Buddha Nature (*Tathagatagarbha*) as merely a metaphor for the potential in all beings to attain Buddhahood, rather than as an ontological reality. She writes of the *Tathagatagarbha* Sutra in particular: "The Tathagatagarbha [Buddha Nature] is here a metaphor for the ability of all sentient beings to attain Buddhahood, no more and no less."

Professor Paul Williams puts forward the Madhyamaka interpretation of the Buddha Nature as Emptiness in the following terms:

"... if one is a Madhyamika then that which enables sentient beings to become buddhas must be the very factor that enables the minds of sentient beings to change into the minds of Buddhas. That which enables things to change is their simple absence of inherent existence, their emptiness. Thus the *Tathagatagarbha* becomes emptiness itself, but specifically emptiness when applied to the mental continuum."

Speaking for the Tibetan Nyingma tradition, Tulku Urgyen Rinpoche sees an identity between the Buddha Nature, *Dharmadhatu* (essence of all phenomena and the noumenon) and the Three Vajras, saying:

"Dharmadhatu is adorned with dharmakaya, which is endowed with dharmadhatu wisdom. This is a brief but very profound statement, because 'dharmadhatu' also refers to sugata-garbha or Buddha nature. Buddha nature is all-encompassing...

This Buddha nature is present just as the shining sun is present in the sky. It is indivisible from the three vajras [i.e. the Buddha's Body, Speech and Mind] of the awakened state, which do not perish or change."

Independent lay yogi lineage of Dzogpachenpo by Chögyal Namkhai Norbu Rinpoche identifies and asserts the primordial non-dual awareness itself as the Buddha Nature, the only non-fabricated and pristine element of our existence. Discussion of the precise nature, meaning and implications of the Buddha Nature doctrine continues to the present day. In Tibetan Buddhism there is the term *dag pa gnyis*, meaning "Twofold purity. Inherent or primordial purity and the purity of having removed all temporary obscurations [ry]".

BUDDHA-NATURE VS. ATMAN

The "*Tathagatagarbha*"/Buddha nature does not represent a substantial self (*atman*); rather, it is a positive language expression of "sunyata" (emptiness) and represents the potentiality to realize Buddhahood through Buddhist practices; the intention of the teaching of '*Tathagatagarbha*'/ Buddha nature is soteriological rather than theoretical. Some scholars favor one interpretation of the Buddha-nature over others. However, other scholars are prepared to take a more nuanced approach. Thus, in discussing the problems with and the inadequacy of much modern scholarship on Buddha-nature and the *tathâgatagarbha*, Sutton states, "one is impressed by the fact that these authors, as a rule, tend to opt for a single meaning disregarding all other possible meanings which are embraced in turn by other texts".

He goes on to point out that the term *tathâgatagarbha* has up to six possible connotations. Of these, the three most important are:

1. An underlying ontological reality or essential nature (*tathâgata-tathatâ-'vyatireka*) which is functionally equivalent to an âtman in an Upanishadic sense,
2. The *dharma-kâya* which penetrates all beings (*sarva-sattve su dharma-kâya-parispharana*), which is functionally equivalent to brahman in an Upanishadic sense, and
3. The womb or matrix of Buddhahood existing in all beings (*tathâgata-gotra-sambhava*), which provides beings with the possibility of awakening.

Of these three, only the third connotation has any soteriological significance, while the other two posit Buddha-nature as an ontological reality and essential nature behind all phenomena. According to Matsumoto Shiro and Hakamaya Noriaki, essentialist conceptions of Buddha-nature are un-Buddhist, being at odds with the fundamental Buddhist doctrine of dependent origination. The Jonangpa School of Tibetan Buddhism, whose foremost historical figure was Dolpopa, sees the Buddha Nature as the very ground of the Buddha himself, as the "permanent indwelling of the Buddha in the basal state".

Dolpopa comments that certain key *Tathagatagarbha* sutras indicate this truth, remarking:

"These statements that the basis of purification itself, the matrix-of-one-gone-to-bliss [i.e. Buddha Nature], is Buddha, the ground of Buddha, and the pristine wisdom of a one-gone-thus [Tathagata] also clear away the assertion by certain [scholars] that the matrix-of-one-gone-to-bliss [Buddha Nature] is not Buddha."

Other sutras which mention the Self in a very affirmative manner include the *Lankavatara Sutra* (in the "Sagathakam" chapter - e.g. "The Self characterised with purity is the state of Self-realisation; this is the Tathagata-garbha, which does not belong to the realm of the theorisers"), the Shurangama Sutra, the Mahavairocana Sutra: "Those who have been initiated into the Mahayana Mandala Arising from Great Compassion, who are honest and pliant, and who always have great compassion... They know their hearts to be the Great Self" and the Sutra of Perfect Wisdom called The Questions of Suvikrantavikramin:

"...one who wisely knows himself (*atmanam*) as non-dual; he wisely knows both Buddha and Dharma. And why? He develops a personality which consists of all dharmas... His nondual comprehension comprehends all dharmas, for all dharmas are fixed on the Self in their own-being.

One who wisely knows the nondual dharma wisely knows also the *Buddhadharmas*. From the comprehension of the nondual dharma follows the comprehension of the Buddhadharmas and from the comprehension of the Self the comprehension of everything that belongs to the triple world. 'The comprehension of self', that is the beyond of all dharmas."

The *Mahaparinirvana Sutra* specifically contrasts its doctrine of the Self with that of the Astikas in order to remove the reifying notion that the Self was a little person or homunculus, the size of a grain of rice or of one's thumb, sitting in the heart of the being, thus: "mundane [philosophers] mistakenly imagine it to be a person (purusa) the size of a thumb, the size of a pea or a grain of rice that dwells shining in the heart." This, the Buddha says, is a misconception of the nature of self, for "that opinion of theirs is a mistaken opinion, one that is transmitted onwards from person to person, but it is neither beneficial nor conducive to happiness." The Self of which the Buddha speaks is said by him to be the "essential intrinsic being" (*svabhava*) or even "life-essence" (*jivaka*) of each person, and this essential being is none other than the Buddha himself - "radiantly luminous" and "as indestructible as a diamond".

Moreover, the Buddhist tantric scripture entitled *Chanting the Names of Mañjusri (Mañjuúrî-nâma-sangîti)*, as quoted by the great Tibetan Buddhist master, Dolpopa, repeatedly exalts not the non-Self but the Self and applies the following terms to this ultimate reality:

- "The pervasive Lord" (vibhu)

- "Buddha-Self"
- "The beginningless Self" (anâdi-âtman)
- "The Self of Thusness" (tathatâ-âtman)
- "The Self of primordial purity" (úuddha-âtman)
- "The Source of all"
- "The Self pervading all"
- "The Single Self" (eka-âtman)
- "The Diamond Self" (vajra-âtman)
- "The Solid Self" (ghana-âtman)
- "The Holy, Immovable Self"
- "The Supreme Self"

In the *Ghanavyuha Sutra* (as quoted by Longchenpa) this immutable, universal and salvific Buddha Essence (the True Self of the Buddha) is said to be the ground of all things, but it is viewed by fools as something changeful and impermanent, whereas in fact it is stated by the Buddha to be the very opposite of such impermanence:

"... the ultimate universal ground also has always been with the Buddha-Essence (*Tathagatagarbha*), and this essence in terms of the universal ground has been taught by the Tathagata. The fools who do not know it, because of their habits, see even the universal ground as (having) various happiness and suffering and actions and emotional defilements.

Its nature is pure and immaculate, its qualities are as wishing-jewels; there are neither changes nor cessations. Whoever realizes it attains Liberation..."

The Buddha in the *Mahayana Mahaparinirvana Sutra* insists that the Self of the Buddha (the Buddha Nature which is present in all beings) is everlasting, pure and blissful and is most definitely not transitory and impermanent:

"The Buddha-Nature is the Eternal, Bliss, the Self, and the Pure... The Buddha-Nature is not non-Eternal, not non-Bliss, not non-Self, and not non-Purity."

The Buddha-Nature is in fact taught in such *Tathagatagarbha* sutras to be ultimate, conceptually inconceivable, immortal Reality. The Buddha-Nature concept remains an important doctrine in Mahayana Buddhism, especially in its Far Eastern manifestations.

THE RIMÉ MOVEMENT OF TIBET

Ringu Tulku says "There has been a great deal of heated debate in Tibet between the exponents of Rangtong, (Wylie: *Rang-stong*) and Shentong, (Wylie: *gZhan-stong*) philosophies. The historic facts of these two philosophies are well known to the Tibetologists."

Jamgon Kongtrul says about the two systems:

Madhyamika philosophies have no differences in realising as 'Shunyata', all phenomena that we experience on a relative level. They have no differences also, in reaching the meditative state where all extremes (ideas) completely dissolve. Their difference lies in the words they use to describe the Dharmata. Shentong describes the Dharmata, the mind of Buddha, as 'ultimately real'; while Rangtong philosophers fear that if it is described that way, people might understand it as the concept of 'soul' or 'Atma'. The Shentong philosopher believes that there is a more serious possibility of misunderstanding in describing the Enlightened State as 'unreal' and 'void'. Kongtrul finds the Rangtong way of presentation the best to dissolve concepts and the Shentong way the best to describe the experience."

In 2006 Khentrul Rinpoche Jamphal Lodro founded "The Tibetan Buddhist Rime Institute" in Melbourne, Australia. It aims to propagate the Rime view of harmony within all Buddhist traditions and to introduce the rare Jonang Kalachakra Tantra lineage teachings in the western world.

ARAHANTS

Arahant (Pali) or *Arhat* (Sanskrit) literally means the "worthy one". It is used in the sramanic traditions of ancient India with each of them having their own definition of the designation.

Arahant in Theravada

In Theravada, it means anyone who has reached the total Awakening and attained *Nibbana, including the Buddha.* Arahant is a person who has destroyed greed, hatred and delusion, the unwholesome roots which underlie all fetters. Who upon decease will not be reborn in any world, having wholly cut off all fetters that bind a person to the *samsara*? In the Pali Canon, the word is sometimes used as a synonym for tathagata.

After attainment of *Nibbana*, the five aggregates (physical forms, feelings/sensations, perception, mental formations and consciousness) will continue to function, sustained by physical bodily vitality. This attainment is termed *the nibbana element with a residue remaining*. But once the Arahant pass-away with the disintegration of the physical body, the five aggregates will cease to function, hence ending all traces of existence in the phenomenal world and thus total release from the misery of *samsara*. It would then be termed the nibbana element without residue remaining. *Parinibbana* is the *Nibbana* that occurs at the death of an Arahant. An Arahant generates no new kamma, but is affected by the fruition of past kamma.

These three awakened beings are classified as Arahant:

1. *Sammasambuddha*, usually just called Buddha, who discovers the truth by himself and teaches the path to awakening to others.
2. *Paccekubuddha*, who discovers the truth by himself but lacks the skill to teach others.
3. *Savakabuddha*, who receive the truth directly or indirectly from a *Sammasambuddha*.

In well known verses in the Pali Canon, the Buddha describes himself as an arahant soon after his enlightenment:

'All-vanquishing, all-knowing am I, with regard to all things, unadhering. All-abandoning, released in the ending of craving: having fully known on my own, to whom should I point as my teacher?

I have no teacher, and one like me can't be found. In the world with its devas, I have no counterpart.

For I am an arahant in the world; I, the unexcelled teacher. I, alone, am rightly self-awakened. Cooled am I, unbound.

To set rolling the wheel of Dhamma I go to the city of Kasi. In a world become blind, I beat the drum of the Deathless.' - *Ariyapariyesana Sutta*

In the Pali Canon, Gotama Buddha is described as thus:

A monk called Gotama...a son of the Sakyans who went forth from a Sakyan clan...Now a good report of Master Gotama has been spread to this effect: 'That Blessed One is such since he is arahant and Fully Enlightened, perfect in true knowledge and conduct, sublime, knower of worlds, incomparable teacher of men to be tamed, teacher of gods and humans, enlightened, blessed...He teaches a Dhamma that is good in the beginning, good in the middle and good in the end...' Now it is good to see such arahants. -*Saleyyaka Sutta*

In the Pali Canon, Arahant qualities are described as thus:

When a monk is an arahant, his fermentations ended, who has reached fulfillment, done the task, laid down the burden, attained the true goal, totally destroyed the fetter of becoming, and is released through right gnosis, he is dedicated to six things: renunciation, seclusion, non-afflictiveness, the ending of craving, the ending of clinging/sustenance, and non-deludedness. -*Sona Sutta*

In the Pali Canon, Arahant qualities are described as thus: ...those monks who are arahants - whose mental effluents are ended, who have reached fulfillment, done the task, laid down the burden, attained the true goal, totally destroyed the fetter of becoming, and who are released through right gnosis - no (future) cycle for manifestation...-*Alagaddupama Sutta*

In the Pali Canon, attainment of arahantship is described as thus: ...dwelling alone, secluded, heedful, ardent, and resolute - he in no long time reached and remained in the supreme goal of the holy life, for which clansmen rightly go forth from home into homelessness, knowing and realizing it for himself in the here and now. He knew: 'Birth is ended, the holy life fulfilled, the task done. There is nothing further for the sake of this world.' And thus Ven. Ratthapala became another one of the arahants. -*Ratthapala Sutta*

For those that have destroyed greed and hatred (in the sensory context) with some residue of delusion, are called anagami (non-returner). *Anagamis* will not be reborn into the human world after death, but into the heaven of the Pure Abodes, where only *Anagamis* live. There, they will attain full enlightenment.

ARHAT IN MAHAYANA

In Mahayana, it usually means anyone who has destroyed greed and hatred, but is still subject to delusion. According to most, but not all, Mahayana authorities, an Arhat must go on to become a *Bodhisattva*. If they fail to do so in the lifetime in which they reach the attainment, they will go to some sort of dormant state, thence to be roused and taught the *Bodhisattva* path, presumably when ready.

7

Mahayana Buddhism

Mahayana is one of the two main existing branches of Buddhism and a term for classification of Buddhist philosophies and practice. It was founded in India. The name Mahayana is used in three main senses:

1. As a living tradition, Mahayana is the larger of the two major traditions of Buddhism existing today, the other being Theravada. This classification is largely undisputed by all Buddhist schools.
2. According to the Mahayana method of classification of Buddhist philosophies, Mahayana refers to a level of spiritual motivation (also known as *Bodhisattva*yana). According to this classification, the alternative approach is called Hinayana, or Shravakayana. It is also recognized by Theravada Buddhism, but is not considered very relevant for practice.
3. According to the Vajrayana scheme of classification of practice paths, Mahayana refers to one of the three routes to enlightenment, the other two being Hinayana and Vajrayana. This classification is the teachings of Vajrayana Buddhism, and is not recognized by Mahayana and Theravada Buddhism.

Although the Mahayana movement traces its origin to Gautama Buddha, scholars believe that it originated in India in the 1st century CE, or the 1st century BCE. Scholars think that Mahayana only became a mainstream movement in India in the fifth century CE, since that is when Mahayanic inscriptions started to appear in epigraphic records in India.

Before the 11th century CE (while Mahayana was still present in India), the Mahayana Sutras were still in the process of being revised. Thus, several different versions may have survived of the same sutra. These different versions are invaluable to scholars attempting to reconstruct the history of Mahayana. In the course of its history, Mahayana spread throughout East Asia. The main countries in which it is practiced today are China, Japan, Korea, and Vietnam and worldwide amongst Tibetan Buddhist practitioners as a result of the Himalayan diaspora following the Chinese invasion of Tibet.

The main schools of Mahayana Buddhism today are Pure Land, Zen, Nichiren Buddhism, Shingon, Tibetan Buddhism and Tendai. The latter three schools have both Mahayana and Vajrayana practice traditions. The historical source of the name Mahayana is polemical, having its origin in a debate about what the real teachings of the Buddha are. As such, its use in any context except as that pertaining to a living tradition is controversial amongst Theravadin practitioners and some scholars.

The earliest known mention of "Mahayana" occurs in the Lotus Sutra between the first century BCE and the first century CE. However, some scholars such as Seishi Karashima suggest the term first used in an earlier Gandhari Prakrit version of the Lotus Sutra was not "*mahâyâna*" but the Prakrit word "*mahâjâna*" in the sense of "*mahâjñâna*" (great knowing).

At a later stage when the early Prakrit word was converted into Sanskrit, this "*mahâjâna*", being phonetically ambivalent, was mistakenly converted into "*mahâyâna*", possibly by contamination arising through proximity to the famous Parable of the Burning House which talks of carts (Skt: *yâna*). Mahayana Buddhism in India can be divided into two periods: early Mahayana Buddhism and late Mahayana Buddhism.

EARLY MAHAYANA BUDDHISM

The period of Early Mahayana Buddhism concerns the origins of Mahayana and the contents of early Mahayana Sutras.

ORIGINS OF MAHAYANA

The origins of Mahayana are still not completely understood. Although the Mahayana movement traces its origin to Gautama Buddha, scholars believe that it originated in South India in the 1st century CE, or the 1st century BCE. Alternatively, some scholars say there is some evidence that Mahayana originated in North-west India in the 1st century CE. Some scholars say that Mahayana could have initially developed in the south-east of India as a non-monastic tradition and that later it underwent a process of monasticization and emerged in the north-west of India as a monastic movement.

Mahayana was first propagated into China by Lokaksema, the first translator of Mahayana sutras into Chinese during the second century CE. Three sources appear to have made significant contributions to the rise of Mahayana Buddhism:

1. The Early Buddhist Schools- Some important Mahayana texts such as the *Prajnaparamita* often refer to doctrines associated with the Sarvastivada, which were mentioned or incorporated into Mahayana texts. In terms of content, however, the Mahasanghika doctrine is closer to Mahayana thought, particularly those of the sub-schools such as the Lokottaravadins.
2. Biographical literature of the Buddha composed by people said to have belonged to 'the vehicle that praised the Buddha'. This literature (comprising the *Jatakas, Avadanas* and other texts describing the life of Buddha) may have had its origins in the various Early Schools, but developed in ways that transcended the existing sectarian lines and contributed to the rise of Mahayana Buddhism. Buddhist poets wrote their work with purposes different from those of scholars who were concerned with doctrinal issues, and they used literary expressions which transcended doctrinal lines between the schools.
3. Stupa worship- Stupas which were initially mere monuments to Gautama Buddha - increasingly became the place of devotion and of spreading Buddhism to the masses, the majority of whom were illiterate laymen. On

the inside wall of the stupa, pictures were drawn or sculpted depicting the life of Buddha and his previous lives as a *Bodhisattva*. This has given rise to devotion to the Buddha and the *Bodhisattvas*, distinct from the purely monastic *sangha* of the Early Buddhist schools. However, this theory has been rejected by a number of scholars. Early Mahayanists may well have used the stupas that were not affiliated with the Early Buddhist Schools as the basis for proselytizing.

The commonly expressed misconception that Mahayana started as a lay-inspired movement is based on a selective reading of a very tiny sample of extant Mahayana Sutra literature. Currently scholars have moved away from this limited corpus of literature, and have started to open up early Mahayana literature which is very ascetic and expounds the ideal of the monks' life in the forest.

A scholarly consensus about the origin of the Mahayana has not yet been reached, but it has been suggested that by the time Mahayana in India became mainstream in the 5th century CE, it had become what it originally most strongly objected to: a fully landed, sedentary, lay-oriented monastic institution. Before that, the Mahayana movement may well have been either a marginalized ascetic group of monks living in the forest, or a group of conservatives embedded in mainstream, socially engaged early Buddhist monasteries. Most scholars conclude that Mahayana remained a marginal movement until the 5th century CE.

EARLIEST MAHAYANA SUTRAS

The earliest sutras which show some Mahayana influence are called the Proto-Mahayana Sutras such as the Ajitasena Sutra. These sutras contains a mixture of Mahayana and pre-Mahayana ideas, and occur in a world where monasticism is the norm, which is typical of the Pali Suttas; there is none of the antagonism towards the úrâvakas or the notion of Arahantship, which is typical of many later Mahayana Sutras such as the *Lotus Sutra*, or *Vimalakirti Nirdesha*.

However, the sutra also has an Arahant seeing all the Buddha fields, it is said that reciting the name of the sutra will save beings from suffering and the hell realms, and a meditative practice is described which allows the practitioner to see with the eyes of a Buddha, and to receive teachings from them that are very much typical of Mahayana Sutras.

The earliest proper Mahayana Sutras were the very first versions of the Perfection of Wisdom series and texts concerning Aksobhya Buddha, which were probably composed in the first century BCE in the south of India. Some slightly later early Mahayana Sutras are the Chinese translations made by the Kushan monk Lokaksema in the Chinese capital of Luoyang, between 178 and 189 CE He translated the following sutras: Astasahasrika, Aksobhyatathagatasyavyuha, Surangamasamadhisutra, an early version of a sutra connected to the Avatamsakasutra, Drumakinnararajapariprccha, Bhadrapa-lasutra, Ajatasatrukaukrtyavinodana, and the Kasyapapari-varta, which were probably composed in the north of India in the first century CE.

Thus scholars generally think that the earliest Mahayana sutras were mainly composed in the south of India, and later the activity of writing additional scriptures was continued in the north. But, to equate evidence for the presence of an evolving body of Mahayana scriptures with the existence at the time of Mahayana as a distinct religious movement, has been described as being an assumption which may be a serious misstep.

EARLIEST INSCRIPTION RELATED TO MAHAYANA

The earliest stone inscription containing a recognizably Mahayana formulation and a mention of the Buddha Amitabha was found in the Indian subcontinent in Mathura, and dated to around 180 CE. Remains of a statue of a Buddha bear the Brahmi inscription:

"Made in the year 28 of the reign of king Huvishka... for the Buddha Amitabha" (Mathura Museum).

However, this image was in itself extremely marginal and isolated in the overall context of Buddhism in India at the time, and had no lasting or long-term consequences. The epigraphical evidence for Mahayana in the period before the 5th century is very limited in comparison to the multiplicity of Mahayana writings transmitted from Central Asia to China at that time.

LATE MAHAYANA BUDDHISM

During the period of Late Mahayana Buddhism, four major types of thought developed: Madhyamaka, Yogacara, *Tathagatagarbha*, and Buddhist Logic as the last and most recent. In India, the two main philosophical schools of the Mahayana were the Madhyamaka and the later Yogacara. There were no great Indian teachers associated with *Tathagatagarbha* thought.

From the 5th century CE onwards, Mahayana was a strong movement in India, possibly owing to support by the Gupta dynasty. It spread from India to South-East Asia and towards the north to Central Asia, China, Korea and Japan. The influence of Mahayana in China seems to have been reached at an earlier time than in India, where Mahayan remained an obscure group until the 5th century. Buddhism (and Mahayana) disappeared from India during the 11th century, and consequently lost its influence in South-East Asia where it was replaced by Theravada Buddhism from Sri Lanka.

DOCTRINE

Few things can be said with certainty about Mahayana Buddhism, especially its early Indian form, other than that the Buddhism practiced in China, Vietnam, Korea, Tibet, and Japan is Mahayana Buddhism. Mahayana can be described as a loosely bound bundle of many teachings, which was thus able to contain the various contrasting ideas found between those differing teachings of whose elements it is comprised.

Mahayana is a large religious and philosophical structure. It constitutes an inclusive faith characterized by the adoption of new Mahayana sutras in addition to the earlier Agama texts, and a shift in the basic purpose and concepts of Buddhism. Mahayana sees itself as penetrating further and more profoundly into the Buddha's Dharma. There is a tendency in Mahayana sutras to regard adherence to Mahayana sutras as generating spiritual benefits greater than those which arise from being a follower of the non-Mahayana approaches to Dharma. Thus the Srimala Sutra claims that the Buddha said that devotion to Mahayana is inherently superior in its virtues to the following of the Sravaka or Pratyekabuddha path.

Mahayana Buddhist schools de-emphasize the ideal of the release from Suffering and the attainment of Nirvana, found in the Early Buddhist Schools. The fundamental principles of Mahayana doctrine were based around the possibility of universal liberation from suffering for all beings (hence "great vehicle") and the existence of Buddhas and *Bodhisattva* embodying Buddha-nature. Some Mahayana schools simplify the expression of faith by allowing salvation to be alternatively obtained through the grace of the Buddha Amitabha by having faith and devoting oneself to chanting to Amitabha.

This devotional lifestyle of Buddhism is most strongly emphasized by the Pure Land schools and has greatly contributed to the success of Mahayana in East Asia, where spiritual elements traditionally relied upon chanting of a Buddha's name, of *mantras* or *dharanis*; reading of Mahayana sutras and mysticism. In Chinese Buddhism, most monks, let alone lay people, practise Pure Land, some combining it with Chan (Zen). Most Mahayana schools believe in a pantheon of quasi-divine *Bodhisattvas* that devote themselves to personal excellence, ultimate knowledge, and the salvation of humanity and all other sentient beings (animals, ghosts, demigods, etc.).

Zen Buddhism is a school of Mahayana which often de-emphasizes the pantheon of *Bodhisattvas* and instead focuses on the meditative aspects of the religion. In Mahayana, the Buddha is seen as the ultimate, highest being, present in all times, in all beings, and in all places, and the *Bodhisattvas* come to represent the universal ideal of altruistic excellence.

Mahayana Buddhism can in general be characterized by:

- Universalism, in that, in those schools of Mahayana that still have large followings, everyone will become a Buddha;
- Bodhicitta as the main focus of realization;
- Compassion through the transferral of merit;
- Transcendental immanence, in that the immortal Buddha Principle is present within all beings.

"Philosophical" Mahayana tends to focus on the first three characteristics (universalism, enlightened wisdom, compassion) and, in some schools, the Buddha-nature, without showing much interest in supernatural constructions, while "devotional" Mahayana focuses mainly on salvation towards other-worldly realms.

UNIVERSALISM

Mahayana traditions generally consider that attainment of the level of an arhat is not final. This is based on a subtle doctrinal distinction between the Mahayana and some of the early Buddhist schools concerning the issues of 'nirvana-with-remainder' and 'nirvana-without-remainder.' The Mahayana position here is similar to that of the early school of the Mahasanghika.

Some of the early schools considered that 'nirvana-without-remainder' always follows 'nirvana-with-remainder' (buddhas first achieve enlightenment and then, at 'death', mahaparinirvana) and that 'nirvana-without-remainder' is final; whereas the Mahayana traditions consider that 'nirvana-without-remainder' is always followed by 'nirvana-with-remainder' – the state of attainment of the Hinayana arhat is not final, and is eventually succeeded by the state of buddhahood, or total Awakening.

This distinction is most evident regarding doctrinal concerns about the capability of a Buddha after nirvana (which is identified by the early schools as being nirvana-without-remainder). Most importantly, amongst the early schools, a *samyaka*sambuddha is not able to directly point the way to nirvana after death.

This is a major distinction between the early schools and some schools of the Mahayana, who conversely state that once a samyakasambuddha arises, he or she continues to directly and actively point the way to nirvana until there are no beings left in *samsara*. Because the views of early schools and Mahayana differ in this respect, this is exactly why some Mahayana schools do not talk about a *Bodhisattva* postponing nirvana, and exactly why the early schools do. However, some Mahayana schools do talk of a *Bodhisattva* deliberately refraining from Buddhahood.

For example, the early schools held that Maitreya will not attain nirvana while Gautama Buddha's teachings still exist. In contrast, some Mahayana schools hold that Maitreya will be the next Buddha manifest in this world and will introduce the dharma when it no longer exists; he is not postponing his nirvana to do so, and when he dies (or enters *mahaparinirvana*), he will likewise continue to teach the dharma for all time.

Moreover, some Mahayana schools argue that although it is true that for this world-system, Maitreya will be the next Buddha to manifest, there are an infinite number of world-systems, many of which have currently active Buddhas or buddhas-to-be manifesting. Because the Mahayana traditions assert that eventually everyone will achieve *samyaka*sam (Buddhahood) or total enlightenment, the Mahayana is labeled Universalist, whereas the stance of the early scriptures is that attaining *nibbana* depends on effort and is not pre-determined.

BODHISATTVA

The later Mahayana school holds that pursuing only the release from suffering and attainment of Nirvana (as held by Pre-sectarian Buddhism and the Early Buddhist Schools) is too narrow an aspiration, because it lacks the motivation of actively resolving to liberate all other beings from *samsara*, as well as oneself. The primary focus of some Mahayana schools is bodhicitta, the vow to strive for Buddhahood or awakened mind both for oneself and for the benefit of all other sentient beings.

As Ananda Coomaraswamy notes, "The most essential part of the Mahanyana is its emphasis on the *Bodhisattva* ideal, which replaces the Arhatta, or ranks before it." According to Mahayana teachings, being a high-level *Bodhisattva* involves possessing a mind of great compassion conjoined with insight into reality (*prajna*), realizing emptiness and/or the buddhic essence of all things. Mahayana teaches that the practitioner will realize the final goal of full Awakening (Buddhahood): an omniscient, blissful mind completely free from suffering and its causes, that is able to work tirelessly for the benefit of all living beings.

Six virtues or perfections (*paramitas*) are listed for the *Bodhisattva*: generosity, morality, patience, energy, meditation, and wisdom. Many "philosophical" schools and Mahayana Sutras have focused on the nature of enlightenment and nirvana itself, from the Madhyamika and its rival Yogacara, to the *Tathagatagarbha* teachings and Zen.

COMPASSION

Compassion, or *Karuna*, is the other key concept of Mahayana, and is a necessity to Bodhicitta. Compassion is important in all schools of Buddhism, but is particularly emphasized in Mahayana. It is also linked to the idea that acquired merit can be transmitted to others. The *Bodhisattvas* are the main actors of compassion, Avalokitesvara (known in East Asia as Guan Yin) being foremost among them. Although having reached enlightenment, *Bodhisattvas* usually make a vow to postpone entering into nirvana until all other beings have also been saved. They devote themselves to helping others reach enlightenment.

This teaching may be a "skillful means" teaching; one strives to liberate all beings only as long as one is under the delusion that there are any actual "beings" to save. The Mahayana idea that liberation is universal also allows for one to focus less on the release of personal suffering and more on humanity's salvation, and is consequently described to be more universally compassionate and caring for the welfare of others than other traditions of Buddhism.

A comparison between the Hinayana and Mahayana Buddhist philosophy approaches, made by the 10th century Tibetan author Jé Gampopa in *The Jewel Ornament of Liberation* follows:

'Clinging to the well-being of mere peace' signifies the lower capacity [Hinayana] attitude wherein the longing to transcend suffering is focused on oneself alone. This precludes the cherishing of others and hence there is little development of altruism. When loving kindness and compassion become part of one, there is so much care for other conscious beings that one could not bear to liberate oneself alone. Master Manjushriikiirti has said: 'A Mahayana follower should not be without loving kindness and compassion for even a single moment', and 'It is not anger and hatred but loving kindness and compassion that vouchsafe the welfare of others'.

SKILLFUL MEANS

The term Skillful Means (Sanskri. *upâya*) is used in the *Lotus Sutra*; the earliest dated Mahayana Sutra, and is a concept accepted in all Mahayana schools of thought. It refers to any effective method which aids the attainment of Awakening. It does not necessarily mean that that particular method is "untrue", but simply refers to any means or stratagem that is conducive to spiritual growth and which leads the various types of beings to Awakening and Nirvana.

A skillful means could thus be certain motivational words for a particular listener or even the noble Eightfold Path itself. Basic Buddhism (what Mahayana would term *sravaka-yana* or *pratyekabuddha-yana*) is an expedient method for getting people started on the noble Buddhic path and allowing them to advance quite far. But the path is not wholly traversed (according to some Mahayana schools) until the practitioner has striven for, and attained, Buddhahood for the liberation from unhappiness of all other sentient beings.

In an ultimate sense, all of verbalised Dharma is a "skillful means", since Dharma or Truth cannot really be expressed in words or concepts. Anything that effectively points the way to liberation can be termed a "skillful means" - an effective method for awakening beings from the sleep of spiritual ignorance. Mahayana often adopts a pragmatic notion of truth: doctrines are "true" in the sense of being spiritually beneficial.

Some scholars have stated that the exercise of skill to which it refers, the ability to adapt one's message to the audience, is of enormous importance in the Pali Canon. In fact the Pali term *upâya-kosalla* does occur in the Pali Canon, in the Sangiti Sutta of the *Digha Nikaya*.

SALVATION

"Devotional" Mahayana developed a rich cosmography, with various Buddhas and *Bodhisattvas* residing in paradisiacal realms. The concept of trinity, or *trikaya*, supports these constructions, making the Buddha himself into a transcendental figure. Dr. Guang Xing describes the Mahayana Buddha as 'an omnipotent divinity endowed with numerous supernatural attributes and qualities...[He] is described almost as an omnipotent and almighty godhead."

Under various conditions, these realms over which Buddha presides could be attained by devotees after their death so that when reborn they could strive towards Buddhahood in the best possible conditions. Depending on the sect, this salvation to "paradise" can be obtained by faith, imaging, or sometimes even by the simple invocation of the Buddha's name. This approach to salvation is at the origin of the mass appeal of devotional Buddhism, especially represented by the Pure Land.

This rich cosmography also allowed Mahayana to be quite syncretic and accommodating of other faiths or deities. Various origins have been suggested to explain its emergence, such as "popular Hindu devotional cults (*bhakti*), and Persian and Greco-Roman theologies, which filtered into India from the northwest" (Tom Lowenstein, "The vision of the Buddha").

BUDDHA-NATURE

The teaching of a "Buddha Principle" (*Buddha-dhatu*) or "Buddha Nature" innate to and inseparable from all sentient beings is a doctrine which according to a number of Mahayana sutras constitutes the "absolutely final culmination" of the Buddha's Dharma. It may be based on the "luminous mind" concept found in the Agamas.

The essential idea (articulated in the *Tathagatagarbha* sutras, but not accepted by all Mahayana) is that no being is without a concealed but indestructible interior link to Awakening (*bodhi*), and that this link is an uncreated element [*dhatu*] or principle deep inside each being which constitutes nothing less than the deathless, diamond-like "essence of the Self" (*Nirvana Sutra*). The Mahaparinirvana Sutra states that: "The essence of the Self (*atman*) is the subtle *Tathagatagarbha*..." while the later Lankavatara Sutra states that the *Tathagatagarbha* might be taken to be atman, but it is not. In the *Tathagatagarbha* class of sutras, the word "atman" is used in a way defined by and specific to these sutras.

According to some scholars, the "*Tathagatagarbha*"/Buddha nature discussed in some Mahayana sutras does not represent a substantial self (*atman*); rather, it is a positive language and expression of *sunyata* (emptiness) and represents the potentiality to realize Buddhahood through Buddhist practices. It is the "true self" in representing the innate aspect of the individual which makes actualizing the ultimate personality possible.

The actual "seeing and knowing" of this *Buddha-dhatu* (co-terminous with the Dharmakaya or Self of Buddha) is said to usher in nirvanic Liberation. This *Buddha-dhatu* or *Tathagatagarbha* is stated to be found in every single person, ghost, god and creature, etc, and uncreated, deathless and ultimately beyond rational grasping or conceptualisation. Yet it is this already real and present, hidden internal element of bodhi (Awakeness) which, according to the *Tathagatagarbha* sutras, prompts beings to seek after Liberation from worldly suffering and enables them to attain the spotless bliss which lies at the heart of their being.

Once the veils of negative thoughts, feelings and unwholesome behaviour (the *kleshas*) have been eliminated from the mind and character, the indwelling *Buddha-dhatu* (Buddha Principle / "Buddha Nature") is enabled to shine forth unimpededly and to transform the seer of it into a Buddha. Prior to the period of these sutras, Mahayana metaphysics had been dominated by teachings on emptiness in the form of Madhyamaka philosophy.

The language used by this approach is primarily negative, and the *Tathagatagarbha* genre of sutras can be seen as an attempt to state orthodox Buddhist teachings of dependent origination and on the mysterious reality of nirvana using positive language instead, to prevent people from being turned away from Buddhism by a false impression of nihilism. In these sutras the perfection of the wisdom of not-self is stated to be the true self; the ultimate goal of the path is then characterized using a range of positive language that had been used in Indian philosophy previously by essentialist philosophers, but which was now transmuted into a new Buddhist vocabulary to describe a being who has successfully completed the Buddhist path.

An exegetical treatise (i.e., interpretive text) on Buddha Nature is the *Uttaratantra,* which sees Buddha Nature (*Tathagatagarbha*) not as that which is caused and conditioned (*samskrta*) but as that which is eternal, uncaused, unconditioned, and incapable of being destroyed, while temporarily concealed within worldly beings by adventitious defilements. According to Buddhist scholar Dr. C. D. Sebastian, the *Uttaratantra's* reference to a transcendental self (*atma-paramita*) should be understood as "the unique essence of the universe," thus the universal and immanent essence of Buddha Nature is the same throughout time and space.

MAHAYANA SCRIPTURES

Like Theravâda Buddhism, Mahâyâna Buddhism takes the basic teachings of the Buddha as recorded in early scriptures as the starting point of its teachings, such as those concerning karma and rebirth, the Four Noble Truths, the Middle Way and the Eightfold Path. Whereas these basic teachings are preserved in the Pali Canon, transmitted by the Theravâdin tradition, Mahâyâna Buddhists use different recensions of these discourses in compilations known as the Agamas, which largely overlap with the Pali Canon in content.

The surviving agamas in Chinese translation belong to at least two schools, while most of the agamas were never translated into Tibetan. In addition to accepting the scriptures of the various early Buddhist schools as valid, Mahâyâna Buddhism also maintains large additional collections of sutras not found or recognized in Theravâda Buddhism. In Mahayana Buddhism, these Mahayana sutras have a greater importance than the *Agamas.*

Although these scriptures claim to be the factual words of the Buddha, scholars believe that they were written by monks who felt the need to restate and change the doctrines of Early Buddhism. The first of the Mahayana-specific writings were written probably around the 1st century BCE or 1st century CE. Some of the Mahayana Sutras, such as certain parts of the Perfection of Wisdom sutras, are presented as actual sermons of the Buddha that had been hidden.

By some accounts, these sermons were passed on by oral tradition, as with other sutras; other accounts state that they were hidden and then revealed several centuries later by some mythological route. In addition to sutras, some Mahayana texts are essentially commentaries. Among the earliest major Mahayana scriptures attested to historically are the Perfection of Wisdom (*Prajna-Paramita*) sutras, the Avatamsaka Sutra, the Lotus Sutra, the Vimalakîrti Sutra, and the Nirvana Sutra.

THREE TURNINGS

Dating back at least to the *Samadhinirmocana Sûtra* is a classification of exoteric corpus of Buddhism into three categories, based on types of understanding the nature of reality, known as the "three turnings of the wheel of dharma". According to this view, there were three "turnings of the wheel of dharma":

1. In the first turning Shakyamuni Buddha taught the Four Noble Truths at Varanasi in the 5th century BC, which led to the founding of Buddhism and the later early Buddhist schools. Details of the first turning are described in the Dhammacakkapavattana Sutta. The oldest scriptures do not mention any further turnings other than this first turning.
2. The Mahayana tradition claims there was a second turning in which the Perfection of Wisdom sutras were taught at Vulture's Peak, which led to the Mahayana schools. Generally, scholars conclude that the Mahayana scriptures (including the Perfection of Wisdom Sutras) were composed from the first century CE onwards,
3. According to the Vajrayana tradition, there was a third turning which took place at Dhanyakataka sixteen years after Buddha's enlightenment. Scholars have strongly denied that Vajrayana teachings appeared at that time, and placed it at a much later time. The first tantric (Vajrayana Buddhist) texts appeared in the 3rd century CE, and they continued to appear until the 12th century CE.

The early Buddhist schools regard the second and third turnings as unauthentic and falsifications of the true teachings of the Buddha contained in the first turning. Mahayana tradition states that the first turning contains the basic doctrines aimed at the initial disciples or *Úrâvakas*. Mahayana claims that the Madhyamika teachings and the *Prajna* Paramita sutras and Yogâcâra doctrines are the most accurate view of reality. Many Tibetan teachers, particularly the Gelugpa School, regard the second turning as the highest teaching. The *Tathagatagarbha* teachings are normally included in the third turning of the wheel. The Chinese tradition has a different scheme.

MAHAYANA AND THE CANON

Scholars have noted that many key Mahayana ideas are closely connected to the earliest texts of Buddhism. The seminal work of Mahayana philosophy, Nagarjuna's *Mulamadhyamakakarika*, mentions the Canon's "Katyayana Sutra" by name, and may be an extended commentary on that work (found in the agamas). Nagarjuna systematized the Madhyamaka school of Mahanaya philosophy. Nagarjuna may have arrived at his positions from a desire to achieve a consistent exegesis of the Buddha's doctrine as recorded in the Canon. In the eyes of Nagarjuna the Buddha was not merely a forerunner, but the very founder of the Madhyamaka system.

Nagarjuna also referred to a passage in the canon regarding "nirvanic consciousness" in two different works. Yogachara, the other prominent Mahayana school which exists in dialectic with the Madhyamaka School, gave a special significance to the Canon's "Lesser Discourse on Emptiness". A passage there (which the discourse itself emphasizes) is often quoted in later Yogachara texts as a true definition of emptiness.

Both the Madhyamakas and the Yogacarins saw themselves as preserving the Buddhist Middle Way between the extremes of nihilism (everything is unreal) and substantialism (substantial entities exist). The Yogacarins criticized the Madhyamakas for tending towards nihilism, while the Madhyamakas criticized the Yogacarins for tending towards substantialism. Key Mahayana texts introducing the concepts of "bodhicitta" and "buddha-nature" use language parallel to passages in the Canon containing the Buddha's description of "luminous mind" and may have been based on this idea.

MAHAYANA AND THERAVADA

Although the Theravada school is usually described as belonging to "Hinayana", some authors have argued that it should not be considered such from the Mahayana perspective. Their view is based on a different understanding of the concept "Hinayana". Rather than regarding the term as referring to any school of Buddhism that hasn't accepted the Mahayana canon and doctrines (such as those pertaining to the role of the *Boddhisatva*), these authors argue that the classification of a school as "Hinayana" should be crucially dependent on the adherence to a specific phenomenological position.

They point out that unlike the now-extinct Sarvastivada School which was the primary object of Mahayana criticism, the Theravada does not claim the existence of independent dharmas; in this it maintains the attitude of early Buddhism. On the contrary, some contemporary Theravadin figures have indicated a sympathetic stance toward the Mahayana philosophy found in the Heart Sutra and the Fundamental Stanzas on the Middle Way.

The Mahayanists were bothered by the substantialist thought of the Sarvastivadins and Sautrantikas, and in emphasizing the doctrine of emptiness; Kalupahana holds that they endeavored to preserve the early teaching. The Theravadins too refuted the Sarvastivadins and Sautrantikas (and other schools) on the grounds that their theories were in conflict with the non-substantialism of the canon. The Theravada arguments are preserved in the Kathavatthu. Thus, according to this view, no form of real "Hinayana" Buddhism survives today.

SCHOOLS OF THE MAHAYANA: PURE LAND, ZEN, TIBETAN, NICHIREN, TANTRA

KOREAN ZEN BUDDHISM

The Korean word for Ch'an or Zen is Son. Buddhism is highly significant in Korea. The latest figures (1991) show 26 Buddhist sects and 9,231 temples with more than 11 million followers in Korea. The largest Son sect today in Korea is the Chogye Order which includes about 90% of Korean Buddhists. The name 'Chogye' is significant in that it was named after the mountain in south China where the great Sixth Patriarch, Hui-neng, had his temple. Koreans say that their tradition is derived directly from Hui-neng.

Buddhism arrived in Korea in the 4th century CE. It spread widely and became the state religion when the three kingdoms that made up the country were united in 688 CE. Son was introduced there in approximately the 7th century CE by a Korean monk named Pomnang, said to have studied under the fourth Chinese patriarch, but little is known of him or of these early times. During the 9th century CE, Son Buddhism became the dominant form of Buddhism in Korea as a result of a steady stream of Korean masters going to China to study Ch'an Buddhism and returning to Korea to teach.

THE 13TH CENTURY MONK CHINUL

One of the most outstanding figures in the history of Son was a man by the name of Chinul. As a young monk he passed examinations necessary to bring him into the monastic hierarchy, but rejected such a lifestyle and instead retreated to the mountains. He devoted himself to study and contemplation, deeply penetrating the Buddhist texts.

In 1190, at the age of 32, Chinul formed a community called the Concentration and Wisdom Community which remained together in retreat for 7 years. Gradually, other monks joined him attracted by the seriousness of the group. The community grew and moved to a place (later renamed Mount Chogye) in about 1200 CE, enlarging a small hermitage into a monastery complex. This temple, Songgwang Sa, exists to this day as an active and thriving Son community.

BUDDHISM RETREATS

Son remained significant in Korea until 1392 CE, when a revolt replaced the pro-Buddhist government with one that favoured Confucianism and regarded Buddhism as an un-Korean influence. Buddhists were still allowed to practise, but official oppression drove them from the centres of power into remote mountain monasteries, changing Buddhism in Korea from a people's religion into a largely monastic practice. This also changed the nature of Buddhism, and the Son tradition moved away from textual study to focusing on meditation practice with the aim of reaching the same state that the Buddha had reached.

THE ESSENCE OF SON

The following hints at the Buddha's truth to which they aspired:

"Heaven and earth cannot cover its body, mountains and rivers cannot hide its light. Nothing of it accumulates on the outside or the inside. Even the 80,000 texts cannot contain or make a record of it. No scholar can describe it, the intellectuals cannot know it, the literati and writers cannot recognise it. Even to talk about it is a mistake, to think about it is an error."

Nevertheless, Son Buddhists see a basic unity between truth as described in Buddhist doctrine and truth as experienced through meditation. In other words, they find the true meaning of the texts through personal experience. Son Buddhism focuses on the enlightenment of a sudden awakening, but even if a person achieves the realisation that they are innately Buddha, that doesn't mean they cease to practise. On the contrary, the sentiment is "sudden enlightenment followed by gradual practise" - the practice of enlightenment, or of being Awakened.

NICHIREN BUDDHISM

Nichiren Buddhism is a Japanese Buddhist movement in the Mahayana tradition. It is also popular in the West and has a fast growing membership in the UK. Nichiren Buddhism differs from other schools of Buddhism in focusing on this world, and in its view that it is the only correct tradition. It also emphasises the importance of individuals taking responsibility for improving themselves.

Although it can be seen as a highly self-focused religion, followers of Nichiren Buddhism believe that individual empowerment and inner transformation contribute to a better and more peaceful world. Instant enlightenment is one of the key elements of Nichiren Buddhism. It teaches that enlightenment is available to everybody. One writer has encapsulated this idea as a "shortcut to salvation". The essence of enlightenment is opening a person's innate Buddha-nature in this world.

PURE LAND BUDDHISM

Pure Land Buddhism offers a way to enlightenment for people who can't handle the subtleties of meditation, endure long rituals, or just live especially good lives. The essential practice in Pure Land Buddhism is the chanting of the name of Amitabha Buddha with total concentration, trusting that one will be reborn in the Pure Land, a place where it is much easier for a being to work towards enlightenment.

Pure Land Buddhism adds mystical elements to the basic Buddhist teachings which make those teachings easier (and more comforting) to work with. These elements include faith and trust and a personal relationship with Amitabha Buddha, who is regarded by Pure Land Buddhists as a sort of saviour; and belief in the Pure Land, a place which provides a stepping stone towards enlightenment and liberation. Pure Land Buddhism is particularly popular in China and Japan.

Pure Land Buddhism is a term that is used to describe both the Pure Land soteriology of Mahayana Buddhism, which may be better understood as Pure Land traditions, and the Pure Land sects that developed in Japan. It is important to understand that Pure Land Buddhism only became a distinct sect/school in the Japanese medieval period (13th century), and that in other countries and times, it merely formed part of the basis of Mahayana Buddhist traditions.

Pure Land oriented practices and concepts are found within basic Mahayana Buddhist cosmology, and form an important component of the Mahayana Buddhist traditions in China, Japan, Korea, Taiwan, Vietnam, and Tibet. Chinese Chan and Tiantai schools, as well as the Japanese Shingon and Tendai sects have strong Pure Land components to their practice and belief. However, Pure Land Buddhism eventually became an independent school in its own right as can be seen in the Japanese Jôdo Shû and Jôdo Shinshû schools. In Japan there are several Pure Land sects, but throughout the history of Mahayana Buddhism, but there was never an independent Pure Land sect in the other Mahayana countries.

One basic Mahayana Pure Land concept is that Nirvana (liberation, awakening, salvation) has become increasingly difficult to attain, and that only through devotion to Amitâbha Buddha and looking towards Amida Buddha for guidance can one be reborn in the Pure Land, a perfect realm in which enlightenment is guaranteed. The Pure Land Path has been popular among both commoners and elite monastics as it provided a straightforward way of attaining salvation. In medieval Japan it was especially popular among those on the outskirts of society, such as prostitutes and social outcasts who, though often denied salvation by the mainstream traditions, were able to find solace in the newly formed Pure Land sect.

Pure Land Buddhism is based on the Pure Land sutras, first brought to China as early as 148 AD, when the Parthian monk Ân Shìgâo began translating sutras into Chinese at the White Horse Temple in the imperial capital of Luòyáng, during the Hàn dynasty. The Kushan monk Lokakœema, who arrived in Luòyáng two decades after An Shìgao, is often attributed with the earliest translations of the core sutras of Pure Land Buddhism. These sutras describe Amitâbha and his Pure Land of Bliss, called Sukhâvatî.

Although Amitabha was mentioned or featured in a number of Buddhist sutras, the Larger Sutra of Immeasurable Life is often considered the most important and definitive. In this sutra, the Buddha describes to his assistant, Ânanda, how Amitabha, as an advanced monk named Dharmakara, made a great series of vows to save all beings, and through his great merit, created a realm called the Land of Bliss (*Sukhavati*). This paradise would later come to be known as the Pure Land in Chinese translation.

Pure Land Buddhism played a small role in early Indian Buddhism, particularly the Mahayana branch, but first became prominent with the founding of a monastery upon the top of Mount Lushan by Hui-yuan in 402. It quickly spread throughout China and was systematised by a series of elite monastic thinkers, namely Tanluan, Daochuo, Shandao, and others. The religious movement spread to Japan and slowly grew in prominence. Genshin (942-1017) made man of power's Fujiwara no Michinaga (966-1028) convert to Amitabha belief. Hônen (1133–1212) established Pure Land Buddhism as an independent sect in Japan, known as Jôdo Shu. Today Pure

Land is, together with Chan (Zen), the dominant form of Buddhism in China, Korea, Japan, Taiwan, and Vietnam.

Contemporary Pure Land traditions see Amitabha preaching the Dharma in his buddha-field (Sanskrit: buddhaksetra), called the "Pure Land" or "Western Pureland", a region offering respite from karmic transmigration. The Vietnamese also use the term *Tây Phýõng Cñc Lịc* for "Western Land of Bliss", or more accurately, "Western Paradise". In such traditions, entering the Pure Land is popularly perceived as equivalent to the attainment of enlightenment. After practitioners attain enlightenment in the Pure Land, they have the choice of becoming a Buddha and entering nirvana or returning to any of the six realms as *Bodhisattvas* to help all living beings in *samsara*.

Thus, adherents believe that Amitabha Buddha provided an alternative path towards attaining enlightenment: the Pure Land Path. In Pure Land Buddhist thought, Enlightenment is difficult to obtain without the assistance of Amitabha Buddha, since people are now living in a degenerate era, known as the Age of Dharma Decline. Instead of solitary meditative work toward enlightenment, Pure Land Buddhism teaches that devotion to Amitabha leads one to the Pure Land, where enlightenment can be more easily attained.

In medieval East Asian culture, this belief was particularly popular among peasants and individuals who were considered "impure", such as hunters, fishermen, those who tan hides, prostitutes and so on. Pure Land Buddhism provided a way to practice Buddhism for those who were not capable of practicing other forms. In fact, in the Larger Sutra of Immeasurable Life the Amitabha Buddha makes 48 vows, and the 18th Vow states that Amitabha will grant rebirth to his Pure Land anyone who can recite his name as little as 10 times. It also states, excluded, however, are those who commit the five gravest offences and abuse the right Dharma.

The Pure Land

The Pure Land is described in the Limitless Life Sutra as a land of beauty that surpasses all other realms. More importantly for the Pure Land practitioner, once one has been "born" into this land (birth occurs painlessly through lotus flowers), one will never again be reborn. In the Pure Land one will be personally instructed by Amitabha Buddha and numerous *Bodhisattvas* until one reaches full and complete enlightenment. In effect, being born into the Pure Land is akin to achieving enlightenment, through escaping *samsara*, the Buddhist concept of "the wheel of birth and death."

Pure Land Practice

Practitioners believe that chanting Amitâbha Buddha's name, or the nianfo, during their current life allows them, at this life's end, to be received with their karma by Amitâbha Buddha. The simplicity of this form of veneration has contributed greatly to its popularity throughout East Asia. This practice is called nembutsu in Japanese, or Buddha recitation, or "Being Mindful of the Buddha."

An alternate practise found in Pure Land Buddhism is meditation or contemplation of Amitâbha or his Pure Land. The basis for this is found in the Contemplation Sutra, where The Buddha describes to Queen Vaidehi what Amitâbha looks like and how to meditate upon him. Visualization practises for Amitâbha are more popular among esoteric Buddhist sects, such as Japanese Shingon Buddhism, while the nianfo is more popular among lay followers.

Some have claimed there is evidence of dying people going to the pure land, such as:

- Knowing the time of death - some prepare by bathing and reciting the name of the Buddha Amitabha.
- The "three saints in the west" (Amitâbha Buddha and the two *Bodhisattvas*, Avalokiteúvara on his right and Mahâsthâmaprâpta on his left), appear and welcome the dying person. Visions of other Buddhas or bodhisttvas are disregarded as they may be bad spirits disguising themselves, attempting to stop the person from entering the Pure Land.
- Records of practicing Pure Land Buddhists who have died

have been known to leave clusters of crystallized bone fragments after [cremation].

The last part of the body to become cold is the top of the head (fontanel). In Buddhist teaching, souls who enter the Pure Land leave the body through the fontanel at the top of the skull. Hence, this part of the body stays warmer longer than the rest of the body.

The *Verses on the Structure of the Eight Consciousnesses*, reads: "to birth in saints the last body temperature in top of head, to deva in eyes, to human in heart, to hungry ghosts in belly, to animals in knee cap, to the hells-realm in sole of feet." The dying person may demonstrate some, but not necessarily all, of these evidences. For example, their facial expression may be happy, but they may not demonstrate other signs, such as sarira and dreams.

Eastern Pure Land

In Mahayana Buddhism, there are many Buddhas, and each Buddha has a Pure Land. For example, Amitabha's Pure Land is understood to be in the Western direction, whereas Aksobhya's Pure Land (Abhirati) is in the East. While recognized by the Japanese Shingon sect, Eastern Pure Land Buddhism is less popular than Western Pure Land Buddhism. Though there are various traditions devoted to various Pure Lands, Amitabha's is by far the most popular.

THE NEW KADAMPA TRADITION

The New Kadampa Tradition is one of the fastest growing Mahayana Buddhist traditions in the West, with 900 meditation centres in 37 countries. Founded by the Tibetan-born meditation master, Geshe Kelsang Gyatso, supporters claim it offers local access to Buddha's teachings, meditation practice and an alternative view to life that promotes peace and harmony.

Kadampa Buddhism was founded in 11th Century Tibet by the Indian Buddhist Master Atisha (982 - 1054 CE). He was invited by King Jangchub Ö, a ruler of Ngari region of

Tibet, to reintroduce Buddhism to Tibet. It had first been introduced by Padmasambhava and Shantarakshita 200 years earlier, but was largely destroyed by the anti-Buddhist purges of the Tibetan king, Lang Darma, who was a follower of Bön, the pre-Buddhist religion of Tibet.

Atisha did revive Buddhist practice in Tibet, and founded what is now the tradition of Kadampa Buddhism. Ka means word and refers to the teachings of the Buddha and dam refers to Atisha's special presentation of them, known as Lamrim or stages of the path to enlightenment. Lamrim literally means Stages of the Path and encompasses all Buddha's teachings. Atisha showed how the paths of Sutra and Tantra were not separate and could be practised together.

Three centuries later (in the 13th century) the Tibetan Buddhist master Je Tsongkharpa, one of Tibet's saints, developed and promoted Kadampa Buddhism throughout the country. He reformed the monasteries, emphasizing the practice of moral discipline, systematic study and meditation, which characterize the three Kadam lineages. He also wrote commentaries to many sacred Buddhist texts, clarifying their meanings, and taught the union of Sutra and Tantra.

His life was an example of purity in body, speech and mind. His followers became known as New Kadampas or Gelugpas (The Virtuous Ones) who strived to become great *Bodhisattvas* and Buddhas themselves, so they could help release others from the suffering of cyclic existence. Kelsang teaches that the deity Dorje Shugden is the Dharma protector for the New Kadampa Tradition and is a manifestation of the Buddha. The spirit Dorje Shugden is described by some as a "wrathful, sword-waving deity with big ears and menacing fangs" or as "a ...warrior figure, riding a snow lion through a sea of boiling blood". This raised concerns among other Mahayana followers, who consider this divinity an evil one.

PUJA IN THE TEMPLE/HOME

In Buddhism, puja (Sanskrit & Pali: *pûjâ*) are expressions of "honour, worship, devotional attention." Acts of puja include bowing, making offerings and chanting. These devotional acts are generally performed daily at home (either in the morning or evening or both) as well as during communal festivals and *Uposatha* days at a temple.

BOWS

In the context of *puja*, bowing refers to the act of raising one's hands together (*anjali*) and lowering one's head in a gesture of homage and humility. As a devotional act, one bows to the Buddha's likeness in a statue, to a *stupa* (a pagoda that enshrines bodily relics of the Buddha) or to the Bodhi tree. Traditionally, one also bows to parents, teachers, the elderly and monastics. When bowing before a sacred object such as a Buddha statue, one usually bows three times, recalling with the first bow the Buddha, then the Dhamma and then the *Sangha*.

One may simply offer a head-lowered bow with palms-together hands held in front of one's heart or forehead, or one may move one's hands in a single flowing movement from the head to the lips to the chest (representing thought, speech and body). More formally, one may bow with a series of head-to-floor prostrations. In Buddhism, a prostration is used to show reverence to the Triple Gem (comprising the Buddha, his teachings, and the spiritual community) and other objects of veneration.

In Buddhism, prostrating has multiple and overlapping benefits for practitioners including:

- an experience of giving or veneration
- an act to purify defilements, especially conceit
- a preparatory act for meditation
- an act that accumulates merit

In contemporary Western Buddhism, some teachers use prostrations as a practice unto itself, while other teachers relegate prostrations to customary liturgical ritual, ancillary to meditation. 'Prostrations' may also be subsumed within sadhana repetitions of various vinyasa forms of yogic discipline, such as Trul Khor, eg. Importantly, vinyasa forms were directly influenced from Buddhist 'impermanence' (*anitya*) as was the language of Patanjali's *Yoga Sutras* informed by Buddhist discourse.

In the Pali canon, laypersons prostrating before the then-living Buddha is mentioned in several suttas. In Theravada Buddhism, as part of daily practice, one typically prostrates before and after chanting and meditation. On these occasions, one does typically prostrate three times: once to the Buddha, once to the Dhamma, and once to the *Sangha*. More generally, one can also prostrate before "any sacred object of veneration."

Theravada Buddhists execute a type of prostration that is known as "five-point veneration" (Pali: *patitthitapanca*) or the "five-limbed prostration" (Pali: *pañc'anga-vandana*) where the two palms and elbows, two sets of toes and knees, and the forehead are placed on the floor. More specifically:

... In the kneeling position, one's hand in añjali [palms together, fingers flat out and pointed upward] are raised to the forehead and then lowered to the floor so that the whole forearm to the elbow is on the ground, the elbow touching the knee. The hands, palm down, are four to six inches apart with just enough room for the forehead to be brought to the ground between them. Feet are still as for the kneeling position and the knees are about a foot apart....

In Theravadin countries such as Sri Lanka, when one goes before one's teacher, in order to "open one's mind up to receive instructions," one bows and recites the phrase, "Okâsa aham bhante vandâmi" ("I pay homage to you venerable sir").

In Zen Buddhism, both half- and full-prostrations are used. Zen master Robert Aitken writes:

The Zen student is taught that in *raihai* [prostration] one throws everything away. Pivoting the forearms on the elbows and raising the hands [palms up] while prostrated is the act of raising the Buddha's feet above one's head.

Roshi Philip Kapleau writes:

The act of unself-conscious prostration before a Buddha is... possible under the impetus of reverence and gratitude. Such "horizontalizings of the mast of ego" cleanse the heart-mind, rendering it flexible and expansive, and open the way to an understanding and appreciation of the exalted mind and manifold virtues of the Buddha and patriarchs. So there arises within us a desire to express our gratitude and show our respect before their personalized forms through appropriate rituals.

Ninth-century Zen Master Huang Po is said to have done prostrations so intensely that he wore a permanent red mark on his forehead.

Zen master Phillip Kapleau recounts his first stay in "a real Zen monastery":

How well, too, I remember the first time I came before my teacher in dokusan. As you know, it is customary to prostrate oneself before the roshi as a sign of respect and humility. But how that went against my grain, and how I resisted it! "... What does all this have to do with Zen?"

My teacher, well aware of these thoughts within me, said nothing, viewing my frustrated maneuvers at each dokusan with an amused smile. Then one day, when I was having a more awkward time than usual trying to prostrate, he suddenly shot at me, "Kapleau-san, when you make prostrations in dokusan you are not bowing down before me but before your own Buddha-nature."

In Vajrayana Buddhism, prostrations are often performed before meditation or teachings, but can form a separate practice by itself. Prostrations are seen as a means of purifying ones body, speech and mind of karmic defilements, especially pride. Prostrations are used in tandem with visualization and can be used to express reverence to Guru Rinpoche and others.

For example, in the context of offering homage to Guru Rinpoche, prostrations are to be performed as follows:

Bring your hands together in the 'lotus bud' mudra (the base of the palm and the fingertips together, and thumbs slightly tucked in) and place them on the crown of the head, then to the throat and heart. As you place your hands on your crown, you offer homage to Guru Rinpoche's enlightened body, purify defilements and obscurations incurred through the avenue of your body, and establish the potential to realize nirmanakaya. At your throat, you offer homage to his enlightened speech, and establish the potential to realized sambhogakaya. Bringing your hands to your heart, you offer homage to his enlightened mind, purify your mind's obscurations, and establish the potential to realize dharmakaya. The actual prostration is performed by dropping the body forward and stretching it full length on the floor, the arms outstretched in front.... Again, with hands in the lotus bud mudra, bend your arms back and touch your hands to the top of your head, a gesture that acknowledges the blessing flowing from Guru Rinpoche. Then stretch your arms out once more and push yourself up.... Bring your hands into the lotus bud mudra for the third time and touch your heart in a gesture of reverence. Then, with a smooth motion, bring your hands to your crown and perform the next prostration....

This type of prostration is often done 3, 7, 21, or 108 times. A prostration mala can be used to facilitate counting. This form of prostration is used with enlightened beings other than Guru Rinpoche as well. Prostrations done in large numbers (like 100,000) can be part of the preliminary practices to the practice of tantra. Other practices like this can be reciting the Refuge prayer, mandala offerings, Vajrasattva mantras and other practices called ngöndro.

Offerings

Symbolic offerings to the Triple Gem are often made prior to meditation. In front of the Buddha are placed the offerings, which may be just seven bowls of water symbolising the eight hospitalities offered to a guest. Another preferred style of offerings contains illumination, flowers, incense, fruit, music and water for washing and drinking. Each represents another aspect of Buddhist teachings and also the five senses.

The flowers for example are a symbol of *Anicca* (everything is impermanent) and *Samsara* (the cycle of birth, death and rebirth), due to their short life span; unless evergreen is used to show eternity. The candles symbolise enlightenment and the sense of sight while the incense is used to show that Buddhist teachings can be spread across the world just like the smell of the incense, which also purifies the air. As water is a necessity of life, a pure sample is also placed on the shrine to show respect and reverence for life. To show the interdependence of all things and gratitude for that fruit is offered-also as a symbol of taste.

A bell is used to indicate when to begin and end puja and to stimulate hearing but also demonstrates the belief of cause and effect and karma. It stimulates hearing and is placed on a lotus shaped cushion once again symbolising enlightenment and the cycle of rebirth, as it flowers and seeds at the same time. In Buddhism, symbolic offerings are made to the Triple Gem, giving rise to contemplative gratitude and inspiration. Typical material offerings involve simple objects such as a lit candle or oil lamp, burning incense, flowers, food, fruit, water or drinks.

Contemporary Western practitioners often find the making of offerings to be occasions for gracious mindfulness. Within the traditional Buddhist framework of karma and rebirth, offerings also lead to:

- A better rebirth in the cycle of birth and death (Pali: *vattagamini-kusala*).
- Progress towards release from suffering (Pali: *vivattagamini-kusala*).

These offerings often act as preparation for meditation. Material offerings nurture generosity (Pali:*dâna*) and virtue (Pali: *sîla*). The act further honors the Triple Gem (the Buddha, Dhamma and *Sangha*) deepening one's commitment to the Buddha's path. Similarly, a traditional Pali incense-lighting verse speaks of the Buddha's "fragrant body and fragrant face, fragrant with infinite virtues."

By contemplating on an offering, one tangibly sees life's impermanence (Pali: *anicca*), one of the three characteristics of all things upon which the Buddha encouraged his disciplines to recollect.

Mahayana material offerings might be imbued with the following symbology:

- The lighting of a candle or an oil lamp represents the light of wisdom illuminating the darkness of ignorance.
- The burning of incense represents the fragrant scent of morality.
- Flowers represent the aspiration to achieve the body of the Buddha with the thirty-two marks of the Buddha as well as the teaching of impermanence. Alternately, a Zen verse expresses the desire for the mind's "flowers" to "bloom in the springtime of enlightenment."
- Food, fruit, water, drinks represents the nectar of Dharma and the wish to achieve it.

In Northern Buddhism, sacred images have set before them:

- Water (representing hospitality, to wash the face and feet).
- Scarves (Tib. *kha-btags*, offering friendship).
- Flowers, incense, lamps, perfume and food (representing one's devoting all their senses to their spiritual practice).

In some traditions, two different types of offerings are identified:

- Material or hospitality offerings (Pali: *amisa-puja* or *sakkara-puja*).
- Practice offerings (Pali: *patipatti-puja*)

In this context, material offerings are considered *external* offerings of "words and deeds."

Practice offerings may be manifested by practicing:

- Giving (Pali: *dana*)
- Moral conduct (*sila*)
- Meditation (*Samadhi*)
- Wisdom (*pañña*)

In the Pali Canon, the Buddha declared practice offerings as "the best way of honoring the Buddha" and as the "supreme" offering. This is primarily an *internal* offering for mental development (Pali: *citta*, *Bhavana* and *Samadhi*).

CHANTING

Typically performed in traditional languages, such as Pali or Tibetan, Buddhist chants assist in the memorization of early canonical formulae and imbue participants with a sense of solemnity and tranquillity. A Buddhist chant is a form of musical verse or incantation, in some ways analogous to Hindu or Christian religious recitations. They exist in just about every part of the Buddhist world, from the Wats in Thailand to the Tibetan Buddhist temples of India (re: Tibetan Government in Exile). Almost every Buddhist school has some tradition of chanting associated with it, regardless of being Theravada or Mahayana.

In Buddhism, chanting is the traditional means of preparing the mind for meditation; especially as part of formal practice (in either a lay or monastic context). Some forms of Buddhism also use chanting for ritualistic purposes. While the basis for most Theravada chants is the Pali Canon, Mahayana and Vajrayana chants draw from a wider range of sources.

In the Theravada tradition, chanting is usually done in Pali, sometimes with vernacular translations interspersed. Among the most popular Theravada chants are:

- *Buddhabhivadana* (Preliminary Reverence for the Buddha)
- *Tisarana* (The Three Refuges)
- *Pancasila* (The Five Precepts)
- *Buddha Vandana* (Salutation to the Buddha)
- *Dhamma Vandana* (Salutation to his Teaching)
- *Sangha Vandana* (Salutation to his Community of Noble Disciples)
- *Upajjhatthana* (The Five Remembrances)
- *Metta* Sutta (Discourse on Loving Kindness)
- Reflection on the Body (recitation of the 32 parts of the body).

In the *Ghitassara Sutta,* the Buddha teaches:

Bhikkhus, there are five dangers of reciting the Dhamma with a musical intonation. What five?

One gets attached to the sound, others get attached to the sound, and householders are annoyed, saying, "Just as we sing, these sons of the Sakyan sing", the concentration of those who do not like the sound is destroyed, and later generations copy it.

These, monks, are the five dangers of reciting the Dhamma with a musical intonation.

In the Mahayana tradition, different schools are known for different chants, often accompanied by melodious chanting, elaborate rituals and utilization of musical instruments (either of which are not used by its Theravadin counterpart):

- Central to daily Nichiren practice is the chanting of the phrase Nam Myoho Renge Kyo (Homage to the Lotus Sutra). Nichiren practitioners will sometimes chant certain chapters from the Lotus Sutra, in particular the 2nd and 16th chapters.
- Pure Land Buddhists chant nianfo, *Namu Amida Butsu* or *Namo Amituofo* (Homage to Amitabha Buddha). In more formal services, practitioners will also chant excerpts from the Larger Sutra of Immeasurable Life or occasionally the entire Smaller Sutra of Immeasurable Life.
- Popular with Zen, Shingon or other Mahayana practitioners is chanting the *Prajñâpâramitâ Hridaya Sûtra* (Heart Sutra). In more formal settings, larger discourses of the Buddha (such as the Diamond Sutra) may be chanted as well. Particularly in the Chinese and the Japanese traditions, repentance ceremonies involving paying deep reverence to the Buddhas and *Bodhisattvas*, as well as executing rituals to rescue and feed hungry ghosts are also occasionally practiced.

In the Vajrayana tradition, chanting is also used as an invocative ritual in order to set one's mind on a deity, Tantric ceremony, mandala, or particular concept one wishes to further in themselves. For Vajrayana practitioners, the chant Om Mani Padme Hum is very popular around the world as both a praise of peace and the primary mantra of Avalokitesvara. Other popular chants include those of Tara, Bhaisajyaguru, and Amitabha.

Tibetan monks are noted for their skill at throat-singing, a specialized form of chanting in which, by amplifying the voice's upper partials, the chanter can produce multiple distinct pitches simultaneously. There are also a number of New Age and experimental schools related to Buddhist thought which practise chanting, some with understanding of the words, others merely based on repetition. A large number of these schools tend to be syncretic and incorporate Hindu japa and other such traditions alongside the Buddhist influences.

While not strictly a variation of Buddhist chanting in itself, Japanese *Shigin* is a form of chanted poetry that reflects several principles of Zen Buddhism. It is sung in the *seiza* position, and participants are encouraged to sing from the gut - the Zen locus of power. *Shigin* and related practices are often sung at Buddhist ceremonies and quasi-religious gatherings in Japan.

PUJA IN DAILY PRACTICE

Personal devotion usually entails first making an offering to a sacred object (such as placing flowers or fruits before a Buddha image). When making the offering, one bows while reciting traditional phrases identifying the offering. Next, the devotee either bows or prostrates three times to the Triple Gem. While continuing to kneel with palms-together hands held before the heart, the devotee then intones various chants typically starting with paying homage to the Buddha, taking the Three Refuges and undertaking the Five Precepts.

CANONICAL REFERENCES

In Buddhism's earliest texts, the Pali Canon, honoring those "worthy" (Pali: *arahant*) of honor is considered one of the "highest blessings," as reflected in the following words attributed to the Buddha (in English and Pali):

With fools no company keeping,With the wise ever consorting,To the worthy homage paying:This, the Highest Blessing.... *Asevanâ ca bâlânampanditânañ ca sevanâpûjâ ca pûjanîyânametam mangalam-uttamam....*

MEDITATION

Buddhist meditation encompasses a variety of meditation techniques that develop mindfulness, concentration, tranquility and insight. Core meditation techniques are preserved in ancient Buddhist texts and have proliferated and diversified through the millennia of teacher-student transmissions. Great religious traditions invariably begin with one person's direct experience. Buddha, who was born in about 560 BC, was a man who investigated his own mind and eventually attained spiritual awakening, or understanding of his own real nature. Buddha is not considered a god to be worshipped. Rather, he was a man who taught that the experiences and realizations that he found through meditation are available to everyone.

The main teaching of the Buddha is that human beings are unhappy because they do not understand their own real identity and potential. From birth, we are taught who we are, how to act and what to think. We come to believe that we are this limited identity. In meditation, our thoughts, which invariably center around this small sense of self, are quieted. We can discover that this sense of small self is a limiting concept. This understanding brings great peace, lightness, joy and understanding.

In general, meditation is a way to quiet the mind. However, "meditation" is a very general term. There are many practices which could be referred to as meditation and all the major religions include some meditative practices. "Buddhist meditation" is also a general term, as there are a multitude of meditation schools and techniques which come out of the various Buddhist traditions. Meditation can also be practiced without religious overtones (*e.g.*, one can meditate with no religious beliefs in mind or one can be a practicing Christian or Jew and employ meditation techniques extracted from Buddhism).

Benefits of meditation include relaxation and stress control, control of blood pressure, pain management, facilitation of psychotherapy and enhanced immune function. These benefits come about chiefly through effects on the autonomic nervous system. In a sentence, the "fight or flight" reaction of the sympathetic nervous system is controlled by the relaxation response of the parasympathetic nervous system. Meditation has also been used through the centuries as a path to self understanding and the most profound and direct spiritual experience.

TWO BASIC TECHNIQUES USED IN MEDITATION

Even though there are hundreds of types of meditation, if examined closely, all techniques fall into one of two categories:

1. Concentration, in which the mind focuses on a mental object (*e.g.*, looking at a candle flame, counting or noticing one's breaths with eye's closed, reciting a chant or mantra with one's mind on the sound, or visualizing certain processes in the body, like the flow of energy).
2. Mindfulness, (sometimes referred to as awareness) in which the mind observes itself (*e.g.*, sitting in meditation or doing a simple task while noticing when one hears a sound, feels a sensation or has a thought arise, without following the thought and becoming distracted).

A specific tradition may use just one of the techniques, or it may integrate the two techniques or use them at different times in a student's practice.

SYSTEMS OF MEDITATION COMMONLY USED IN THE WEST

Of the many types of meditation derived from Buddhism, three are most widely used in the United States. The following view of these schools (of necessity, in a short overview) contains many broad generalizations but should be useful:

1. Insight Meditation: This style of meditation may also be referred to as Mindfulness or Vipassana. It comes out of the Theravada Buddhist tradition of primarily Thailand and Burma. In this method one watches her or his bodily sensations and thoughts come and go. When one's attention wanders, one returns to this watching. This is a

simple technique (but not that easy to do) which has far-reaching implications. Watching oneself can lead to profound insights about one's real identity. This type of meditation has been brought to the West with minimal cultural and religious trappings.

Well known centers include the Insight Meditation Society in MA, Spirit Rock in CA, and the *Bhavana* Society in West Virginia. Typically, a student of this type of practice spends some time in silent retreat settings and sits in meditation for a short period each day. The use of this type of meditation for pain management was pioneered by Jon Kabot-Zinn at UMASS Medical Center.

2. Zen: This school comes from the Mahayana school of Buddhism in Japan and Korea. It was popularized in the United States in the 1950's and 60's by Alan Watts and D.T. Suzuki and poets of the Beat Generation. Zen schools place great emphasis on direct, non-verbal, non-conceptual perception. In one type of Zen, the student just sits with thought suspended ("sitting quietly doing nothing"). In another, the student just watches sensations and thoughts as they arise and disappear (this is akin to Mindfulness). In a third type of Zen, the student's teacher gives him or her a koan or word puzzle to ponder. There are many Zen Centers in the United States. A Zen student typically attends intensive retreats from time to time at residential Zen centers and also meditates for a set period each day.

Oh house-builder, you are seen!

You will not build this house again.

For your rafters are broken and your ridgepole shattered.

My mind has reached the Unconditioned;

I have attained the destruction of craving.

Non-Buddhists use these techniques for the pursuit of physical and mental health as well as for non-Buddhist spiritual aims. Buddhist meditation techniques are increasingly being employed by psychologists and psychiatrists to help alleviate a variety of health conditions such as anxiety and depression. As such, mindfulness and other Buddhist meditation techniques are being advocated in the West by innovative psychologists and Buddhist meditation expert teachers such as Jon Kabat-Zinn, Jack Kornfield, Joseph Goldstein, Tara Brach, Alan Clements, and Sharon Salzberg, who have been widely attributed with playing a significant role in integrating the healing aspects of Buddhist meditation practices with the concept of psychological awareness and healing.

Buddhists pursue meditation as part of the path toward Enlightenment and Nirvana. The closest words for meditation in the classical languages of Buddhism are *bhâvanâ* and *jhâna* (Pâli; Skt.: *dhyâna*). The accounts of meditative states in the Buddhist texts are largely free of dogma, so much so that the Buddhist scheme has been adopted by Western psychologists attempting to describe the phenomenon of meditation in general. Given the large number and diversity of traditional Buddhist meditation practices, this article primarily identifies authoritative contextual frameworks - both contemporary and canonical - for the variety of practices.

TYPES OF BUDDHIST MEDITATION

While there are some similar meditative practices - such as breath meditation and various recollections (*anussati*) - that are used across Buddhist schools, there is also significant diversity. For example, in the Theravada tradition alone, there are over fifty methods for developing mindfulness and forty for developing concentration, while the Tibetan tradition has thousands of visualization meditations. Most classical and contemporary Buddhist meditation guides are school specific. Only a few teachers attempt to synthesize, crystallize and categorize practices from multiple Buddhist traditions.

FROM THE PALI CANON

In terms of the vast Pali canon, meditation can be contextualized as part of the Noble Eightfold Path, explicitly in regard to:

- Right Mindfulness (*samma sati*) – exemplified by the Buddha's Four Foundations of Mindfulness.
- Right Concentration (*samma Samadhi*) – culminating in *jhanic* absorptions through the meditative development of *samatha*.

And implicitly in regard to:

- Right View (*samma ditthi*) – embodying wisdom traditionally attained through the meditative development of *vipassana* founded on *samatha*.

Classic texts in the Pali literature enumerating meditative subjects include the Satipatthana Sutta (MN 10) and the Visuddhimagga's Part II, "Concentration" (*Samadhi*).

THE BUDDHA'S FOUR FOUNDATIONS FOR MINDFULNESS

In the Satipatthana Sutta, the Buddha identifies four foundations for mindfulness: the body, feelings, mind states and mental objects. He further enumerates the following objects as bases for the meditative development of mindfulness:

- Body (*kâyâ*)
    1. Breathing
    2. Postures
    3. Clear Comprehending
    4. Reflections on Repulsiveness of the Body
    5. Reflections on Material Elements
    6. Cemetery Contemplations
- Feelings (*vedanâ*)
- Mind (*cittâ*)
- Mental Contents (*dhammâ*)
    1. The Hindrances
    2. The Aggregates
    3. The Sense-Bases

4. The Factors of Enlightenment
5. The Four Noble Truths

Meditation on these subjects develops insight.

SWIFT MESSENGERS OF NIBBANA: SERENITY AND INSIGHT

The Buddha is said to have identified two paramount mental qualities that arise from wholesome meditative practice:

- "Serenity" or "tranquillity" (Pali: *samatha*) which steadies, composes, unifies and concentrates the mind;
- "Insight" (Pali: *vipassana*) which enables one to see, explore and discern "formations" (conditioned phenomena based on the five aggregates).

Through the meditative development of serenity, one is able to suppress obscuring hindrances; and, with the suppression of the hindrances, it is through the meditative development of insight that one gains liberating wisdom. Moreover, the Buddha is said to have extolled serenity and insight as conduits for attaining *Nibbana* (Pali; Skt.: *Nirvana*), the unconditioned state. For example, in the "Kimsuka Tree Sutta" (SN 35.245), the Buddha provides an elaborate metaphor in which serenity and insight is "the swift pair of messengers" who delivers the message of *Nibbana* via the Noble Eightfold Path.

In the "Four Ways to Arahantship Sutta" (AN 4.170), Ven. Ananda reports that people attain arahantship using serenity and insight in one of three ways:

1. They develop serenity and then insight (Pali: *samatha-pubbangamam vipassanam*).
2. They develop insight and then serenity (Pali: *vipassana-pubbangamam samatham*).
3. They develop serenity and insight in tandem (Pali: *samatha-vipassanam yuganaddham*), for instance, obtaining the first *jhana* and then seeing in the associated aggregates the three marks of existence, before proceeding to the second *jhana*.

In the Pali canon, the Buddha never mentions independent samatha and vipassana meditation practices; instead, samatha and vipassana are two qualities of mind to be developed through meditation. Nonetheless, some meditation practices (such as contemplation of a *kasina* object) favor the development of samatha, others are conducive to the development of vipassana (such as contemplation of the aggregates), while others (such as mindfulness of breathing) are classically used for developing both mental qualities.

FROM THE PALI COMMENTARIES

Buddhaghosa's forty meditation subjects are described in the Visuddhimagga. Almost all of these are described in the early texts. Buddhaghosa advises that, for the purpose of developing concentration and "consciousness," a person should "apprehend from among the forty meditation subjects one that suits his own temperament" with the advice of a "good friend" (*kalyana mitta*) who is knowledgeable in the different meditation subjects. Buddhaghosa subsequently elaborates on the forty meditation subjects as follows:

- Ten kasinas: earth, water, fire, air, blue, yellow, red, white, light, and "limited-space".
- Ten kinds of foulness: "the bloated, the livid, the festering, the cut-up, the gnawed, the scattered, the hacked and scattered, the bleeding, the worm-infested, and a skeleton".
- Ten recollections: the Buddha, the Dhamma, the *Sangha*, virtue, generosity, the virtues of deities, death, the body, the breath, and peace.
- Four divine abodes: *metta, karuna, mudita,* and *upekkha.*
- Four immaterial states: boundless space, boundless perception, nothingness, and neither perception nor non-perception.
- One perception (of "repulsiveness in nutriment").
- One "defining" (that is, the four elements).

When one overlays Buddhaghosa's 40 meditative subjects for the development of concentration with the Buddha's foundations of mindfulness, three practices are found to be in common: breath meditation, foulness meditation (which is similar to the Sattipatthana Sutta's cemetery contemplations and related to reflections of bodily repulsiveness), and contemplation of the four elements. Of these, according to Pali commentaries, only breath meditation can lead one to the equanimous fourth jhanic absorption. Foulness meditation can lead to the attainment of the first *jhana*, and contemplation of the four elements culminates in pre-*jhana* access concentration.

ZONGMI'S "FIVE TYPES OF ZEN"

In the early ninth century, Zongmi (Chinese; Guifeng Zongmi or Kuei-feng Tsung-mi; Jap. Kei-ho) grouped Zen practices into five categories. While this typology is best known to Zen practitioners, it is applicable to all Buddhist meditation practices and is thus used here.

According to this typology, the outward appearance of all meditation practitioners is the same, but their substance and purpose differ. Thus, for instance, most who practice mindfulness of breath would have a similar posture, meditative subject and level of concentration. But while some use the practice for mental quietude others use it to transcend all suffering. More specifically, Zongmi's five categories of meditative practices are:

1. "Ordinary" (Chinese, *bonpu*; Jap. *bonpu* or *bompu*) – meditation pursued for mental and physical well-being without any spiritual goal.
2. "Outside way" (*gedô*) – meditation pursued for non-Buddhist purposes, such as in tandem with Hindu yoga or Christian contemplation or for the pursuit of supernatural powers.
3. "Small vehicle" (*shôjô*) – the pursuit of self-liberation, nirvana.
4. "Great vehicle" (*daijô*) – the pursuit of self-realization to experience the unity of all things and working for the benefit for all beings.

5. "Supreme vehicle" (*saijôjô*) – the realization of buddha-nature as immanent in all beings.

While the relative merits of the last three categories is open for discussion among various branches of Buddhism, it is useful to see that the same Buddhist meditation practices have been used for many centuries by Buddhists and non-Buddhists alike, for different ends. Contemporary Western examples of *bonpu* meditation include the psychotherapeutic use of Buddhist mindfulness techniques in Kabat-Zinn's Mindfulness Based Stress Reduction (MBSR) and Linehan's Dialectical Behavioral Therapy (DBT).

WESTERN BUDDHIST ORDER'S "FIVE BASIC METHODS"

Western Buddhist Order meditation teacher Kamalashila identifies "Five Basic Methods" as "a traditional set of meditations, each one an antidote to one of the five principal obstructions to Enlightenment."

Kamalashila's Five Basic Methods are:

1. Mindfulness of Breathing
2. *Metta Bhavana* (including all four *Brahma-viharas*)
3. Contemplation of Impermanence, including:
    - contemplation of a decomposing corpse
    - reflection on death
    - reflection on the Tibetan Book of the Dead's "Root Verses"
    - contemplations of mental states and external objects
4. Six Element Practice (earth, water, fire, air, space, "consciousness")
5. Contemplation of Conditionality

In addition, he discusses three other meditations as "among the most important" not identified above:

- Visualization, including:
    1. visualizations of *Bodhisattvas*

2. *kasina* meditations
3. recollection of the Buddha
4. visualization of the Six-Element *Stupa*

- Just Sitting
- Walking Meditation

An important (although not universally accepted) theme throughout Kamalashila's guide is that the various methods of meditation can be divided into samatha meditation (tranquillity meditation) and vipassana meditation (insight meditation). In such a schema, Kamalashila identifies *anapanasati* (mindfulness of breathing) and *mettâ bhâvanâ* (development of loving kindness) as samatha meditations.

The vipassana meditations include contemplation on impermanence, the six element practice, and contemplation on conditionality. Some meditations (such as Tibetan visualizations) have elements of both samatha and vipassana. Samatha meditations usually precede and prepare for vipassana meditations.

Limitations of Kamalashila's systemization of Buddhist meditation include:

- Breath meditation is widely considered a method conducive to developing vipassana as well as samatha.
- Only passing references to auditory meditations, such as mantras which are particularly important to Pure Land and Nichiren practitioners.
- The omission of visualizations from the Five Basic Methods, given for instance the salience of *kasina* objects in the Pali literature and centrality of visualizations to Vajrayana traditions.

Nonetheless, it should be noted that Kamalashila's explicit aim is not to create an exhaustive systemization of pan-Buddhist meditation practices but to create a useful meditation guide.

Bibliography

Auboyer, Jeannine, *Buddha: A Pictorial History of His Life and Legacy*. New York: Crossroad, 1983.

Bapat, P. V., ed., *2500 Years of Buddhism*. New Delhi: Government of India, Publications Division, 1956.

Basham, A. L., *History and Doctrines of the Ajivikas*. London: Luzac, 1951.

Bechert, Heinz and Richard Gombrich, eds., *The World of Buddhism: Monks and Nuns in Society and Culture*. London: Thames and Hudson, 1984.

Cabezon, Jose Ignacia, ed., *Buddhism, Sexuality, and Gender*. Albany: SUNY Press, 1992.

Charles S. Prebish, ed., *Buddhism: A Modern Perspective*. University Park: Pennsylvania State University Press, 1975.

Conze, Edward, *Buddhism: Its Essence and Development*. New York: Harper Torchbooks, 1965.

Conze, Edward, ed., *Buddhist Texts through the Ages*. New York: Harper Torchbooks, 1964.

Horner, I. B., *The Living Thoughts of Gotama the Buddha*. London: Cassell, 1948.

Jayatilleke, K. N., *Early Buddhist Theory of Knowledge*. London: George Allen & Unwin, 1963.

Joseph M. Kitagawa and Mark D. Cummings, ed., *Buddhism and Asian History*. New York: Macmillan, 1987.

Karetsky, Patricia Eichenbaum, *The Life of the Buddha:*

Ancient Scriptural and Pictorial Traditions. Lanham: University Press of America, 1992.

Keown, Damein et.al., eds. *Buddhism and Human Rights.* London: Curzon, 1998.

Kohn, Michael H., trans., *The Shambhala Dictionary of Buddhism and Zen.* Boston: Shambhala, 1991.

Lamotte, Etienne, *History of Indian Buddhism: From the Origins to the Saka Era.* Louvain-La-Neuve: Institut Orientaliste, 1988.

Lopez, Donald S., Jr, ed., *Buddhist Hermeneutics.* Honolulu: University of Hawaii Press, 1988.

Lopez, Donald S., Jr., ed., *Buddhism in Practice.* Princeton: Princeton University Press, 1995.

Malalasekera, G. P., ed., *Encyclopedia of Buddhism.* Colombo: Government of Sri Lanka, 1961.

Morgan, Kenneth W., ed., *The Path of the Buddha.* New York: Ronald Press, 1974.

Nakamura, Hajime, *Gotama Buddha.* Los Angeles: Buddhist Books International, 1977.

Ñanamoli, Bhikkhu, *The Life of the Buddha.* Kandy, Sri Lanka: Buddhist Publication Society, 1972.

Narada Thera, *The Buddha and His Teachings.* Kandy, Sri Lanka: Buddhist Publication Society, 1988 (reprint).

Prebish, Charles S., ed. *Buddhist Ethics: A Cross-Cultural Approach.* Dubuque: Kendall/Hunt, 1992.

Thomas, E. J., *The Life of the Buddha as Legend and History.* London: Routledge & Kegan Paul, 1927.

Warder, A. K, *Outline of Indian Philosophy.* Delhi: Motilal Banarsidass, 1971.

Warder, A. K., *Indian Buddhism,* 2nd ed. rev. Delhi: Motilal Banarsidass, 1980.

Warren, Henry C., *Buddhism in Translations.* New York: Atheneum, 1963.

INDEX